PRAISE FOR *BENNELONG & PHILLIP*

'In this highly experimental double portrait we see two famous men face to face, each shaped by demands of culture, gender, place and time. The result is contact history of a wonderfully vivid and interesting kind.'

Alan Atkinson, author of *Elizabeth & John: The Macarthurs of Elizabeth Farm*

'Kate Fullagar has achieved something astonishing with this dual biography of the eighteenth-century Eora warrior, emissary Bennelong, and colonial governor Arthur Phillip. The complexities of their relationship stand as a leitmotif for Australian race relations. It started dramatically with kidnapping and detention, developed into an attempt to understand and negotiate, then moved on to mutual (mis) understandings before eventually being subdued by the exertion of colonial power and finishing in silence. In a clever retelling of Bennelong and Phillip's shared history, Fullagar moves us deftly both forward and back through time. This is reconciled history at its very best.'

Distinguished Professor Lynette Russell AM

'Bennelong and Phillip: two exiles, one in Sydney, one in London, struggling to make sense of utterly alien worlds. They meet, baffle, recoil, reconcile, drift apart. With insight and empathy, Kate Fullagar adds new depth and meaning to this old story of nation-building and imperial dispossession.'

Bill Gammage AM, author of *The Biggest Estate on Earth*

'History is usually written moving forward, from past to present. But Kate Fullagar's *Bennelong & Phillip* is a rare feat of imagination; a narrative that is true to the way we discover history – through a backward glance. Fullagar's determined, searching and courageous approach challenges our assumptions about the past and its relationship with the present. The backward pairing of Bennelong's and Phillip's lives expands the horizon of their histories. Unshackled from their conventional walk-on parts as cross-cultural negotiator and founding father, their lives become richer, their histories at once more anchored and more diffuse. At a moment of profound uncertainty for future relations between Indigenous and non-Indigenous Australians, *Bennelong & Phillip* is essential reading.'

Mark McKenna, author of *Return to Uluru*

'Sadly, bias and inaccuracy in portraying Australia's history have been reinforced and justified over two centuries of dispossession, dispersal and discrimination. For many generations of Australians, Bennelong's story and his contribution to our nation's story has not been taught. Not been mentioned. Bennelong became the stereotype of the defeated 'native', a victim scarred by dispossession and cultural loss who could not adapt to European 'civilisation'. In *Bennelong & Phillip* Kate Fullagar smashes the many myths of one of the most mythologised Aboriginal men of those early settlement times. She comprehensively investigates, tracks and details the intricate relationship between Bennelong and Phillip across two continents. *Bennelong & Phillip* is the foundation story of us – the story of Country – the story of our nation.'

John Paul Janke, co-host of NITV's *The Point*

Bennelong & Phillip

ALSO BY KATE FULLAGAR

The Warrior, the Voyager and the Artist: Three Lives in an Age of Empire

The Savage Visit: New World People and Popular Imperial Culture in Britain, 1710–1795

As editor
Facing Empire: Indigenous Experiences in a Revolutionary Age
(ed. with Michael A. McDonnell)

The Atlantic World in the Antipodes: Transformations and Effects since the Eighteenth Century

Bennelong & Phillip

A History Unravelled

KATE FULLAGAR

SCRIBNER

SCRIBNER

First published in Australia in 2023 by Scribner,
an imprint of Simon & Schuster Australia
Suite 19A, Level 1, Building C, 450 Miller Street, Cammeray, NSW 2062

Sydney New York London Toronto New Delhi
Visit our website at www.simonandschuster.com.au

SCRIBNER and design are registered trademarks of The Gale Group, Inc.,
used under licence by Simon & Schuster Inc.

10 9 8 7 6 5 4 3 2 1

© Kate Fullagar 2023

All rights reserved. No part of this publication may be reproduced, stored in a
retrieval system, or transmitted in any form or by any means, electronic, mechanical,
photocopying, recording or otherwise, without prior permission of the publisher.

A catalogue record for this
book is available from the
National Library of Australia

9781761108174 (hardback)
9781761108181 (ebook)

Cover design by John Canty
Maps © by Erin Greb Cartography
Typeset by Midland Typesetters in 11.5/17 Adobe Caslon Pro
Printed and bound in Australia by Griffin Press

The paper this book is printed on is certified against the
Forest Stewardship Council® Standards. Griffin Press holds
chain of custody certification SCS-COC-001185. FSC®
promotes environmentally responsible, socially beneficial
and economically viable management of the world's forests.

To Rohan

What is required is not so much progress as recovery from the imaginary of progress ... We might tell new, more encompassing, perhaps more chaotic stories that will return us to the fullness of time.
PRIYA SATIA, *TIME'S MONSTER* (2020)

In settler history we seem to be searching constantly for beginnings ... But in Aboriginal history in the colonial period so often the search is for endings.
GRACE KARSKENS, *THE COLONY* (2009)

Since we choose to broaden our reality backwards ... we must find a way of dealing with known facts and worse still with truths which may not be compatible with our desirable round present.
ERIC WILLMOT, 'THE DRAGON PRINCIPLE' (1985)

Contents

Recognitions, Audiences, Words — xii
Maps — xiv
Timeline — xvi

Introduction: The Past Two Hundred Years — 1
Endings: Kin and Country, 1823–1796 — 21
Journeys: At Home and Abroad, 1796–1794 — 54
London: Journal of a Metropolitan Year, 1794–1793 — 86
Détente: Forging Order, 1793–1790 — 120
Gayamay: Drama at Manly Cove, 1790–1789 — 154
Decisions: Enduring History, 1789–1783 — 183
Beginnings: Saltwater People — 212
Conclusion: Stories and Futures — 240

Notes — 247
Acknowledgements — 285
Picture Credits — 289
Index — 291

Recognitions, Audiences, Words

Bennelong & Phillip was written on the unceded lands of the Ngambri people and of Ngunnawal-speaking First Nations, which include the plains and riverways of what is now also called Canberra. The book was conceived while I was living on Gadigal Country and working on Wallumedegal Country, two places in today's Sydney that were especially close to Bennelong's heart. I acknowledge the Elders of all these lands, past and present, and extend through them my respect to any First Nations readers.

As most Aboriginal people will gather, this work is written from a settler perspective, as much as it attempts to offer a fresh historical critique of settler foundations. It is intended for a global audience. It does not pretend to say new things to those Aboriginal people who have known about Bennelong all their lives, though it does seek to offer the first full account from obtainable sources to those who have relied until now on frustratingly fragmented or dated scholarship. Readers should be aware that the book alludes to women's birthing customs and male initiation ceremonies, which were restricted practices: they are sketched in a deliberately incomplete way here out of respect for those restrictions, offering only the partial glimpses afforded to colonists at the time.

Any book that deals with words and writing from the eighteenth century faces a series of difficult linguistic decisions. For British words, I have mostly cleaned up the capitalisations favoured by eighteenth-century writers but otherwise retained their idiosyncratic spellings. For the spelling of Darug words – those spoken by Bennelong and his wider community – I have relied chiefly on Jakelin Troy's phenomenal *The Sydney Language* (Aboriginal Studies Press, 1994). However, for some Darug names, I have opted for versions that at the current time seem more recognisable. This means I have opted, to give the main examples, for Bennelong, Boorong, Burramatta, and Warrane, where Troy recommends Banilung, Burung, Buramada, and Waran.

The hardest decision I have made is to use the word Yiyura for the coastal clans of the Darug-speaking people – a people whose Country stretches from the Pacific Ocean to today's Hawkesbury River, Blue Mountains and Appin River. Yiyura (often spelled Eora) is simply the Darug term for 'people', but it was used by the early colonists as a collective noun for the clans who lived nearest to the harbour. I retain such a use here, partly because it respects the fine cultural differences between the coastal and hinterland clans, and partly because it remains a preferred word among many Sydney-based Aboriginal communities.

Europeans referred to the colony of New South Wales interchangeably as Sydney, Botany Bay and New Holland. For a guide to how this volume treats relevant place names, both British and Darug, I direct readers to the maps that follow.

History shows that no protocol endures through all times. Several of the decisions I have discussed above will inevitably soon look archaic. I trust they appear at least reasonable to contemporary readers.

Phillip's Britain in the eighteenth century

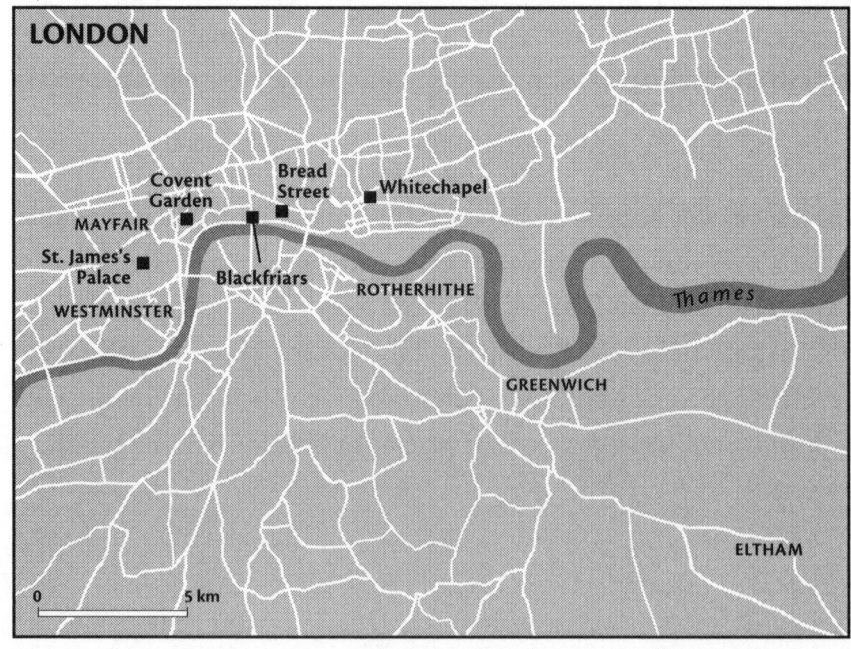

Phillip's London

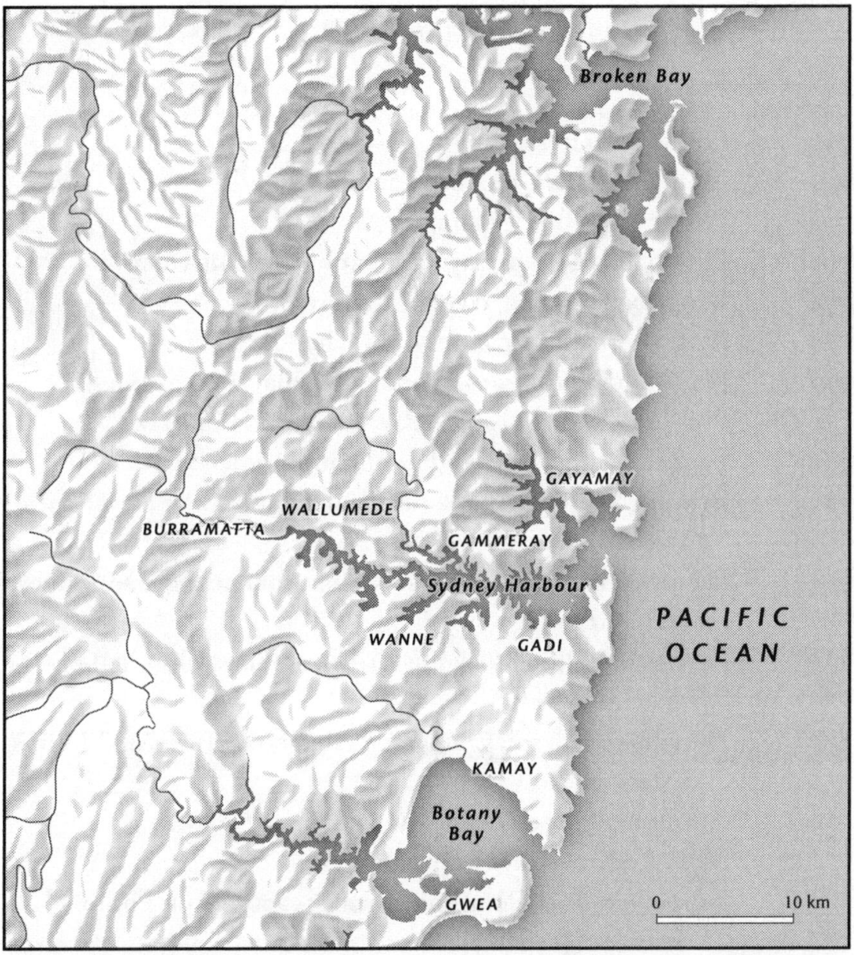

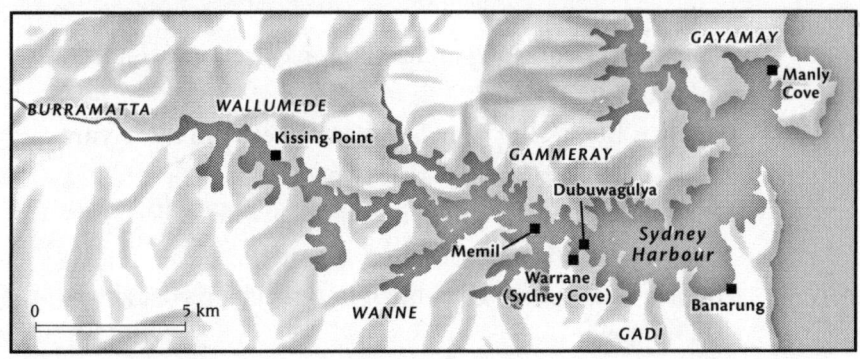

Some key Yiyura clan-sites of the Darug-speaking people in the eighteenth century

Closer view of Sydney Harbour and the Parramatta River

Timeline

1738	Phillip born in London
1751	Phillip starts at Greenwich naval school
1755–63	Phillip serves in British navy
1763	Phillip leaves navy, marries Charlott Tibbott Denison
1764	Bennelong born on Wangal Country
1769	Phillip formally separates from Charlott
1770	James Cook's *Endeavour* lands at Kamay/Botany Bay
1774–78	Phillip seconded to allied Portuguese navy in Brazil
1783	Bennelong undertakes adult initiation rituals about now
1786	British government appoints Phillip governor of New South Wales
1788	January: First fleet arrives at Kamay, soon to move to Sydney Harbour
	February: Phillip proclaims British authority over half of current Australia
	December: Gayamaygal man Arabanoo captured on Phillip's orders
1789	April: smallpox epidemic rife in Sydney Harbour
	May: Arabanoo dies from smallpox
	November: Bennelong and Colebee captured on Phillip's orders at Gayamay
1790	May: Bennelong leaves Government House, marries Barangaroo
	September: Bennelong orchestrates payback spearing of Phillip at Gayamay
	October: Bennelong signals a détente between the Yiyura and colonists (lasts roughly two years)
	December: Bennelong acquires another wife, called Kurubarabula
1791	August: Barangaroo gives birth to Bennelong's daughter Dilboong

	November: Barangaroo dies, buried near Government House
	December: Dilboong dies, buried at Government House
1792	December: Phillip and Bennelong leave Sydney for London, with Wangal man Yemmerrawanne
1793	May: Phillip, Bennelong and Yemmerrawanne arrive in London
	October: Yemmerrawanne sickens
1794	May: Phillip marries Isabella Whitehead; Yemmerrawanne dies
1795	March: Bennelong departs Britain with John Hunter
	September: Bennelong arrives back in Sydney, separates from Kurubarabula
	October: Bennelong moves to Wallumedegal Country
1796	March: Phillip restarts active service in navy
	April: Bennelong on a short trip to Norfolk Island
1797–1806	Bennelong engaged in many local battles and initiation ceremonies
1798–1801	Phillip put in charge of a local unit of the Sea Fencibles
1801–05	Phillip made an inspector of naval impressment throughout Britain
1803	Bennelong has a son, Digidigi, born to his last wife, Boorong
1805	Phillip retires from all government services
1806	Phillip and Isabella move to their last house in Bath; Bennelong steps back from warrior life
1813	January: Bennelong dies, buried in Wallumedegal Country
1814	August: Phillip dies, buried at Bathampton
	December: current governor of New South Wales opens Parramatta Native Institution
1815	Boorong is buried by now with Bennelong
1816	Bennelong's son Digidigi enrols in the Parramatta Native Institution
1823	January: Digidigi dies, aged about twenty, buried in Burramatta
	March: Isabella Phillip dies, buried with Phillip

INTRODUCTION

The Past Two Hundred Years

They died within one year of each other, even though more than two decades separated them in age. Arthur Phillip, the first governor of New South Wales, died in 1814 in Bath, southwest England, after serving the British empire around the globe for more than forty years. Bennelong, a Wangal man from today's Sydney region, died in 1813, a member of a group of Indigenous people living along the northern shore of Parramatta River.

Their burial sites are some seventeen thousand kilometres apart, but the men are linked in contemporary Australian memory as key figures in the development of Britain's colony at New South Wales. Bennelong and Phillip were the most influential leaders of their respective peoples during the initial period of contact from 1788 – those first few difficult years of claiming, defying and misunderstanding. They watched, taught and negotiated with each other on behalf of their communities. Because modern Australia deems this period foundational to its sense of self, Phillip and Bennelong have come to assume outsized roles in the national imagination, representing something essential about both settler arrival and Aboriginal possibility.

For many, these men are also emblems of broader settler–Indigenous encounters. Phillip stands for the colonial forces that quadrupled their presence around the globe between the late eighteenth and early nineteenth centuries, while Bennelong symbolises the First Nations people who confronted them.

Two hundred years after their deaths, tussles over the men's respective remains reflect their standing in the public consciousness. In 2018 the New South Wales state government purchased a plot of land in a western Sydney suburb upon advice from a committee which claimed that it contained the grave of Bennelong. The committee's geomorphologist, Peter Mitchell, located the site after extensive cross-referencing of historical texts and maps, photographs and surveys, and some 'ground-penetrating radar work'.[1] By the time of the purchase, the municipal council that initiated the research was floating the prospect of a full-scale 'trench excavation'.[2] The council hurriedly noted that any such work would of course require comprehensive consultation with relevant Aboriginal groups.

The motivation for the research and the acquisition was mixed. Most public observers in the past couple of decades have been keen to honour Bennelong because they now see he was important to Phillip's endeavours. But many also believe that this honour is owed because Bennelong suffered terminally as a result of his collaboration. In 2007 the member of parliament for the significant federal electorate of Bennelong asserted that, for the man himself, 'there was no happy ending ... he was scorned by the Europeans and by his own people'.[3] When the board of the Sydney Opera House, located on Bennelong Point, applied for World Heritage listing a year earlier, it stated that the Wangal leader had died 'alienated from both Aboriginal and European cultures'.[4] Official recent interest in Bennelong, then, has been undertaken as an act of atonement for his apparently miserable later life.

Phillip's remains have been under threat of exposure for longer than Bennelong's but with an equally partial understanding of the man's history. In 2013, high-profile Australian barrister Geoffrey Robertson argued for the relocation of Phillip's body from St Nicholas' church, near Bath, to Sydney's botanic gardens. He wanted the Australian government to give 'our founding father' a state funeral in gratitude for his 'enlightened genius . . . humanity, egalitarianism, and moral vision'. Robertson managed to get successive New South Wales premiers, from opposing parties, interested in this project and was even charged by one to start making enquiries.[5]

Robertson's proposal was not in fact original. Back in 1937, on the eve of the sesquicentenary of Phillip's arrival in New South Wales, several newspapers argued for the former governor to be 'disinterred and conveyed to Sydney'.[6] Before that, in 1907, *The Sydney Morning Herald* insisted that 'our brave pioneer [and the] first maker of Australia' should be reinterred in the lands he helped to colonise.[7] Today's interest in Phillip, as with Bennelong, is thus animated by strong emotions. Here, though, a particular kind of progressive settler nationalism drives the responses.

Neither plan, it should be noted, appears destined for success, due to the conventions surrounding both men against disturbing sacred grounds.

Neither plan, though, needs to succeed if the fundamental aim is to honour each man's legacy, to gain deeper knowledge about the roles they played, or to understand the history of modern settler–Indigenous relations in a fresh way. As *Bennelong & Phillip* will show, all these aims can be achieved not by digging up the men, but by digging back through the multiple sources available on them, including their chosen burial sites.

That Phillip should be buried under slate in an English church and that Bennelong should rest with kin close to Wangal Country reflects the most telling truths about them. The five years Phillip spent establishing the colony at New South Wales constitute only a small part of his near half-century of dedication to the British imperial state. His service included fighting rival empires during the Seven Years' War,

INTRODUCTION

being seconded to allies to help preserve British power in the Atlantic, supporting the war against American democratic independence, spying for the government at various times on the European continent, and guarding the English coastline against French republican invasion. This book will reveal that Phillip was far less a moral father to a single settler nation than he was loyal servant of a reactionary and escalating superpower. He was lucky to end his days where his heart had always remained, at the centre of the British empire.

Bennelong's burial site is likewise apt. It is not the lonely grave of an outcast who is only now finding recognition and respect, for Bennelong shares his resting place with at least two other individuals – his last wife, a woman called Boorong; and one of his first protégés, a man called Nanbarree. Long after his death, admirers and relations continued to visit his grave, mourning a man who had worked valiantly in maintaining local rituals, performing leading roles in social ceremonies, and protecting his region as best he could from the newcomers.

Phillip's burial place at St Nicholas' church, Bathampton, c. 1845

All the visitors to Bennelong's grave were Yiyura – the collective name used in this book for the fifteen or so clans located around Sydney Harbour in the eighteenth century.[8] As such, they were increasingly unnoticed by the colonists, whose records still dominate perceptions of early Australia. Colonial observers then did not see that Bennelong was widely appreciated at the time of his death. He received deep acknowledgement for his life when he passed – just not by the kind of people who would determine the course of his public memory.

History in reverse

Finding the most telling truths about Phillip and Bennelong in their gravesites leads me to the unusual narrative approach taken in this book. It starts at the end of the men's lives – so close in time – and unravels them back to their beginnings. The emphasis is on plotting key events in roughly reverse order rather than on making time itself run backwards. The rest of this introduction thus steps back through the different ways that Phillip and Bennelong have been remembered

Burial place of Bennelong, shown in Kissing Point, *Joseph Lycett, c. 1825*

over the past two hundred years. The following chapters unspool their respective legacies and retirements, their final journeys and ponderings, their time together in England and Sydney, their difficult meeting, their backstories, and finally their origins in blood and place. (For readers unfamiliar with the main events of this story, a forwards-running timeline is shown on pages xiv–xv.)

If a back-running method feels counterintuitive it nevertheless suits the two overarching ambitions of this book. My first ambition is to offer a new picture of Phillip and Bennelong. Most accounts of these long-twinned men, which are always told forwards, focus on the decade or so surrounding the formation of the New South Wales colony. Because this colony spurred the creation of others on the continent, which then became a nation, its inaugural leader tends to be depicted in a patriotic light. Phillip is made to express the qualities that the resultant nation most identifies with – 'humanity, egalitarianism, and moral vision', as Geoffrey Robertson would have it. Because Bennelong represented the people hit hardest by Phillip's colony, and by the nation that rose over it, his image has been coloured more by loss. Sometimes Bennelong has been blamed for that loss and sometimes he has been pitied for it, but loss is what prevails overall.

Telling the story from the end of the men's lives back to their beginnings upturns how we arrive at their most commonly told decade. Once we learn, for example, about Phillip's extensive counter-revolutionary activities in Europe after his governorship, it becomes harder to see his short stint in New South Wales as the pinnacle of an especially liberal career. Likewise, once we trace through the final two decades of Bennelong's life, thoroughly immersed as they were in his rich and complex Indigenous culture, it becomes less feasible to believe he lost his connections to kin.

After reconsidering the supposedly defining era of the men's lives, our method also enables a reassessment of their earlier years, before they even met. It queries once again what is the real centre of their stories. Too often modern histories assume the first chapters of a life are just the prelude to a main event. What new things can we see in Bennelong and Phillip if we don't read their earlier years as preliminaries to colonial settlement and their later years as a fading aftermath? What emerges as the main event in their lives if it's not the foundation of New South Wales? Can we now grasp each era more on its own terms? Can we discern different worlds and priorities informing the actions of both men?

I hope to show with this approach how deeply embedded the famed governor was in a galloping global empire, and, equally, how much his best-remembered Indigenous counterpart managed to defy that empire. Shifting the frame of Australia's two most foundational figures away from a narrow settler context, away from myths about preternaturally liberal values, and away from a sense of Aboriginal doom changes how we think about the nation's origins and about its future.

The second ambition of this book is to answer the mounting calls for new 'temporal scripts' to represent the past.[9] Recently, historian Priya Satia has made the clearest case for new modes of history-writing. In her sweeping account, *Time's Monster*, she exposes the way in which the 'historicist imagination' of the past three centuries was implicated in the development of empire.[10] She shows how European historians, with their conventional belief in events moving always towards greater liberty, have helped to exculpate empire's terrible violence by depicting it as the unfortunate means to a justifiable end. The modern historical mode, in other words, tends to license imperial injustices by presenting them as the necessary if sad cost of modernity itself. Instead, 'what is required', Satia writes, 'is not so much progress as recovery from the imaginary of progress'.[11]

A principal plank of the imaginary of progress has been its forwards-moving narrative style. Turning that style on its head helps us resist seeing Phillip's life in light of the later nation's grandest ideas about itself, and it helps us question the notion that Bennelong's fate was the dismal but inevitable price to be paid for modernisation.

In settler-colonial settings, one peculiar effect of much modern history-writing is what Ojibwe scholar Jean O'Brien calls Firsting and Lasting.[12] In those places where settlers have sought to displace Indigenous peoples permanently, a progressing sense of history has emphasized settler *firsts* and Indigenous *lasts*. Stories of the settlers' first battles, first famines, first crops, and so on imply that their destiny can only grow more capacious. Conversely, tales of last Indigenous chiefs, last Indigenous performances, or last Indigenous language-speakers naturalises the idea that such people are incompatible with the future. As Grace Karskens puts it in the Australian context, 'in settler history we seem to be searching constantly for beginnings ... but in Aboriginal history in the colonial period so often the search is for endings'.[13] Tracing the lives of two key Australian historical figures in contrary order tests the assumptions that emerge from thinking in terms of firsts and lasts.

In sum, *Bennelong & Phillip* is an experiment in trying to move beyond the limitations of typical Western ways of writing about the past – ways that have often seemed so innocent of politics but which have long privileged the coloniser over the colonised. This book does not claim to embody how someone like Bennelong would have approached the past – which was hardly linear at all – but it does at least mean that his and Phillip's histories now share an equally unfamiliar framing. The European character is no longer favoured over the non-European by the very way their stories are told.

Afterlives

The afterlives of Phillip and Bennelong have fared differently over the past two centuries. Phillip's reputation has enjoyed the most consensus.

When Geoffrey Robertson insisted on Phillip's 'enlightened genius' he was repeating the view given in most memorials and accounts since the Second World War. Bennelong's image during the same period has been more varied: even though he is usually portrayed in terms of deficit, this sometimes appears as tragedy and sometimes as farce.

The same impressions also pertained, on the whole, back through the nineteenth century. Both men, however, provoked fewer representations of any kind before the 1930s, ever lessening as history reversed past federation and into a colonial era that identified more with contemporary British events than with its own troubled beginning.

Notably, in a sweeping survey of posthumous reputation, every single account of Bennelong offers also a portrait of Phillip, since he has never been conceivable outside of colonial history. But only some histories of Phillip include a mention of Bennelong, since the governor's achievements have always been considered his own.

The view of Phillip as Enlightenment paragon has been so sturdy it even withstood the furore over colonial statues that ignited globally in the late 2010s. To be fair, this was also partly due to James Cook taking much of the heat in that contest. Phillip has been fortunate to share his status as founder with another eighteenth-century man – the navigator who sailed up the Australian east coast eighteen years before Phillip's arrival. In fact, Cook has usually overshadowed Phillip for the title, even though he spent less than nine months in Australian waters compared to Phillip's five years of active colonisation. This is because in the era of national-identity formation in the nineteenth century, Cook appeared further removed than Phillip from the taint of the first fleet's convicts.[14]

Still, even Cook's reputation survived better than that of many other colonists around the world. What saved his image from being toppled, literally to the ground, was his strong association with the Enlightenment. Cook's image only took a beating when it was sundered from notions of scientific discovery or navigational prowess – when, for example, protesters remembered that Cook occasionally shot at Indigenous people and certainly declared possession over them.[15]

Phillip's reputation has suffered fewer such sunderings because his link to the Enlightenment has been steadier. His memorialists have not bothered with the details of his racial interactions or possessive declarations to the degree that they have with Cook.

The kind of Enlightenment attributed to Phillip usually boils down to three key notions, as Robertson intimated: humanitarianism, egalitarianism and rectitude. This consensus view reached its apogee during the bicentenary of Phillip's death in 2014, when the Britain-Australia Society convinced Westminster Abbey in London to lay a commemorative stone in the floor of its nave. The stone read, 'founder of modern Australia'. Then-sitting New South Wales Governor Marie Bashir presided at its dedication, which described Phillip as an 'extraordinary humanitarian'.[16] In the same year, a new biography appeared. Penned by judge Michael Pembroke, it concurred that Phillip was a man of 'Enlightenment', 'integrity' and 'benevolent egalitarianism'.[17]

Earlier, Lyn Fergusson's 2009 biography uncovered new data on Phillip's family origins, but similarly expressed the view that he was, in essence, an 'honest', 'caring' and 'humanitarian' man.[18] Before Fergusson, Inga Clendinnen's *Dancing with Strangers* (2003) claimed to offer a radically new account of Sydney's first decade. While it did attend more assiduously to Indigenous agency than most histories at the time, the book's portrayal of Phillip turned out to be remarkably familiar. Clendinnen felt he was 'close to visionary'. The scourge of 'racist terror would come soon enough', she declared, 'but not in Phillip's time'.[19]

Both Fergusson and Clendinnen, and indeed all later biographers of Phillip, owed greatly to Alan Frost's *Arthur Phillip* of 1987. This work laid a bedrock of research about the man and was the first to delve meaningfully into Phillip's other activities besides his colonial governorship. Frost, however, as did most everyone else, concluded that Phillip was at his core respectful, humane and kindly.[20] Frost in fact went further in this vein because he was one of the few writers also to narrate Phillip's sporadic flares of authoritarianism. These he explained as due either to bouts of severe illness or, more often, to a particularly thorough egalitarianism: 'just as Phillip would not tolerate theft or acts of violence from the Europeans, so too would he not tolerate dishonesty or mindless violence from the Aborigines, for whom his government had made him also responsible'.[21]

The consensus view was established more than a generation prior to Frost's scholarly tome. In time for the sesquicentenary of Phillip's arrival in New South Wales, two huge biographies appeared. The literary duo of Marjorie Barnard and Flora Eldershaw, writing as M. Barnard Eldershaw, published *Phillip of Australia* in 1938. It is a slightly muddled work that claimed Phillip was both 'an unusual man in his own or any day', who insisted on governing 'along lines of equity', and inevitably a creature of the eighteenth century, which explained why he 'had no scruples about taking the dark man's country from him'.[22] The general point was to honour a man who founded, nonetheless, a 'civil, democratic' state.[23] Getting in just ahead of Barnard Eldershaw, George Mackaness produced *Admiral Arthur Phillip* in 1937. It is nearly five hundred pages long, but a degree less florid than its competitor. Mackaness, too, ultimately admired his subject, concluding that Phillip was compassionate, tactful and forbearing.[24]

The only two major settler scholars to directly question this near-century-long trend have been the historian Grace Karskens in 2009 and the anthropologist W.E.H. Stanner in 1963. Karskens' book *The*

Colony was in many ways a response to Clendinnen's work. It sought to remind readers that all Phillip's actions, despite the dancing with strangers, 'were underwritten by the threat of violence and guns'.[25] There was no quarantining Phillip from the racism or the terror of early New South Wales, she implied. Stanner was similarly sceptical of the constant 'eulogies' to Phillip. He was happy to leave Phillip's reputation as a convict manager intact, but stressed how often the governor seemed 'wrong-headed' when it came to race relations. 'One is hard put', he wrote, to ignore his 'raids' on and 'trickery' of Aboriginal people.[26]

An indirect challenge emerged in Alan Atkinson's *Europeans in Australia* in 1997. Less focused on pointing out the ferocity and the hubris that occurred alongside the vision and the care, Atkinson instead tried to explain how these things were not necessarily contradictory. Phillip was indeed a type of Enlightenment figure, Atkinson suggested, but in the eighteenth century, Enlightenment did not reduce to humanitarianism, egalitarianism or rectitude. In Phillip's era it was chiefly about taking a rationalist approach to worldly matters. Phillip believed in 'nourishing' governments because they produced better subjects, not because they were kinder. He disliked slavery, despotism and unfair rationing because they produced chaotic behaviours, not because they were inhuman.[27] In Atkinson's book, it becomes possible to see that Phillip could be both meditative and ruthless, both thoughtful and unbending.

My book builds on Atkinson's contextual approach to Phillip, assessing the actions and views of the man within a consistent eighteenth-century global frame. It does not doubt Phillip's Enlightenment values, but it questions how these have been defined in modern memorials to him. Enlightenment thinking in Phillip's era had some positive effects for some people, but it did not yet assume that all humans had the same capacity to realise their destinies. The notion of granting all humans equal rights just because they were human barely existed in the British intellectual landscape in the eighteenth century.[28] My intent is less to denigrate the idea of Phillip as a dignified humanitarian democrat than to reveal how extremely unlikely that label was in his period. Instead, I explore his persona as more or less typical of Enlightenment attitudes as they existed within his contemporary British empire. In this world, compassion to others went only as far as it logically furthered the aims of conquest; equity could never be extended to the people that empire needed to suppress; and the idea of virtue had to find room for shackles, dispossession and forced labour.

Through Phillip, we catch an individualised glimpse of how empire operated in his era. We see how empire interacted with Indigenous peoples, who were always its greatest problem; how empire's world-spanning ambitions brought a global resonance to every outpost; and how all this left legacies which deserve urgent reappraisal today.

Bennelong's depiction over the past eighty years has been more complex than Phillip's. Loss has stuck to the image of Bennelong as often as Enlightenment has stuck to that of Phillip, but Bennelong's primary quality has seen different representations. The most common way of understanding Bennelong's loss is as tragedy, where Bennelong is the victim of all-encompassing colonial manipulations. The slightly less prevalent way is loss as foolishness, the apparent consequence of Bennelong's selfish drive to ingratiate himself with the colonists, lacking all foresight and resulting in no social benefit.[29]

That said, loss has not been the whole story. Glimmers of a stronger and more estimable Bennelong have broken through to public audiences on occasion, especially in the past fifteen years. His greatest settler advocate, Keith Vincent Smith, started publishing pieces of neglected evidence in 2005. Smith's work suggests that Bennelong found more respect among his own people in old age than has been acknowledged. These findings were only quietly and partially received, however, and never found an outlet for a whole-of-life biography.[30] In 2012 the Indigenous writers Wesley Enoch and Anita Heiss dramatised this shift in perception in their play *I Am Eora*. At the start of the play Bennelong is disliked and rejected, but by the end he is valued and even revered. The character of Bennelong here, though, represented the change in image rather than in the man himself. And as with Smith's work, the play has not yet penetrated the cultural mainstream.[31]

Earlier, of course, many Indigenous people had suspected that the pervasive image of Bennelong as a tragic or foolish figure was wrong, but most found it difficult to bin completely, given its entrenched power. Dharawal Elder Gavin Andrews recalls suggesting to fellow Dharawal man John Lennis around 2001 that Bennelong might in fact have been a hero for representing – not for selling out – his people to Phillip. Andrews remembers that Lennis was surprised at the time, because the narrative he'd been told was of Bennelong as a drunken opportunist. Lennis had been commissioned to condense Bennelong's biography for a plaque in the Sydney botanic gardens. He felt compelled to opt in the end for a middle path, heading the plaque with the question, 'Bennelong: hero or traitor?'[32] Aboriginal novelist Eric Willmot wove a similarly ambiguous tale about Bennelong in his 1987 novel *Pemulwuy*. Even though his portrayal was mostly sympathetic, Willmot closed the book with Bennelong dying in an alcoholic stupor.[33]

Although 'Competent Bennelong' has some lineage, then, this is still far from the dominant perception of the man. The overriding image of him in modern times remains that of tragic victim; a character doomed by colonial taint, often signified by alcohol addiction, and who additionally bears the weight of symbolising the future of all Aboriginal peoples. This figure was most powerfully represented in 2017 by the Indigenous dance troupe Bangarra. Their rendition of Bennelong, in their eponymous main show for that year, was intense and moving. Bennelong appeared more immersed in his Yiyura culture and with a greater depth of character than he had ever enjoyed before. Notably, though, Bangarra made his ending bleak: Bennelong returns home after spending three years overseas unable to 'belong in either world'. He dies encased in a literal box on stage, 'mourning his own spirit'.[34]

To be clear, Bangarra was up-front about diverging from 'a literal translation of historical events'. It is a sobering indictment of settler audiences that an Aboriginal arts group in 2017 found more purchase in repeating a story of Indigenous ruination than in exploring the idea that Bennelong might have had a better fate than is usually assumed. Bangarra estimated that instructive stories about all that was lost through colonisation – stories that Bennelong has for so long epitomised – still need clarifying before Indigenous storytellers can move on to visions of who and what defied it.[35]

The portrait of Bennelong in this book is not meant to dismiss the despair of later Indigenous generations that he has been made to exemplify. Nor is it an attempt to suggest that Indigenous life over the past two centuries has been rosier than claimed. It is instead an experiment in imagining what else might be seen when Aboriginal characters finally get to be more than lost.

'Tragic Bennelong' reached his height in the early 2000s. Along with the federal MP for the electorate of Bennelong, and the board of the Sydney Opera House on Bennelong Point, other voices advocating this version of the man included several bestselling writers. Thomas Keneally, in *Commonwealth of Thieves*, thought Bennelong was eventually an addict accepted by no one.[36] Lucy Hughes Turnbull, in her biography *Sydney*, found Bennelong to be, at length, uneasy and lonely.[37] And Inga Clendinnen, in her book that so stridently defended Phillip, agreed that Bennelong wound up drunk and violent. 'At fifty,' she declared, he 'fumed his way to an outcast's grave. He should have died earlier, in the days of hope.'[38]

The tragedians of the early 2000s inherited an image of outcast Bennelong that had been shaped by some of the most illustrious Australian intellectuals of the twentieth century. In the 1980s, art critic and Boyer Lecturer Bernard Smith lamented Bennelong's fate to live 'between two cultures . . . fraught with terrible tensions'.[39] A decade earlier, economist and leading public servant H.C. Coombs penned a foreword to a brief biography of Bennelong where he decried the man's 'sombre . . . incompatibility' with his 'conquerors'.[40] Another decade earlier still, Australia's most famous historian, Manning Clark, intoned that Bennelong 'disgusted his civilisers and became an exile from his own people, [rushing] headlong to his own dissolution'.[41] Clark had been inspired by the novelist Eleanor Dark, who perhaps inaugurated the tragic vision of Bennelong in her 1941 historical novel *The Timeless Land*. Dark rescued Bennelong from a period of almost complete erasure, but in her resurrection she locked him into a gloomy role. At first, Dark's Bennelong is vibrant and plucky but soon Europeans corrupt his all too corruptible soul. The novel concludes with him passed out from drink: 'the merciful, swift twilight of his land crept up about him to cover his defeat. The End.'[42]

In the twentieth century, 'Tragic Bennelong' sometimes tussled with 'Foolish Bennelong'. This version of the man has not been seen much since the 1980s, though he did make a brief appearance in Matt Murphy's 2021 *Rum: A Distilled History of Colonial Australia*. Here, Bennelong exists only as described by some early British sources: a man 'so savage . . . as to be capable of any mischief' and remembered chiefly for his 'propensity for drunkenness'.[43] In 1973 this same unpleasant Bennelong starred in Isadore Brodsky's *Bennelong Profile*, in which he was a 'Stone Age' primitive – an impulsive unwanted child who could not grow up.[44]

The figure of Bennelong as fool has in fact two sides. As evidenced in Murphy's and Brodsky's books, one side comes directly from early sources, and particularly from the derogatory *Sydney Gazette* obituary of Bennelong published in 1813.[45] The other, more curiously, comes from a misfired ambition to shine positive light on some Aboriginal characters by denigrating others. Two otherwise strong advocates for Aboriginal history, John Mulvaney and W.E.H. Stanner, both fell into this trap. In 1984, Mulvaney, in an effort to praise the rebellious warrior Pemulwuy, conjured a dishonourable Bennelong, describing him as a parasite compared to his peer.[46] Nearly twenty years before, Stanner had done the same thing, even while also criticising Phillip's behaviour towards Indigenous people. Imploring his audiences to consider the many 'outstanding' characters to be found in the Aboriginal past, Stanner added that he 'was not thinking of mercurial upstarts like Bennelong', who was a 'volatile egotist . . . a trickster and eventually a bit of a turncoat'.[47]

This book eschews both tragic and foolish renditions of Bennelong, exploring further the suggestion that he maintained his most cherished quality – his personal sovereignty – throughout life. Perhaps the greatest loss Bennelong ever sustained was that to his reputation, inflicted partly in his later years and especially after his death. Questioning that loss offers a view into how sovereignty endured for at least one Indigenous person in this era of imperial infiltration. This is a crucial history to recall during present-day efforts to conciliate, for the first time, descendants of that momentous time.

Back into the nineteenth century
Before the Second World War, and arguably before the true consolidation of the Australian nation, the reputations of both

Bennelong and Phillip were hazier. Between the 1930s and 1900, no extended biographies appeared, though each man featured in local newspaper columns devoted to bite-sized history. Phillip popped up around once a week; Bennelong surfaced about once a year.[48] These snippets were almost all gleaned from the *Historical Records of New South Wales*, which were published in seven volumes by the government during the 1890s. Nearly every one offered the same sentiments about Phillip being a worthy modern leader and Bennelong (if rated at all) being his sometimes helpless but mostly hopeless sidekick.

Phillip enjoyed a brief moment in brighter light in the final years of the nineteenth century, when a burgeoning nationalist movement was searching for a historical anchor point. In 1899 the popular writers Louis Becke and Walter Jeffrey produced the first ever full-length biography of him. Sadly, as many reviewers noted, their minimal research meant little advance could be made on the already published *Historical Records of New South Wales*.[49]

In 1897 an altogether more original interpretation had materialised. This was the statue of Phillip by Italian sculptor Achille Simonetti, erected in Sydney's botanic gardens. Then-premier of New South Wales, Henry Parkes, had commissioned Simonetti to make the monument in 1889, just after the centenary celebrations of Phillip's landing. It was meant at first to be a realist work, though it changed under the directions of Parkes' successor to a classical style. The resultant statue is a remarkable jumble soaring over fifteen metres high. A venerable and realist Phillip holding a flag and papers stands on top of three classical friezes depicting justice, patriotism and education. Below him recline mythical figures representing agriculture, commerce, navigation and mining, but wedged beneath these are a series of unidentified Aboriginal people less than a metre high.[50] Despite the stylistic mixing, this Phillip is still figured as an honourable leader of modern industry.

Bennelong featured in schoolteacher Richard Sadleir's 1883 *The Aborigines of Australia*, where, intriguingly, he is first described as a 'hero'.[51] Within one page, however, he has descended into the prototypical fool, not through the tragic means of colonists but through the chuckle-worthy mechanism of his own 'troublesome' peers.[52]

In the mid-nineteenth century, before the rise of a strong nationalist movement, Phillip and Bennelong shared minimal attention. This was due partly to a general British disdain then for the supposed corruptions of the eighteenth century, and partly to a desire among Antipodean colonists to distance themselves from their rough start. At a time when colonists sought to be free of both convict transportation and continued frontier massacres, they did not want to recall their origins as a penal settlement on other people's lands.[53]

More accounts exist prior to the 1830s, when commentators could still personally recall Phillip and Bennelong. Many return us once more to the men's graves. In 1823 the slab covering Phillip's remains in St Nicholas' was temporarily removed in order to bury those of his last wife, Isabella. The slab had been engraved with the words, 'Underneath lies the remains of Arthur Phillip, Esq., Admiral of the Blue, who died 31st of August 1814 in his 76th Year.'[54]

It's noticeable that at the time of his death only his naval credentials marked Phillip, not his governorship. Dozens of newspapers observed Isabella's passing, mentioning that she was the widow of 'the late Admiral Arthur Phillip', but again, few referred to New South Wales.[55] Soon afterwards, the slab was covered by a mat, and the Phillips' mutual spot in an English church was neglected for many decades.[56]

Also in the 1820s, a clergyman living in western Sydney observed an ageing Yiyura man frequently visiting the site of Bennelong's grave.[57] This man was Bidgee Bidgee, a relative of Bennelong's, and in some ways his successor as a leader of the conglomerate clan they had

INTRODUCTION

both helped to form in the early 1800s. The clergyman heard Bidgee Bidgee express 'a wish, after his death, to be buried by the side of his friend Bennelong . . . amidst the orange trees of the garden'.[58]

No records indicate if Bidgee Bidgee was granted his wish, though some reported that by 1821 both Nanbarree and Boorong were lying beside Bennelong.[59] Nanbarree had been a member of the Gadigal clan, an occasional enemy of Bennelong's Wangal clan. Boorong was the mother of his surviving son, Digidigi.

None of these additional facts was remembered by colonists, who had largely moved on from their hunger for Yiyura knowledge. But the memory of Bennelong still thrived quietly among kin. In this same decade another clergyman visited the people living near Bennelong's grave. He showed them a portrait of their deceased leader. 'They were astonished, and wept aloud,' he recalled. '"It is Bennellong!" they cried . . . "He was our brother and our friend!"'[60]

The 1820s is often seen as the start of a new era in the West – a time, finally, of peace after the tumult of the American, French, and Industrial revolutions. It heralded the coming of liberalism, free settlers and free trade. It was also, though, the start of a great forgetting, the erasure from mind of how much peace and liberty in the West had depended on earlier coercive imperial forces to fuel its victories and resource its economies. Equally, the era now doubled down on forgetting the roles that Indigenous people had played in the formation of stability – their suffering during the invasions, their care of the lands now dispossessed, and their survival through it all regardless. This is a book about remembering the twin pillars upon which the Western world rests: the never-repealed incursions of global empire and the always-enduring sovereignty of Indigenous peoples.

ENDINGS

Kin and Country, 1823–1796

*The last wives of Phillip and Bennelong • Their respective next of kin
• The hour of their deaths • Phillip's retirement in Bath • Bennelong's
final years on Wallumedegal Country • Phillip battles the French
Revolution while Bennelong also engages in conflicts*

When Isabella Phillip's remains joined those of her husband, nine years after his death, the covering slate slab was amended accordingly. 'Also of ISABELLA relict of above Admiral PHILLIP,' it now read, 'who died the 4th of March 1823, in the 71st Year of her Age.'[1] It was actually the seventy-third year of her age, but as with the reference to Isabella as a relict of someone else, interest in the details of British women in this period was never as deep as it was for British men.[2]

Bennelong did not have to wait so long for company in his grave – or buma, as the Yiyura called it. Within two years he was joined by his last wife, Boorong. A British sailor in Sydney in 1815 reported that 'old Bennelong is dead … he died after a short illness about two years ago, & … they buried him & his wife at Kissing point'.[3] In life, Boorong may have shared Bennelong with another wife, since Yiyura men at that time often had two partners while women usually had just one. Like Britain's, Yiyura society often favoured men over women, though as we shall see, its gender conventions operated quite differently.[4]

The posthumous reunions of Phillip and Bennelong with their wives represent one way their stories could end. There are others. They might end instead with their next of kin. Or more prosaically, with the expiration of their natural bodies. Or they might end well before death, with their respective retirements among specific communities. Some might choose to close the stories of such politically loyal men with their last acts of service to their beloved countries.

Each of these finales is narrated here, to emphasise the variety that can exist in telling life stories. More significantly, they are assembled together at the beginning of our history because as a collection they summarise the men's loftiest objectives. The endings of Phillip's story show that his ultimate priority in life was Britain's wider imperial aspirations rather than any one particular colony, or indeed any one particular person. The endings of Bennelong's indicate that his largest life goal was the preservation of kin networks, in which he remained always embedded.

In addition, these endings – involving family, community and work – introduce some of the most fundamental elements of the two societies: gender norms, social norms, economic norms, the role of religion, and the function of war. These elements give crucial context to any attempt at grappling with character or motivation.

Last wives

Isabella and Arthur were married for two decades. They wed when both were in middle age: she was forty-three and he fifty-five. Their final few years together, living in a grand townhouse in Bath in the 1810s, appeared relatively happy. Friends wrote that they were almost always in each other's company and usually 'in very good spirits'.[5] They maintained a congenial circle of acquaintances around Bath and its close surrounds.

The pair's earlier years, however, had been more fraught. When widowed in 1814, Isabella may have looked back on her marriage and remembered mostly this trickier time – a period during which one acquaintance implied she was uncheerful and another described her as 'mad as a March hare'.[6] Two letters from the turbulent era, recently discovered, intimate a wife beset with insecurities and a husband curt with frustration at their irrationality. 'Say which situation you like best,' Phillip wrote in one letter in 1803, regarding their future abode, 'and for godsake let me hear no more doubts for which there is no reason.' He went on to declare himself injured by 'the word afflicted at the conclusion of your letter & if that is repeated, I shall think I have too good reason to conclude myself an afflicted husband'.[7]

A couple of years earlier, in the other letter, Phillip had admonished Isabella for persisting in 'groundless ideas, that your husband and all your friends are plotting against your happiness, ideas which make you miserable as well as myself'. He told her that her own letters to him 'are painful to read' and that she should no longer send them 'unless you can write in a different language'. He urged her not to 'drive [your friends] from you [and instead to] think more justly of your affectionate husband, A Phillip'.[8]

A few different causes may have been behind these troubles. The first might have been Isabella's slightly higher class background compared to Phillip's. She was the daughter of a successful cloth merchant who was later a sheriff, while he was the son of an obscure plebeian immigrant. But by the time of his marriage, when Phillip was in his fifties, he had mingled with pretty much every level of society, from navvies to kings, and achieved substantial prestige himself, so a class antagonism seems unlikely. Both had also lived fairly independent lives until their marriage; thus they may just have been too set in their ways to adjust readily to each other. The norms of British society at this time, however, deeply favoured the married over the single, which means they probably knew there were few better alternatives.[9]

Most likely, the difficulties stemmed from Phillip's chronic absences throughout their initial decade together. For nine of their first ten years of marriage, Phillip was largely away from Isabella, serving on naval or para-naval missions for the British Admiralty. These were all missions he had sought and from which he was released only because of his age. Isabella would have known that Phillip's imperial pension as a retired governor was more than sufficient to keep them. She could only have wondered at how vigorously her husband still applied to work for his country elsewhere.

She may have wondered even more deeply about Phillip's mysterious first marriage. In the 1760s, when furloughed for the first time from the navy, Phillip had been married briefly to a Margaret Charlott Tibbott Denison, known always as Charlott. He was twenty-four when they wed, to her forty-two. This made their age difference greater than that between Phillip and Isabella, and with a far less common gender ordering.

Nothing in fact seemed typical about this union. Charlott made Phillip sign a marriage settlement before the wedding, overriding English law at a time in which all of a wife's wealth was consigned permanently to her husband.[10] She also got him to agree to a judicial separation six years later, something which occurred in less than one per cent of marriages and was the closest thing to divorce that existed for ordinary people.[11]

The irregular legalities, however, were still not the most unusual thing about Phillip's marriage to Charlott. A close examination of the documents shows that another woman lived with them throughout their time together: a Mrs Anna Maria Cane. Anna ended up co-habiting with Charlott for close to five decades and shared her grave after death, described on the tombstone as Charlott's 'companion'.[12]

Whatever the status of Charlott and Anna's relationship, Phillip did not seem to pose much of a challenge to it. There is no evidence of hostility in any of the legal papers, and in fact Phillip actively sought to secure Anna's share of Charlott's will when Charlott died in 1792.[13] He appears in the sources less thwarted husband than amenable helpmate. Phillip's first marriage thus looks to have been an unconventional arrangement of convenience. The two women in it found a capable young farm manager to run their estate through their middle age, and Phillip found something to do during a rare episode of peace in Britain's war-filled eighteenth century.

A survey of Phillip's two marriages highlights how much his society normally privileged men over women, from the styling of gravestones to the customs of family law. It also begins to uncover Phillip's deep-seated preference for serious public service over traditional private life. For him, domesticity was what you made do with when the grander work of national advancement was not possible. Phillip was hardly a typical patriarch, but neither does he appear to have been a very easy kind of husband.

Bennelong's relations with women were warmer than Phillip's, though equally complex. The colonial records indicate that he had at least four wives through his life. Boorong was his last. There were two others during Phillip's time in Sydney, Kurubarabula and Barangaroo, and one who'd died before Bennelong ever met the colonists, never to leave a name in European records.

The settler identification of Boorong as Bennelong's last wife is relatively recent, pieced together by scholar Keith Smith after some ingenious sleuthing. By connecting remarks in some unrelated sources, he realised that the mother of Bennelong's surviving son was also the sister of Bidgee Bidgee, the old friend of Bennelong who frequented his grave in the 1820s. Bidgee Bidgee's only sister by the 1800s was Boorong (whom he was also doubtless visiting when he made those trips to the burial site).¹⁴

Boorong was from the Burramattagal clan, a group adjoining Bennelong's Wangal people. Her relationship with Bennelong exemplified the Yiyura custom against marrying within clans. In this period, Yiyura society had much stricter rules against endogamy than did British society, which still often condoned marriage between first cousins. The relationship also exemplified the tendency among the Yiyura to strengthen bonds between certain clans through marriage. Before the arrival of the colonists, Boorong's Burramattagal people had often combined with Bennelong's Wangal – they both lived along the shores of the same huge river, both shared a fishing-based economy, and both nursed a cautious antipathy to the more eastern-lying clans.¹⁵

Boorong was around twelve years younger than Bennelong, which was the same age difference as between Isabella and Phillip. Unlike the Phillips, though, Bennelong and Boorong had known each other since they were youths, and probably since Boorong's birth. The colonial sources reveal that Boorong was friendly with all three of Bennelong's sisters and that one of them, Worogan, ended up marrying a brother of hers, Yeranabe.¹⁶ By the time Bennelong and Boorong partnered in the late 1790s, their families and fates had long been intertwined.

We don't know how Bennelong and Boorong got on with one another, though there would perhaps have been few surprises between them after such entangled histories. Bennelong would have known that Boorong's name meant 'star', and that she possibly had a gift for prophesying events via the stars. One evening she had tried to warn the colonists of impending problems after witnessing a certain shooting star.¹⁷ Bennelong would also have known that Boorong had a particularly loving nature. He'd been present at several of the recorded moments when she showed affection for her first husband, the Gammeraygal man Garradah (who died after they'd been married three years); for her oldest brother Baludarri, who died when she was young; and for her father, the renowned Elder Maugoran.[18] Boorong, in turn, would have known all about Bennelong's struggles to forge a détente with the colonists in those initial years of the invasion. And she'd have known especially about his deep passion for his main former wife, Barangaroo. In the early 1790s, when still only a teenager, Boorong had been a constant witness of that two-year marriage.[19]

Like the colonists, Boorong had seen some of Bennelong's more volatile interactions with Barangaroo (who, like Charlott, was older than her husband). Several times he was said to have slapped Barangaroo on the face or cut her about the head.[20] Barangaroo, though, often hit Bennelong back and successfully forbade many of his ambitions when it came to accompanying colonists on excursions.[21] She solicited great adoration from him too. There are numerous accounts of the pair laughing and teasing each other, and of Bennelong caring for her through illness, childbirth and an untimely death.[22]

The deeper meanings of Yiyura gender norms in the eighteenth century may be one of those things that remains irrecoverable to non-Yiyura readers. Inga Clendinnen once wisely noted that, given their equal opacity and durability, 'I think we have to assume a compelling, shared understanding of a network of rights, liberties and infringements [that is today] simply invisible to us.'[23] It bears remembering, of course, that some aspects of eighteenth-century British gender norms also now seem impenetrable. The automatic loss of all of Isabella Phillip's wealth to her husband upon marriage, for instance, is inconceivable to modern Britons – and possibly to the Yiyura of any period.

Bennelong and Boorong might also have had a stormy relationship. On the other hand, eight years after his marriage to

Barangaroo, Bennelong was probably a different kind of husband. In the intervening years he'd led his people to a fragile peace with unprecedented newcomers, become the first Aboriginal person to travel around the world, lost one wife to a rival, buried another, and mourned the death of an infant daughter. Events had come at him fast. They may also have mellowed him. So, too, Boorong's softer nature no doubt produced a different dynamic.

Like Phillip's marriages, Bennelong's offer glimpses into some of the key elements of his society. They suggest that, as in Britain, the Yiyura afforded significant privileges to men, but also that comparatively it was less gendered overall. There were evident rules about who could marry whom, who could wield violence, and who did the caring, but these were governed less by gender than by clan, seniority or personal disposition. Most of all, Bennelong's two main marriages, when considered from Boorong's perspective, show how the question of public versus private, so pertinent for Phillip, was essentially irrelevant for Bennelong. All his endeavours – with kin or with others – included his wives in ways that Phillip's did not. Bennelong never had to juggle domesticity and work because each was part of the other: maintaining marriage customs was a central aspect of preserving culture, rather than any kind of obstacle. For too long historians have overlooked how Bennelong's embrace of his Yiyura marriages for his entire adult life was a sign of his continued commitment to his own society.

Next of kin

Perhaps unsurprisingly, given the conditions of his two marriages, Phillip had no children by either wife. His will, however, names more than twenty individuals as legatees upon his death. After seventy-five years of life, which included a globe-spanning career and a rather complex origin story, Phillip had evidently accrued a dense network of family, friends, patrons and dependants. Tracing just a few of those mentioned in his will indicates something of Phillip's professional debts. It also shows how kinship worked within the British empire, and how the wealth gained from imperial expansion was consolidated back home.

Phillip's estate at probate in 1814 was estimated at around £25,000, which equates to around £2–3 million today.[24] This placed Phillip firmly in the narrow band of the upper-middle class at the time of his death, but very far off the £100,000-plus estates left by typical aristocrats.[25] Isabella, naturally, obtained the lion's share: a comfortable annuity for the remainder of her life and their Bath residence, along with most of the home's contents. The only contents that were to be disposed of on Phillip's death were 'my drawings made in New South Wales which I direct to be sold by my ex[ecut]ors immediately after my decease'.

Why Phillip should have singled out these items is mysterious. There's no evidence that he had lined up a buyer for his memorabilia. Nor is there evidence that they were objects particularly distressing to his widow. The drawings were sold at an estate auction eleven months later, though their whereabouts are now vague.[26] What stands out as most intriguing is that Phillip did not see his effects from New South Wales as being of value to his survivors. Cash and goods obtained from his other sorties around the world were deemed the important legacies.

The first important legacy mentioned in his will was what Phillip called 'my brazil diamond', left to him by the late aristocratic Charles Duncombe. Upon Isabella's death, it was to be given to the descendants of Sir Evan Nepean. The history of the Brazil diamond is as murky as the precise nature of Phillip's relationships with Duncombe and Nepean. But the sources that survive open up the world of commerce and favours upon which Britain's empire relied and grew. Biographer Michael Pembroke speculates that Phillip first acquired the diamond in the 1770s when he was seconded to the Portuguese navy.²⁷ One of his duties had been to help transport a cargo of diamonds from the Portuguese colony of Brazil, for which a single diamond may have been a perquisite. Phillip appears to have given this diamond to Duncombe, who later gifted it back to him in his own will of 1803.²⁸ Phillip's connection to the Duncombe family could have dated to his marriage to Charlott; their estates were close by one another. After his marital separation, when Phillip was virtually penniless, he spent some unspecified time in Flanders, where the Duncombes had business interests and from which Phillip emerged much wealthier.²⁹ Another possibility is that Duncombe acquired the diamond independently and gave it to Phillip as some form of payment. Either way, it stands here for the commercial trade that always shadowed Britain's eighteenth-century naval history.

Nepean was a closer connection. He probably met Phillip around 1780 when both men served as naval officers during the American Revolution. Two years later, Nepean became under-secretary of Home Affairs, responsible not only for naval intelligence but also, eventually, the planning of the penal colony at New South Wales. Nepean recruited Phillip first as a spy in France and then as the first governor of the Australian settlement. While both appointments served Nepean well, they grew out of personal friendships rather than open applications.³⁰ Phillip's reward to the Nepean family of the jewel he'd acquired through trade turned the legacy into a symbol of imperial patronage.

The next goods itemised in Phillip's will were numerous pieces of expensive silverware, presumably purchased with his sizeable earnings from his various imperial services. These he left to Isabella's nephew. After that, there were multiple bequests of cash, ranging from £10 to £2,000. The legatees included many people whom Phillip named as cousins, seemingly all from his mother's clan. The biggest cash bequest was to John Lane, a long-time banker friend who had known Phillip since he'd married one of Phillip's relatives, Eleanor Everitt, in the 1770s. Eleanor was the daughter of naval captain Michael Everitt, who had appointed a teenaged Phillip to his first naval position. Everitt continued to play a strong paternal role for Phillip for the rest of his life. He was Phillip's mother's cousin through marriage, which made him only distantly related, but his continued influence offers at least two pertinent insights.[31] One, it suggests that Phillip's actual father was absent from an early age; and two, it shows how naval advancement often worked through family connections.

Phillip's service to the British empire for over forty years earned him a satisfactory share of the spectacular profits that this empire gathered from every corner of the world. Upon death, that share did not die with him, but went on to enrich the lives of his own contacts in Britain, further amalgamating the wealth that had come from elsewhere into one small region on earth. So, too, Phillip's will reveals how positions within the empire, from humble cabin boy to trading go-between to spy to governor, depended more on associations than merit. They privileged insider knowledge and bloodlines over any transparent ability.

With very different attitudes to the accretion of material wealth, Bennelong's survivors likely buried his most valued belongings with him. Modern archaeologists have often found what they call 'burial goods' in Yiyura graves.[32] This is not the case with the graves of all Aboriginal groups, and scholars disagree as to what it says about the beliefs of a society that practises this custom. But many have argued that groups which bury personal valuables with a deceased person are exercising a form of social equalisation. The goal is to prevent the uneven build-up of wealth, and thereby power, in select pockets.[33]

Ironically, the identification of the social inequalities produced by familial inheritance was becoming a major philosophical concern for Europeans at exactly this time. Jean-Jacques Rousseau's *Discourses of Inequality* had centred on the issue in the mid-1700s, and was finding popular traction in Europe from the late 1700s.[34] This is also when Europe's own division between rich and poor was stretching wider due to the wealth now pouring in from imperial endeavours and pooling in particular circles. The dispersal of Phillip's imperial wealth among his network exemplified Rousseau's problem with the issue. Bennelong's survivors, on the other hand, were possibly enacting one solution to it.

If Bennelong did not bequeath many noteworthy goods, he did, unlike Phillip, leave behind at least one offspring. This was Digidigi, commonly called Dicky in the colonial records: 'the son of Bennelong, of notorious memory', so said the *Sydney Gazette*.[35] Digidigi was the son of Bennelong and Boorong. He survived his parents by less than a decade.[36]

When Digidigi died in 1823, aged just twenty, he had lived quite a different life to his father, even aside from its distressing shortness. For one thing, he was baptised as a Christian. For another, he had spent five years in a colonial residential school for Aboriginal children, learning how to read and write in the colonisers' language.

But Digidigi's was not, for all that, a story of total assimilation. Just before he died he married a Darug-speaking woman called Maria, indicating a commitment to Aboriginal continuation that had been undertaken by his Ancestors for millennia. Even more telling, he appeared to be a vocal advocate for Aboriginal people. 'He ever seemed greatly interested in the present unenviable condition of his hapless race,' claimed his *Sydney Gazette* obituary, 'and often fervently prayed that their case should never be allowed to droop.'[37] It is not clear what precise case Digidigi invested in – their case to stay where they were? to benefit also from colonial literacy? to be allowed to survive? – but a sense of connectedness to his own people over his would-be assimilators stayed with him until the end.

Before his marriage, Digidigi lodged with the freshly arrived Wesleyan missionary to the colony, William Walker. It was Walker who baptised Digidigi and in the process gave him a new name, Thomas Walker Coke – after both himself and the founder of the Wesleyan mission, Thomas Coke. Around this time, Walker accompanied the clergyman whose visit to Bennelong's survivors with his portrait had been so emotional. Walker was said to have found the scene 'so affecting' that he started to weep with them.[38] Whether this was his spur to locate Bennelong's son or whether it came about because Walker already knew Digidigi by then is unknown. What it says about Digidigi is that he had tender kin around him through his life, even if he didn't reside with them and even if he journeyed along a different path.

Digidigi had met his wife Maria when they were students at the same residential school.[39] This was the Native Institution at Parramatta, the first such facility in the colony, designed, so the British officials said, to 'effect the civilization of the Aborigines [and] render their habits more domesticated and industrious'.[40] The school was not just for orphans like Digidigi; in the beginning, several Aboriginal parents sent their children to it for a range of reasons. Maria's father, an important leader called Yarramundi, was alive when he enrolled her. He perhaps decided, as Bennelong had so many years before, that understanding colonial power was sometimes more beneficial than outright defiance. All the same, Digidigi, unlike Maria, was an orphan when he entered the institution at the age of thirteen in 1816. Bennelong and Boorong had died a few years before. His aunts and uncles evidently believed, for better or for worse, that their nephew should take this novel course.[41]

Digidigi was nine years old when his father died. He may not have known at that age the full story of Bennelong's achievements, but growing up he would have seen him serve as a leader among his own group and also attract admiration from other Yiyura. That admiration was most evident in the size and vehemence of the battle waged in Bennelong's honour after his death. Like every Yiyura child, Digidigi would have been familiar with these ritualised battles. Death among the eighteenth-century Yiyura, as scholar Val Attenbrow puts it, 'was rarely considered a natural event'.[42] Instead, it was seen as a transgression against nature, a crime to be remedied through corporal punishment. The kin of the deceased fought proclaimed enemies, who were sometimes revealed through supernatural means like dreams, but more often by the secular record of mutual hatreds. Yawuru historian Shino Konishi explains that while these battles could be violent, they were also a form of closure. They entailed genuine risk but through their very ritual they helped to knit kin back together after the devastation wrought by loss. In this way, they 'contributed to maintaining social order'.[43]

Usually, a battle to avenge a death might involve around two dozen men, which would account for all the leaders of two average-sized clans.[44] The battle following Bennelong's death involved about two hundred men. This figure was estimated by an unnamed passing trader in April 1813, roughly three months after Bennelong died. The anonymous British observer witnessed the battle that took place 'in consequence of the death of the celebrated Bennelong'. He had heard a garbled explanation for it. 'On the death of any one,' he understood, 'the nearest relation is obliged to stand punishment for *permitting him to die*; he stands at a distance with a shield made of hard wood, and the rest throw spears with great dexterity at him, while he defends himself, till wounded, or perhaps killed, and there the affair ends.'[45] Records show that targets were rarely in fact direct relatives and they infrequently died themselves. On the other hand, many did notice the typical involvement of shields and spears.[46]

In the battle fought for Bennelong, the observer saw that 'the spears flew very thick, and about thirty men were wounded'. He spotted children 'running backwards and forwards, behind the hostile parties', and women shouting encouragement to the battlers. The huge numbers and energetic pageantry involved spoke to the deeply acknowledged significance of Bennelong at the end of his life, even if most British officials did not see it by then. Digidigi grew into manhood without a father, but always in the knowledge that his had been loved.

The hour of their deaths

Phillip's and Bennelong's deaths, like all their various endings, reveal significant differences between their worlds. More than the other finales, though, death affords a view into some of their similarities too. One of these similarities was 'a gut aversion', as the historian Thomas Laqueur puts it, 'to the bare, bereft dead body'.[47] An eighteenth-century compatriot of Phillip's explained this instinct with greater drama: 'the dead naturally tend to destroy the life of others; and that is really the reason men abhor the sight or the touch of the dead'.[48] The Yiyura of Bennelong's era certainly knew the feeling. 'None of the natives . . . would touch [a dead] body, or even go near it,' commented one colonial official in 1793: they say, 'the *Mawn* would come; that is literally *the spirit of the deceased would seize them*'.[49]

As a result, both Phillip and Bennelong were buried quickly after their deaths, and for each man certain rituals were enacted in order to restore the normality upended by death's intrusion. In Bennelong's case, we know already that restoration came in the form of a large revenge battle. Prior to the battle, there would have been specific practices that are today called sorry business – probably, in Bennelong's community, involving much vocal keening and some minor bloodletting.[50] Phillip's death was countered in a less demonstrative manner. Still, the custom of wearing sombre black dress for weeks and of refraining from smiling or laughing for a longer period were also ordeals borne by kin to mark and end the reign of death.[51]

In slightly more coincidental fashion, Phillip and Bennelong in death shared some other experiences. Both were likely to have been fully extended in their graves, Phillip in either formal clothes or a simple linen sheet, Bennelong covered in skins or, more probably, bark.[52] Both interments also likely followed a short procession. Phillip's cortège was modest, with only two vehicles to take mourners the two miles from his home to the grave. Some later Australians have lamented that Phillip was not given a grander send-off, preferably at the empire's premier burial lot in Westminster Abbey. His chosen grave site, however, accorded with that of many imperial leaders of his age, such as the colonial adviser Joseph Banks and the statesman Edmund Burke.[53] There are no records of Bennelong's cortège, but one that he himself led twenty years earlier involved a procession of mourners holding the corpse aloft on their heads. When they reached the grave spot, women and children were waiting, and a senior mourner then threw down two spears to indicate that the death would eventually be avenged.[54]

Of course, there were a few noticeable differences as well between the deaths of Phillip and Bennelong. Phillip was interred in a Christian church, even though he'd shown little interest in religion during his life. His grave was oriented eastwards, in keeping with ancient Christian beliefs that Christ's resurrection will occur from this horizon, and it was surrounded by many other graves. Eighteenth-century Britons preferred to bury their dead all together, either in old-fashioned church settings or, increasingly, in secular cemeteries.[55]

Bennelong, on the other hand, had lived in a significantly more animistic society, making him prospectively a more spiritual person than Phillip. Even so, or perhaps in consequence, he didn't need a special structure in which to commemorate his earthly relationship with the divine. Bennelong was buried near where he had recently lived, in open ground, where family could visit easily. Yiyura graves have been found oriented in all directions. Research with Indigenous communities suggests that orientation was linked to a person's individual totem, which was an emblem from nature awarded by an Elder and the means through which people accessed spiritual levels. Bennelong once told the colonist David Collins that his personal totem was a kind of 'large fish'. What this entailed for his burial, though, goes unrecorded. At the least, it appears that his grave was not part of a cluster. Very few Aboriginal clans grouped their dead together, preferring instead to keep them within the vicinity of living kin.[56]

We don't know the exact hours of the deaths of Phillip or Bennelong, but we do know the days. Phillip died on the last day of August 1814. Bennelong died on the third day of January 1813. Both appeared to be 'at home' when they passed. Phillip died in the house he'd bought eight years earlier in Bath. Bennelong died on Wallumedegal Country where he'd been living for seventeen years, a few miles north of his birthplace on Wangal Country.

Final years

Phillip spent the last decade of his life retired from public service, a situation dictated more by infirmity than desire. He lived for almost the whole of his retirement in fashionable Bath, which lay just over a hundred miles west of London. Phillip had no familial connection to Bath, though at least two of its main attractions had pulled him there earlier in life. These were its reputation for healthfulness and for naval sociability.

Phillip had suffered episodes of ill health since his teens, which were partly responsible for what others described as his 'little figure' and his 'shrivelled' face.[57] In his letter of resignation from the New South Wales governorship in 1796, he mentioned that this appointment had amounted to 'six years' care and anxiety'. It had not been helped by a serious spearing during that time, clean through his right shoulder. Phillip sought some respite, he said in the resignation letter, in the town of Bath, though he had 'given up all hopes' that its famed waters specifically would cure him.[58] The natural sulphurous springs that so many people came to immerse themselves in and drink from also drew large numbers of healers, therapists, and promoters of leisurely pastimes.[59] These might prove more useful to his recovery.

In addition, Phillip knew that many naval officers spent their home leave in Bath, a trend started perhaps by Horatio Nelson's first stint there in the 1780s. What had begun, though, as a short trip for health and conviviality turned into his retirement town because it was in Bath that Phillip met Isabella. She was living there as a carer for her father, Richard Whitehead, who was a similarly convalescing older gentleman.[60] Isabella's partiality for the town no doubt played a role in where the Phillips spent their last ten years.

Another well-known attraction of Bath at the beginning of the nineteenth century was its reputation for consumerism and the performing arts. By the time Phillip bought his Bath residence, the town was one of the ten largest in Britain. The other nine towns were either manufacturing centres or ports, reflecting the twin drivers of Britain's economy – industry and the navy.[61] Bath flourished from what that industrial and naval strength had produced: an explosion of luxury goods, disposable cash, and a new will to display personal status at balls, theatres and music rooms. Here, remarked one tourist in the 1810s, 'the shops are tastefully laid out; capacious and elegant . . . [The streets] afford to the utmost extent every thing towards supplying the real or imaginary wants of the visitors.'[62] Bath stood for the way in which imperial power elsewhere had created not only new markets back home, but also new hungers.

Whether Phillip himself hungered for the flashier aspects of Bath is not clear. Most of his adult life choices had pointed to a rather abstemious personality, not given to the trinkets, dances and concerts on offer in his retirement town. He seemed to place more value on professional titles, such as naval honours, than on stuff or high culture. Certainly he was proud to receive the series of maritime sinecures granted him after leaving the service, ending with Admiral of the Blue just three months before death.[63] At the same time, though, Phillip did collect through these years an assortment of fine wines, a carriage replete with horses, and all those many silver items noted in his will. Bath's consumerism may have worked its magic on him in the end, as it did with so many people freshly flush with funds.

Phillip's everyday life in retirement can be glimpsed in the diaries left by one of his frequent callers, Miss Fanny Chapman. She was the daughter of his close friend Henry Chapman. Fanny was in her early thirties when she described her many visits to the ageing Phillips. She wrote of their shared 'luncheons' and strolls to 'the Grove', her gifts of 'nosegays' to them, and their loan, in turn, of the fortnightly 'Bath paper' to her.[64] Fanny's delight in quotidian details recalls a far more famous former Bath resident, Jane Austen, who had lived near to the Phillips' address just a few years earlier. Fanny's sober activities with the Phillips conjures the character of Anne Elliot in Austen's *Persuasion*, who doted on a distinguished Admiral but never really thought that Bath 'agreed with her'. Fanny's activities without the Phillips, however – which included gossiping about duels, listening to music bands, and shopping for comforts – evokes more the character of Catherine Morland in Austen's *Northanger Abbey*, whose 'head runs too much upon Bath, [its] balls and plays'.[65]

Fanny witnessed Phillip struggle with his health throughout the year of 1808. He suffered a stroke in February and it took him many months to recover. During that period, Fanny remarked on his 'feeble' bearing, his many 'bleedings' as treatment, and even his voluble tears.[66] One of Phillip's closest naval protégés, Philip Gidley King, called on him that year too. King was appalled at Phillip's state. 'He is very much altered,' he wrote in a letter, 'having lost the entire use of his whole right side, arm, and leg . . . He may linger on some years . . . but from his age, a great reprieve cannot be expected.'[67] As it turned out, Phillip did get better; it was King who died within three months of his visit.

The Phillips' home in Bath was located at 19 Bennett Street, a couple of blocks from the town's architectural centrepiece, The Circus. Phillip bought the house in 1806 for £2,200: a substantial residence of five floors, including a basement kitchen and an attic with servants' quarters.[68]

Documents produced after Isabella's death reveal something of the home's contents: fine furniture, many books, a portrait of the master of the house.[69] Interestingly, very little of the contents related directly to New South Wales. Other than the drawings that Phillip wanted sold upon his death, the only other connections seemed to be a wooden cabinet made in Botany Bay and a landscape print of Sydney Cove.[70] The landscape print foregrounded an Aboriginal man and his family sitting around a fire. Perhaps it reminded Phillip of his one-time associate Bennelong? Then again, it was found wedged among discarded papers in an abandoned room at the top of the house, where new tenants came upon it accidentally more than seventy years after Phillip's death. Its survival may have been more a symbol of neglect than nostalgia.

Since Bennelong's society distinguished less between public and private life, it's harder to say that he ever had a European-like retirement. Nevertheless, colonial records suggest he participated in fewer observable activities from 1806 (coincidentally the same year that Phillip relinquished his formal roles). Bennelong spent the remainder of his years where he had lived ever since returning from England in 1795: on a portion of Wallumedegal Country known by the colonists as Kissing Point.

Why Bennelong should not have returned instead to his birth land of the Wangal, on the southern side of the river, encapsulates the story of colonial invasion into the Yiyura world thus far. On the outskirts of Sydney Harbour, well into the 1800s, Aboriginal life carried on in significant defiance of the 3500-plus newcomers. This continuity was symbolised, as historian Stephen Gapps notes, by the thousands of campfires that ringed the colony every evening.[71] But closer in to the Sydney Cove settlement in this era the effects of dispossession were starker. The five nearest clans – the Gadigal, the Gammeraygal, the Wallumedegal, the Wangal, and the Burramattagal – had experienced the most disorder over the preceding twenty years. Colonial bodies, violence, and pathogens had intruded on their sense of place, their understanding of boundaries, and their numbers. This did not mean that these five clans had vacated their Ancestral homes – Phillip's forgotten print of Sydney Cove illustrates the ongoing presence of Aboriginal people even in the midst of colonial edifices. But it did mean that these clans had begun the process of reweaving everyday practices of belonging with the threads of knowledge that still survived.

Reformation had occurred especially among the Wangal, the Burramattagal and the Wallumedegal – three clans that had historical links predating colonists through their shared custodianship of the region's central river.[72] One result was the creation of a new, clan-like community on a small spot of Wallumedegal Country. There is evidence that some Burramattagal people had sought refuge there from as early as 1790.[73] By the time Bennelong returned from Britain in late 1795, the community included some Wangal people like himself, too, and presumably some accommodating Wallumedegal. The diverse group became such an identifiable entity that even colonists recognised its existence, calling it the Kissing Point Tribe, after the peninsula where boat keels 'kissed' the river bottom. Outsiders saw that after one generation its members had developed so strong an attachment to the area that they appeared to be among those clans 'most bigoted . . . to the ground'.[74]

In the early 1800s, the convict farm manager Joseph Holt described Bennelong as the 'chief or king' of the Kissing Point Tribe, which he numbered at around 'a hundred of both males and females'.[75] As much as this group was a new conglomeration shaped by unprecedented times, it had certainly not taken up European roles like chief or king. Yiyura clans were typically headed by several Elders at a time. Holt's comment suggests rather that Bennelong, now over forty years of age, was among the leadership circle. As such, it seems he had been not only welcomed into the new community at Kissing Point, but was also looked up to as a guide, mentor, or special carrier of Law.

It's possible that the position Bennelong held was not in fact Elder, but instead something even less transparent to colonial observers. This was the role of Garadyigan, or healer, undertaken by people who also officiated at initiation and other ceremonies.[76] We know that Bennelong presided over several ceremonies in later life.[77] As well, Phillip's men had in earlier years often encountered him far away from Wangal Country, which might be evidence that Bennelong was a Garadyigan even as a young adult, since healers were permitted more rights than most people in entering or crossing the land of other clans.[78] Being a Garadyigan, whose healing powers were revered, would further explain why Bennelong was so readily accepted into the new grouping at Kissing Point.

Garadyigan or Elder, in these greying years, Bennelong still sometimes visited the colony at Sydney Cove. Significantly, though, this happened far less often than it once did. Bennelong lived to see four British governors succeed to Phillip's position. The last was

Lachlan Macquarie: he had succeeded William Bligh, who succeeded Philip Gidley King, who succeeded John Hunter. Bennelong called on all of them, at the same Government House that Phillip's men had built in 1788.

During Macquarie's tenure, legal official Ellis Bent noticed that Bennelong was among the many 'Natives ... in Town [who] paid ... visits'. In Bligh's time, the emancipated convict David Dickenson Mann remarked that Bennelong 'sometimes... holds intercourse with the colony'. The printer George Howe saw Bennelong visit King more regularly, adding that the governor clothed him and gave him dinner 'at the servant's table'. Bennelong knew Hunter, Phillip's immediate successor, the best and visited him the most often. Hunter's surgeon, John Washington Price, recorded that Bennelong lodged with the governor whenever at the cove.[79]

Despite his high connections, the vast majority of the colonial comments about Bennelong from this era were pejorative. Ellis Bent thought he always overstayed his welcome and that the Yiyura in general were unpleasant, with 'the appearance of being half famished'. Both Mann and Howe found Bennelong peculiarly resistant to 'improvement' and 'civilization'.

Price alone refrained from negativity, remarking that Bennelong seemed 'exceeding polite & agreeable'. Price's full comment, however, shows why he stood out from the other observers. Price had thought Bennelong 'polite & agreeable' because 'he speaks English tolerably well [and] admires the English customs'. When Bennelong was observed speaking his own language or exercising his own culture, colonists interpreted this as a rejection of themselves. Earlier, they might have tolerated the difference of Yiyura ways but now, after a decade or so of settlement, they expected Aboriginal people to be more like them. They especially expected Bennelong to be more like them. Mann, for example, had thought Bennelong unimprovable and uncivilisable because 'he prefers to taste of liberty among his native scenes'. Howe had felt the same because 'in spite of everything that could be done ... he fell off spontaneously into his early habits'.

Many other Europeans joined in the disparagement of Bennelong in this period. The missionary William Pascoe Crook was amazed to discover in 1805 that even though Bennelong had 'been quite civilized [and] in England' he later chose to be 'wandering stark naked in the bush living on worms insects &c'.[80] The sailor John Turnbull that same year was even more dumbstruck to learn how Bennelong had been lavished with prestigious introductions and 'every attention' but now had 'thrown away' them all. Turnbull went on to indulge his disgust for several pages. Bennelong 'was no sooner re-landed in his own country', he wrote, 'than he forgot, or at least laid aside, all the ornaments and improvements he had reaped from his travels, and returned as if with increased relish, to all his former loathsome and savage habits ... He is in truth a savage beyond all hopes of amelioration by any mode of culture.'[81]

The myth of Bennelong's deterioration began in these comments from the early nineteenth century. Such remarks were simply not common before 1800, but thereafter the myth flourished. At length, colonists added that Bennelong was a drunk and even that he was disliked by his own people. These accusations were powered by a strengthening assumption, backed by the colonists' accumulating years in New South Wales, that anyone who rejected British culture had to be universally rejected in turn. Critically, these slurs overrode the scattered observations by more marginal observers of Bennelong's evident leadership and beloved status among the Yiyura.

Final battles

Before being ensconced in their retirement communities, both Phillip and Bennelong were engaged in complex battles for their wider societies. In Phillip's case these were the many battles that Britain waged against the French Revolution. Parisians had first rebelled against their absolutist monarchy when Phillip was still governing New South Wales. The conservative British government back home had looked on with unease, not because they opposed the reforming of autocratic power, but because they feared popular means of doing so. As early as 1791, the British state gingerly backed other European monarchies who threatened to attack France in defence of their counterpart, Louis XVI. In 1793, when Louis XVI was decapitated for treason and a democratic republican government installed in his place, Britain officially joined the alliance to defeat the revolution. Apart from a short peace in 1802, Britain remained at war with France for the next twenty-two years.

Phillip's political persuasion was never explicitly stated but it seemed most aligned to the faction that elevated him to his greatest official appointments. This was the Pittite conservative faction which had dominated parliament since 1783. Prime Minister William Pitt called himself a Whig but ended his days canonised by what might be termed Modern Toryism.[82] Pitt served two periods as prime minister: both his governments continued the relentless imperial expansion begun by eighteenth-century Whigs but gradually abandoned the Whiggish commitment to increasing political liberties. This meant that during the French Revolution they combined the bellicose attitude and enlarged state powers of old Whigs with the royalism, xenophobia, and restrictions of traditional Tories.

Many times through these years, Phillip voiced his desire to serve the British empire in its quest to crush revolutionary forces. 'I hope,' he once wrote in a letter to Lord Sydney, 'that Europe will be rescued from what you so justly name an insulting captivity.' Phillip likened the democrats to a spider who 'when one web is destroyed, immediately begins another, until destroyed by their own work'.[83]

Phillip's chief desire was to join active naval service against the liberal spirit of French popular democracy. He reasoned, argued, and even on occasion begged with officials to grant him a command like he had enjoyed as a younger man.[84] In the end, what he got was seven years on land supervising naval impressment and the sea fencibles, after two years in formal home and trade defence. It was better than nothing.[85]

Naval impressment was a deeply controversial tool of the burgeoning British empire. Deployed since the late sixteenth century, it involved gangs of regulating captains who pressed unsuspecting men into compulsory naval service. It escalated in the eighteenth century when the navy trebled in order to cope with the greater number of wars and the protection of ever-increasing colonial assets. Technically, press gangs were meant to recruit only seafaring men below the age of fifty-five who were of legal repute. In reality, they often corralled prisoners, the infirm, and the totally inexperienced. Ordinary Britons loathed press gangs, believing them to contravene age-old claims that British subjects could never be enslaved. At the same time, though, British liberties were supposedly defended by the navy, which needed by the 1790s a force that was almost fifty per cent pressed.[86]

Phillip was an important inspector of impressment for the four years prior to his retirement in 1805. He travelled the length of the nation, from Scotland to Cornwall, to carry out his duties.[87] It was an awkward assignment for someone of his disposition. As a naval man above all other things, he would have preferred to ditch impressment and staff his beloved force with skilled and loyal volunteers like himself. But as someone who had experienced decades of the navy's inability to recruit enough men, he also sought to make pressing as efficient as possible. His reports to the Admiralty advised various ways to circumvent exemptions among the pressed, avoid corruption among the pressers, and increase the likelihood of acquiring people who had some knowledge of boats.[88]

Supervising the sea fencibles was a similarly tricky task. The sea fencibles were a non-military corps raised explicitly to defend the British coast from potential French Revolutionary invasions. It included fishermen, shipwrights, ferry captains, and any other essential maritime provider who could not be pressed into naval service. They were armed to act as an additional line of shore defence, and numbered at their peak some thirty thousand men.[89]

Phillip supervised all southern units of the sea fencibles for the three years prior to 1801. As with impressment, the sea fencibles posed a dilemma to a man like Phillip. If the men in the corps were any good, they should have been serving in the real navy; if they were no good, they were likely just wasting the navy's time and perhaps even obstructing the war effort.[90] Phillip's last official recommendation to the Admiralty, reflecting his methodical yet patriotic approach in all things, was to merge formally the oversight of impressment with that of the sea fencibles. This, he argued, would simultaneously broaden the pool for recruitment and give the state greater power to punish shirkers.[91]

Phillip's supervisory years were recompense – inadequate, he always felt – for being denied naval commands after 1798. His dismissal from his last active post that year had burned acutely. Phillip described it in a letter to the Admiralty Secretary as 'mortifying', especially after 'having served so many years, & I trust in a manner that has never given a shadow of reason for censure'.[92] The decision to dismiss him does seem to have resulted from miscommunication – the under-secretary was surprised to hear of it – but notably it was never rectified. The Admiralty wanted younger men in charge during such high-stakes conflict as revolutionary repression.[93]

Phillip received his discharge orders while commanding a ship in allied Portuguese waters. He had been stationed there for nearly a year. Initially he'd been part of Horatio Nelson's dramatic blockade of Spanish revolutionary sympathisers in 1797, but after six months and without explanation, he was transferred to a less seaworthy vessel that required extensive repairs in Lisbon. While others around him set off to secure further victories against liberal spread, Phillip was left preparing for a Spanish counterattack that never came.[94]

His active service the previous year had been no less deflating. Most of it was spent in charge of vessels patrolling southern home shores.[95] Throughout the entire decade preceding his retirement, Phillip asked for more or harder commands than he was given. When the war looked like it might expand to South America he offered the Admiralty copies of his personal charts of the region. When it spilled into the Caribbean he reminded them that he knew that area too. Even when in charge of the sea fencibles he proposed turning a fleet into ad hoc units of the navy proper, a request that was admonished in no uncertain terms for trying to usurp naval authority, and for which he was reminded 'to confine himself solely to . . . his Instructions'.[96]

Phillip's last official endeavours on behalf of an empire he'd served for forty years were, then, tinged with disappointment. His idea of a just reward for such service was to be given more chances to serve. Instead he was eased out in favour of a new generation. The pleasures of retirement with Isabella and friends were never going to match the satisfaction, as he once put it, of doing 'great [and] essential . . . service to this Country'.[97]

During the years that Phillip was involved in British efforts to fight the French Revolution, Bennelong was also taking part in battles. These were not, though, conflicts aimed at the suppression of unprecedented ideas, but rather sought to maintain a balance of power between long-standing neighbours. Local Indigenous battles could have numerous causes. In addition to avenging the unnatural crime of death, they were also fought to redress adultery, murder, disrespect and other violations. Their enactment not only maintained stability, but also, literally, realised Aboriginal Law.[98]

The processes of charging, judging and sentencing were often puzzling to outsiders, but they seemed clear enough to the Yiyura. Early colonists saw that most parties readily accepted their punishment. One offender, for example, understood that he was allowed a single bark shield to withstand the flying spears, but must not display 'too much defensive skill'. Later, the offender submitted to having one arm pinned behind him 'without making any resistance'. The observing colonist in this scenario, the officer David Collins, was baffled: 'What rendered this sort of contest as unaccountable as it was extraordinary was that friendship and alliance were known to subsist between several that were opposed to each other.' The Yiyura appeared to fight 'with all the ardour of the bitterest enemies', but when it was over they could pronounce their opponents 'to be good and brave, and their friends'.[99]

Bennelong was seen both exacting and suffering these punishments, with a similar acceptance in each. His last known battle occurred in January 1806, punishment for a murder committed by a Gweagal man from the Kamay (Botany Bay) region. It's unclear what relationship Bennelong had to the other punishers, who included Kamaygal and Gadigal warriors – not his normal allies. The *Sydney Gazette* reported that this conflict 'nearly proved fatal to Bennelong'. Narrowly escaping a direct spearing from one Gweagal warrior, he was then ambushed by four – two in front and two behind. Those in front 'obliged him to stand, and he had scarcely warded off their spears, when turning with surprising agility, he [stopped] those also of the two hindmost'. The *Gazette* reported that Bennelong's survival in this contest 'with [only] a single wound was a matter of astonishment to all present'.[100]

Just two months earlier Bennelong had been the one facing punishment. It's less obvious this time what the crime had been, but again the foes were Gweagal. The contest occurred at a place known as the Brickfields, a favoured site believed to be today's Hyde Park. Bennelong 'withstood numerous flights of spears with his accustomed *sang froid*', reported the *Gazette*, 'but narrowly escaped [death], as seldom less than three spears were thrown at once, and most of his adversaries [were] peculiarly skilled in the deadly sciences'.[101]

The *Gazette* identified Bennelong in local battles three more times in 1805 – twice as an avenger, once as an offender.[102] Always, the newspaper reported these incidents with a mixed tone of titillation and fascination.

If the colonial press didn't outright censure local battles, why, we might ask, didn't they read Bennelong's involvement in them as evidence of his integration in Yiyura society? The answer lies in the same rationale that lay behind the colonists' darkening views of Bennelong himself. Now into their second decade of settlement, the colonists were becoming more confident of their presence in New South Wales, and, equally, less interested in those who still obstructed it. Most colonists had initially accepted inter-Indigenous fighting as part of a legitimate if obscure justice system that ran parallel to theirs.[103] Even by 1803, however, the *Gazette* was remarking that these same contests were not so much legal instruments as proof of the Yiyura's 'unconquerable attachment to . . . barbarous usages'.[104] Soon afterwards, the colony's governor forbade their practice, decreeing them 'repugnant to British laws'.[105]

Colonists saw Bennelong partake in local actions, then, just as their attitudes towards them were changing. They were becoming less likely to read Bennelong's participation in ritual battles as an exercise in law. Instead, they were more inclined to view it as mere scrapping.

Further entrenching this colonial perception was Bennelong's apparently mysterious refusal to engage in any battles against the colonists themselves. This was not due to a lack of conflict between the Yiyura and the British: Gapps suggests that settler–Indigenous violence occurred pretty much yearly during this period.[106] (The delicate détente that Bennelong had helped to forge with Phillip was long gone by the late 1790s.) During his senior years, though, Bennelong avoided direct combat with the colonists.

This stance was quite unlike, for example, that of his compatriot the Bidjigal man Pemulwuy, who organised surprise raids on the British for nearly a decade. The British of course loathed Pemulwuy for his armed defiance, yet they could at least understand him. Pemulwuy became their antihero while Bennelong, off-stage and focused elsewhere, became an object of scorn. Later revisionist historians incorporated more colonial assumptions than they knew when they flipped Pemulwuy from antihero to hero but maintained Bennelong as a man without purpose.[107]

The fact that Bennelong eschewed what Gapps calls 'the Sydney Wars' speaks to a hugely important but under-recognised shift in his thinking at this time. Earlier, he had worked hard to excel as a negotiator with the newcomers, believing this to be the most effective strategy for his cherished wider interests. It is now his best-remembered role. But nearly ten years on, Bennelong turned further and further away from this position. Colonists read that turning as proof of a peculiarly resistant savagery. Later commentators reached for the tropes of tragedy to explain it. But all along it was a deliberate reorientation on Bennelong's part to achieve the same ends he'd always sought: the preservation of Yiyura customs in the face of massive disruption. How exactly he came to this decision is explored in the following chapter.

It is enough here to observe that by 1798 Bennelong's mind seemed to be made up. His performance in a battle fought between the Kamaygal and the Gadigal that year illustrated the extent of his embrace of Yiyura ways, as well as the degree to which this was encouraged by other Yiyura people. This battle was also fought at the Brickfields, a Kamaygal punishment for a crime committed by the Gadigal man Colebee. Bennelong took part as an ally of Colebee, his long-time associate. An American voyager witnessed the noonday combat, which involved the usual flurry of spears and defensive moves. 'At length,' the American wrote, a spear pierced Bennelong in the side and came out 'at his Belly'.

What most struck the American outsider, but perhaps bypassed the resident colonists altogether, was the depth of the emotions that Bennelong's injury provoked. The women from all the different clans watching from the sidelines started 'howling' in horror. They beat themselves in distress. Friends flocked to Bennelong to extract the spear, and onlookers rushed to kneel beside him to begin 'sucking the blood from his wound'.[108] This fighter was no outcast soul, damned for his past doings, suspicious in his motives, or untrusted as a future leader. He was instead highly valued, much admired and sorely needed. Bennelong's contributions, the participants knew that day, were part of what held Yiyura life together.

As with Phillip, Bennelong understood himself primarily as a servant of his community. For Phillip, this community was the whole insurgent British empire rather than any one single colony. For Bennelong, it was the intersecting and ancient world of Yiyura clans, who faced harsh trials with the British invasion but never total collapse. These long underplayed or neglected endings, placed at the start of our story, offer keys to unlock the meaning of what came before.

The various endings of Phillip and Bennelong also illuminate the men's most abiding characteristics. Measured by his marriages, Phillip emerges as a rather aloof and cerebral figure, uncomfortable with domesticity and showing some workaholic tendencies. His last legacies and activities confirm his devotion to public service, his reliance on patronage to perform it, his relatively reactionary outlook, and his overall rationalist attitude. Conversely, from the perspective of Bennelong's wives, we discern in Bennelong a man with a richer and more integrated family life. His last years reveal a person thoroughly enmeshed in old kin networks, committed to keeping the Yiyura intact by whatever means necessary.

JOURNEYS

At Home and Abroad, 1796–1794

Two letters written in 1796 • Bennelong's first year back home after England • Phillip reflects on his governorship • Bennelong's voyage home • Phillip's much earlier travels in Brazil • Both men together during the summer of 1794

In the last week of August 1796 Bennelong dictated from Yiyura Country a letter to Phillip in London. He had been back from England for just under a year. The letter was written down by a scribe of the new colonial governor, John Hunter. Bennelong's English was excellent by this time, so it likely represented his direct words.

'Sir, I am very well,' the letter began. 'I hope you are very well. I live at the governor's. I have every day dinner there.' It went on to relate that his most recent wife, Kurubarabula, had left him during his three-year absence in England, but that all his other friends were thriving. He sent his best wishes to Isabella Phillip, mentioning her care of him when he was sick. He similarly asked Phillip to 'give my duty' to the man whom he understood to be Phillip's boss, Lord Sydney. He requested that Phillip send him a few items: 'two pair of stockings . . . some handkerchiefs for pocket [and] some shoes'. He hoped all of Phillip's family was healthy, then he closed the letter with his name, 'Bannelong'.[1]

Today, this letter holds great significance for many Aboriginal people. Wuthathi man John Paul Janke celebrates it 'as the first [published] use of English by an Aboriginal author'. Tahjee Moar – a Meriam, Barkindji, and Malyangapa woman – likewise values the way it shows Bennelong 'as an author rather than a subject of the colonial gaze'.² The letter also has bearing on the history of Phillip. Since the copier of the original (which sadly no longer exists) scrawled at the top that it was written to 'Mr Phillips Lord Sydney's steward', scholars had long thought it was meant for someone other than Arthur Phillip. They searched fruitlessly for some minion of the former Home Affairs Minister called Phillips whose wife might have looked after Bennelong. However, given the number of times Arthur Phillip's name was written as Phillips by reporters, officials, and even his good friends during his lifetime, it seems clear that the copier made a spelling mistake. The reference to 'Mrs Phillip' later in the letter gets the name right, and moreover the word 'steward', meaning a person who supervises or manages something public on behalf of another, describes perfectly how Bennelong viewed Phillip's occupation. The letter was meant for Phillip.³

The text reveals several important details about Bennelong at this point. First, that upon immediate homecoming he resumed the practice he'd started with Phillip, which was to reside occasionally in Government House. This had been a fundamental aspect of Bennelong's role as mediator for the Yiyura. That he left Hunter's Government House permanently soon after dictating the letter, however, signals he was now on the verge of his momentous change in strategy.

Second, the letter shows that Bennelong had learned from the British many specific customs and routines. Bennelong's multiple references to Phillip's wife as 'Madam' and his deliberate directive to send a polite representation to Phillip's former boss reflect detailed attention to particular imperial social practices. Bennelong understood deeply the culture he was about to forsake.

Third, it suggests a subtle understanding of how much the British valued such items as clothing and footwear. Most observers record that Bennelong shunned these things himself, even when they were available; he rarely wore much European apparel after 1796. His request for them in this letter was not, then, an expression of his own material wants. Instead, it was likely a further display of Bennelong's deep comprehension of British mores: he knew that the British enjoyed their consumables inordinately and he sought to demonstrate the extent of his knowledge. The scholar Penny van Toorn has argued that Bennelong requested these things in exchange for the friendship, data and even land that Phillip had taken from him. But if this was the case, surely he would have asked for something he also valued.[4] It seems rather that Bennelong was confirming in the letter his expertise in British culture.

Fourth, the letter's closing signals the name Bennelong preferred for himself by 1796. Some years earlier, he had told the colonists he had several names, recorded as various versions of Bennelong, Wollarawarre, Boinba, Bunde-bunda and Wogletrowey.[5] At least three colonists had heard him say he favoured the name Wollarawarre. All, however, called him a variation of Bennelong, probably because they heard other Yiyura use it the most. Whether from conformity or desire, Bennelong also decided on this usage in the end. Notably, Bennelong did not sign the letter 'durung', one of the terms he had offered to Phillip during their early negotiations. Durung means son-figure, the counterpart to the term biyanga, or father-figure, which Bennelong had in turn used for Phillip. By now Bennelong saw that the colonists misunderstood these titles. They had been intended to formalise the relationship between Bennelong and Phillip in a way that also respected their age difference. They were not intended to signify a supplicant or childish position for Bennelong.[6] After learning more about British thinking, Bennelong decided it was wiser to stick to stable rather than relational names.

Given what we now know about Bennelong's later life, the most essential part of the letter is its middle line: 'Not me go to England no more. I am at home now.' This line ensured that Bennelong's familiarity with British customs in the letter would not be mistaken for longing. Read in the light of his behaviour after this time, Bennelong was, rather, revealing his progression to some reconfigured thinking. After 1796, Bennelong evidently believed that the best way to protect his world was to be solely Yiyura-focused, rather than to engage seriously any longer with the colonists.

In the year following his voyage home from Britain, Bennelong undertook several other momentous journeys. Some were literal, others were more emotional or political. He went to Norfolk Island and back, travelled between Hunter's Government House and Kissing Point several times, and vacillated over which approach he should now take with the colony. The year before had been similarly dynamic. He'd journeyed to and from the global city of Rio de Janeiro, to and from multiple British port-towns, and to and from elation and despair in his heart.

Collectively, these journeys reflect the back-and-forth that Bennelong travelled in his mind in order to arrive, finally, at his decision to look only towards his own.

In the same fortnight that Bennelong dictated his now-famous communiqué, Phillip was also in letter-writing mode. As a long-serving official of an extremely text-driven empire, however, this was not so unusual. The note he now sent was written in London, and addressed to the naturalist Sir Joseph Banks, then living in the same city.

A quarter of a century earlier, Banks had made his name as a key personality of Cook's first voyage to the Pacific. Banks was an early advocate for a British settlement in New South Wales and remained an influential adviser to the government on its running.

'My Dear Sir,' Phillip's note began. 'While at Plymouth I received several letters from N.S. Wales, where I understand they go on as they have done for some time past.'[7] Phillip had been in Plymouth in the lead-up to his reactivated naval service. What he understood of colonial officials 'going on' in New South Wales was that they had been in the same mode since he'd left four years before, and none of it sounded good.

Chiefly, Phillip was concerned that those in charge were 'making fortunes at the expense of the Crown' instead of 'labouring for the public'. These comments summarised his attitude to colonial governance in general, an opinion that did not seem to alter over time. He raised this now with Banks, he explained, not to plead for an overhaul of all who currently led the New South Wales colony, but to point out that the only person reliably continuing in the correct manner was his old protégé Philip Gidley King.

At the time, King was Lieutenant-Governor of Norfolk Island, an auxiliary settlement of New South Wales situated some thousand miles northeast off its coast. Phillip was keen for King to be paid his due salary – £450 a year in addition to his naval half-pay – which was as yet undelivered. 'Can you, my Dear Sir, render him any service?' Phillip queried. He sent along King's own petition, which Phillip conceded was inadequate. 'He writes badly, but he is an honest man, who is faithfully discharging the trust reposed in him.'

Two intriguing points emerge from Phillip's note. The first is its postscript, where Phillip advised of a possible interruption to his usual practice of sending Banks the botanic specimens still arriving from the colony. Soon to be on active service against revolutionary France, he recommended that Banks send a letter with any directives on the matter to Mrs Phillip at their temporary address in Bath.

Banks famously collected specimens for the Royal Botanic Gardens, Kew from around the world, and especially from New South Wales. In later histories, his collecting mania and the scientific advancement it offered has featured as a kind of counterpoint to imperial devastation. In Banks's own time, however, as Banks would have been the first to affirm, scientific investigations were inextricably bound with imperial growth. Increased knowledge led to the empire's relentless expansion, and the empire's relentless expansion led to increased knowledge. Banks was a fan of both endeavours and understood their correlation. As Phillip had earlier experienced, Banks's hunger for greater knowledge and empire did not always stop at botany or at Sydney Cove. As we shall see, Banks's requests sometimes verged on the macabre.

The other, and perhaps greater, insight from Phillip's letter lies in what followed it, or rather what didn't follow. King eventually received his outstanding earnings, for which he acknowledged Phillip's efforts.[8] What did not ensue were further exertions on Phillip's part regarding other New South Wales matters. Certainly, this note was his last correspondence with Banks. The connections he maintained from his time in New South Wales were personal: King until his death; John Hunter, his successor; and Henry Waterhouse, his loyal assistant. He also kept tabs on young William Chapman, who became an official in the colony, because he was the son of his old family friend Henry Chapman. And there is a rumour that in 1811 Phillip recommended leniency for the convict-architect Francis Greenway after a chance meeting, but this has never been proved and seems an uncharacteristically indulgent move for Phillip.[9]

No letters exist after 1796 between Phillip and the British government on the running of New South Wales. This is not to suggest that Phillip no longer cared about empire's progress; arguably, he cared for nothing more deeply for the remainder of his life. But it does intimate that New South Wales did not remain at the centre of his concern. Instead of a founding father of one colony, Phillip understood himself far more as a representative of a world-stretching superpower that spawned many interconnected colonies.

Like Bennelong, Phillip undertook various literal and metaphorical journeys in the two years leading up to 1796. Unexpectedly, though, we know less about his doings in this phase than we do about Bennelong's. The peculiarities of colonial archives mean that a non-writing Indigenous person occasionally emerges more clearly than a Great White Male. In this instance, the vagaries are compounded by what look to be sustained ill health, and thus quietude, for Phillip. His resignation from the governorship had noted that he suffered from a 'complaint [that] may in time require assistance which cannot be found in a distant part of the world'.[10]

From the scatterings of his correspondence through this period, it seems that Phillip and Isabella journeyed frequently between London and Bath. Newly married, they were perhaps trying out which option suited them best. His writings included a few final missives about New South Wales, written against a backdrop of the developing French Revolution, as well as some ongoing petitions to be allowed back into the navy just when Britain appeared to be once more muscling up to protect its world supremacy.

Bennelong's first year back

In April 1796, after eight months in Yiyura Country, Bennelong was on another British ship on another exploratory mission. This vessel was not traversing the earth but sailing instead to the tiny colonial satellite of Norfolk Island. The Norfolk settlement, situated on otherwise uninhabited and rich volcanic soil, had been created on Phillip's orders as a potential resource base. Bennelong knew the British leader there, Phillip's dear friend Philip Gidley King, very well.

He had in fact almost voyaged with King to Norfolk five years earlier. Back then, Bennelong had been enticed by the reminiscences of another Aboriginal person – a boy called Bondel – who'd visited the island in 1791. Bondel boasted of excellent hunting on Norfolk as well as great opportunities to learn more of the colonists' language and ways. Bennelong was eager to experience those things himself, but personal circumstances thwarted his plans.[11]

Now, these many years later, Bennelong took his second chance to go to Norfolk. King recorded that he stayed on the island for five days between 3 and 8 April 1796.[12] This seems a remarkably brief stopover considering the ten or eleven days of sailing it took each way. Bennelong's motives for the visit had evidently changed in the interim. He may still have been keen to enjoy the hunting but he no longer needed to improve his English or his understanding of colonial culture. Instead, the trip was likely a circuit-breaker; the previous several months had been wearying to say the least, and he needed some time out from domestic and diplomatic troubles.

The most recent trouble was an altercation with one of his oldest associates, the Gadigal man Colebee. Bennelong and Colebee had been through a lot together. It was Colebee who shared Bennelong's first, unhappy encounter with the British in 1789. While Bennelong had decided to stay with the colonists to learn their ways and ambitions, Colebee quickly escaped. Through it all, the two men – from not always easily allied clans – had respected each other's choice.

Doubtless if he'd been in Bennelong's position Colebee would have declined Phillip's invitation to travel to Britain – or Berewal as the Yiyura called it.[13] He had always been more suspicious of British motives. What Colebee saw in Bennelong's conduct after his immediate return from Berewal confirmed this view. Bennelong might have explained his behaviour in this period as that of someone undergoing complicated readjustment. Colebee, though, only registered erratic nonsense. In this in-between time, it was no longer clear to him what plan Bennelong was enacting with the British. As we will see, sometimes he seemed to be continuing his negotiator role, sometimes not. Colebee's confusion came to a head in March 1796 when Bennelong made an overt play for one of his own wives.

The woman escaped Bennelong's clutches, but the breach of trust and honour, like all indiscretions among the Yiyura, now required formal punishment. Colebee undertook the lead role in the consequent ritual. No colonist witnessed it, but afterwards the officer David Collins saw that Bennelong had sustained a split lip and two broken teeth. He also heard that Colebee had sarcastically asked Bennelong if he meant his inappropriate overture 'to be a specimen of English manners?'[14]

Bennelong sent word to Hunter that he would not be attending Government House until his wounds were healed, evidently embarrassed to be seen by his colonial counterparts in a disfigured way. It may have been Hunter who suggested a short spell on Norfolk Island to clear the air. However it came about, the trip seemed to do the trick. Perhaps during his respite, Bennelong came to realise that he'd rather show an honourable face to Colebee than to any colonist. What is plain is that he returned from Norfolk a much steadier man, ready to face his future differently.

The most difficult part of Bennelong's readjustment phase was coming to terms with what had become of his Wangal kin. In his three-year absence, the colonists' diseases and greed had ravaged the clan. There were simply fewer Wangal bodies and fewer unsullied Wangal spaces than there had been. He saw, too, that the neighbouring Wallumedegal and Burramattagal people were suffering similarly. Where he'd left a colony that showed some semblance of co-operation with Aboriginal Law and use of land, now he found that Phillip's successors had encroached further on

Aboriginal fisheries, forests and boundaries. The colonial population around the harbour was in 1796 outnumbering the Indigenous population for the first time.[15] It was as a result of these factors that many Wallumedegal, Burramattagal and Wangal converged north of the river on Wallumedegal Country and began the wrenching process of rebraiding their lives. This was the amalgam later referred to as the Kissing Point Tribe.

Upon his return from Berewal, Bennelong faced a few different options for his future place of residence. He knew that Hunter felt obliged to continue Phillip's invitation to live with him in Government House. And he also had the brick hut that Phillip's men had built for him on a promontory called Dubuwagulya. Or he could join his kin at that spot on Wallumedegal Country. Bennelong went back and forth on his decision before plumping in the end for the last option.

A problem with the first two options was that they were both on Gadigal Country. Bennelong knew, as did most Gadigal by now, that the colonists were not leaving any time soon, but it still might have felt improper to him to claim the two locations from a clan who had no special love for the Wangal. An additional problem with the Dubuwagulya hut was that colonists seemed to view it as a shared resource rather than just for the Yiyura. Bennelong learned that Europeans had used his hut without permission during his absence, despite the colonists naming the site Bennelong Point. He was right to be cautious. Hunter had the building demolished for its bricks in October 1795.[16]

The main issue with the Government House option, of course, was the message of rapprochement it would send to both Yiyura and colonists – a message Bennelong wasn't sure he wanted to send any more. To re-enact the conditions he'd had when forging a détente with the colony five years earlier would be to signal that he wanted to do this again. But if Bennelong's final experiences in Berewal had not entirely turned him off the idea of engaging with the empire, then his first months back home surely did.

What Bennelong saw around him wherever he went were British people becoming less and less interested in recognising the Yiyura's existence. He'd sensed the decrease in attention to Yiyura needs while still in Berewal. In the colony the indifference was heightened by the ever-creeping spread of settlers, and mirrored in the slowly escalating impatience with Aboriginal customs. Even Collins noted that by 1795 the settlers were displaying increasing 'misconduct' and attacking Yiyura 'wantonly'.[17] To Bennelong, this changed situation demanded a change in outlook. By late 1795 he was approaching his new strategy of quitting all serious colonial connections.

British observers started noticing Bennelong's absences from around October of that year. One of the first fleet officers, John Shortland, wrote to Lord Sydney that 'Banilong . . . absconded from the Governors about a week ago.' Shortland could only account for such behaviour by describing Bennelong as being 'in his Sulks'.[18] Two days earlier, another first fleeter, Henry Waterhouse, wrote to Phillip that Bennelong now 'goes away with the Nativs for days together'. Waterhouse clearly disapproved of the situation, for while it persisted he decided to withhold Phillip's gift of money to Bennelong: 'I shall have the sum you mention [given to] Benalong whenever I can see any opportunity of it rendering any service.'[19] These comments were precursors of the derisive views that dominated after 1800.

The clergyman's wife, Mary Johnson, seemed initially to view Bennelong's absence with sympathy. 'The native man that went to England with Governor Phillip,' she noted in a letter home, 'has been in the woods several times.' She had 'no doubt' that he would soon depart the colony for good, since the Yiyura 'prefer their own way of life'. She went on to say, though, that such preference was proof that he was, after all, just 'a Savage'. Intriguingly, in the same paragraph, she mentioned that her own particular acquaintance, Boorong the Burramattagal girl, had taken off permanently 'into the woods' at this time.[20] Bennelong and Boorong may have begun their marital relationship as early as 1795, if their new wooded abodes were the same.

Wherever Boorong was at the time, Bennelong's woods were that parcel of Wallumedegal Country known by colonists as Kissing Point. Just a few months before, in July, the acting governor had granted 30 acres of this land to an emancipated convict called James Squire. Within five years Squire would start brewing and serving beer at Kissing Point, and within twelve years his annexation of Wallumedegal Country would increase tenfold. Retrospectively, he was said to have been a great friend to Bennelong because he let him live on his property.[21] Bennelong may have understood the question of who was being hospitable to whom a bit differently.

Before Kissing Point, which was before his fight with Colebee, which was before the clarifying time-out on Norfolk Island, Bennelong experienced the crushing lows and joyous highs of homecoming. The worst blow was finding that his third wife, Kurubarabula, had left him for another man. Their marriage had never been very tender – Bennelong had claimed her back in 1790 more as a political victory against her father, one of his Gweagal enemies, than as an object of affection. For their first year, too, while Bennelong's primary wife Barangaroo was still alive, Kurubarabula lived predominantly with her father. Still, she had been visibly distressed when Bennelong departed for Berewal in 1792, and Bennelong had clearly longed for her on his arduous six-month passage home. He was looking forward to presenting her with some souvenirs from his travels.[22]

Collins recorded that the first thing Bennelong asked for upon his return in September 1795 was the whereabouts of Kurubarabula. She soon turned up in Sydney Cove and at first accepted his presents of hat, jacket and rose-coloured petticoat. Within a 'few days', however,

Kurubarabula dumped the trinkets and went back to her new lover, a Gadigal man called Caruey. Bennelong hunted Caruey down and demanded a contest. Caruey obliged, though he was said to be annoyed that Bennelong seemed to fight like an Englishman, with his fists, rather than in the Yiyura manner with 'the weapons of his country'. It's not clear if Bennelong lost to Caruey or if he simply gave in to his wife's preference; either way, the marriage concluded that afternoon. Its dissolution foreshadowed some wrenching times ahead.[23]

All the same, the happiness Bennelong felt when his British ship sailed through the heads of Sydney Harbour hinted at some future pleasures, too. Later, the French voyager Pierre Milius learned of Bennelong's deep delight upon seeing Yiyura Country again. It had become the stuff of legend. 'At the sight of New Holland's shores,' repeated Milius, Bennelong 'almost went crazy, so intense was his joy'.[24] Whatever lay ahead, at least he was among kin again. As he would come to explain to Phillip within the year, 'I am at home now.'

Taking stock of Phillip's governorship

Records do not indicate whether Phillip ever received Bennelong's letter. It would have reached Britain in early 1797, when Phillip was back onboard a warship, patrolling British coastlines. The two years prior to his military reinstatement, on the other hand, were spent shuttling between Bath and London, nursing his ailments, and chasing re-entry to the navy. He had more than enough time to take stock of what had just been against all that he now saw.

Only when Phillip rejoined the navy did Britain, coincidentally, start to make any headway in its war against revolutionary France. The first few years of its campaign had been lacklustre. Phillip had come home to a nation miserably unprepared for a long and novel war. Not only had armed personnel been reduced to around fifty thousand men (soon to be compared to half a million in the French citizen armies), but Britain had a feeble comprehension of the challenge the revolution would pose to its political life. Phillip would have seen – though certainly would not have participated in – the blooming of reform-minded clubs in every major town. Inspired by ideas of popular democracy from across the channel, radicals of every stripe created or recreated groups that asked increasingly hard questions of their own rulers. Phillip would also have seen a government reacting in ruthless fashion to these radical agitators. By 1795, Pitt's parliament had passed acts that prevented any assembly of more than fifty people, that redefined treason as the mere critique of the state, and that suspended the century-long right to a fair trial.[25]

The polarisation of British politics felt even more extreme than it was due to a combination of philosophical and material factors. Philosophically, the stakes were unusually high, given how the French Revolution prompted a fundamental reconsideration of the contract between governors and the governed. Radical pamphleteer Richard Price, for example, claimed that current events were not just an amendment to French affairs but 'a general amendment . . . in human affairs'.[26] Materially, these debates played out alongside a rise in both complex warfare and unforeseen food shortages. To Phillip, lofty social theorising, complicated conflicts, and the threat of famine were eerily familiar. They had constituted the three core themes of his time in New South Wales.

Of course, Phillip never had to contend with visions of radical secular republicanism when establishing the Sydney colony, but he had been aware of several competing grand schemas for how that colony should proceed. His official superior, the Home Secretary Lord Sydney, dreamed of a self-sufficient agrarian utopia, free of the corrupting cosmopolitanism of modern commerce. Lord Sydney imagined that the convicts would be emancipated quickly, reformed in character by the absolving experience of tending their own land,

and soon enough running at least a partial form of representative government within the empire.[27]

Rather more lowly administrators foresaw instead a public-works operation processing natural resources like timber and flax for their insatiable expansionist needs. These bureaucrats assumed an unfree labour base so were less troubled by the minutiae of political representation.[28]

Commentators in the press had added their two pennies as well. Some emphasised the value of a Southern Hemisphere port to supply 'our ships'. Others envisaged an artificially created hunger 'for acquiring the various enriching articles of [Britain's] Eastern Commerce'. Many just liked the idea of having a new place to dump society's undesirables, now that British North America was so diminished.[29]

In practice, Phillip could reflect that in his five years in New South Wales he had planted a colony that included parts of all these theories. He'd never had any time for the idea of emancipating the convicts too early, and had deployed them as best he could on public farms and public building sites. But at the same time he was opposed to formal slavery and had allowed most to work to task rather than to time.[30] Furthermore, if convicts had served out their sentences and wished to settle in the colony, he apportioned them British-claimed land and resources as maximally as possible. All these stances accorded with the 'resolved judgement' and commitment to state oversight that he mentioned now in his 1790s letters to government as ideal values.[31]

The environment in New South Wales had proved more challenging than expected, making self-sufficiency difficult, let alone major exports viable. Again, Phillip's letters now from London show that he believed still in the constant need for a metropolis to top up supplies in peripheries.[32] That said, the beginnings of a regional port and consumer settlement were seeded during Phillip's reign. As he also reflected upon his return to London, 'industry [and] resources' were of course to be maximized as much as possible, even if within a state-led economy.[33]

Phillip had been obliged to send back to Britain all convicts who desired to return at the completion of their sentences, thereby thwarting those Britons who wanted to be rid of them entirely. He could have rightfully claimed, however, that transportation made many prisoners into more useful subjects of the empire than they would otherwise have been.

Not a single theory in regard to New South Wales had given much nuanced thought to what role the Indigenous inhabitants were meant to play. In the more abstract versions of both the pastoral and mercantile visions, First Nations simply didn't feature. In fairness to the British theorists, the issue of Indigenous sovereignty didn't trouble the French Revolutionaries or their radical sympathisers much either.[34] At best, the British officials who appointed Phillip had hoped the Aboriginal people might just fade away. At worst, they'd assumed they could be dealt with by a treaty.[35]

On the ground, the Indigenous presence posed a much bigger problem to the colonists than anticipated. 'The natives are far more numerous than they were supposed to be,' Phillip had noted immediately to Lord Sydney.[36] If he had once thought his main problem would be securing order among the convicts, Phillip soon learned that at least half his energies would be taken up with securing a stable relationship with the Yiyura. Now, years later, the former governor may have identified ruefully with those British officials back home who were coming to a similar realisation about fighting a dual rather than single front against revolutionaries. The British government in the early 1790s had believed that popular democracy threatened only from abroad. These days it saw that radical ideas could also disrupt from within.

The problem from New South Wales that Phillip would have least expected to find echoed in Britain was food scarcity. For its first three years, the colony had been under constant threat of famine, with the failure of crops and the death of livestock dogging every action Phillip took. It had even meant sending out a ship to southern Africa to acquire more familiar supplies. Doubtless he'd hoped never to repeat such an experience. Yet through the mid-1790s, Phillip found London in a similar crisis. The causes in Britain were more complex. Harvest failure for two consecutive years had hit the freight train of the wartime interruption to trade, which had then smashed into a poor regulation of prices. The resultant panic, though, surely felt the same.

Like everyone in Britain, Phillip witnessed the dramatic ways this panic played out. In October 1795, the poor of London were so angry they mobbed the king's coach near St James's Palace, throwing a rock through its window and yelling, 'No King! No Pitt! No War! Bread! Bread!'[37] Earlier in the year, strikes had destabilised the provision of other goods, and smaller riots everywhere demonstrated an accumulating fury. The government's punitive measures against radical activity were by the winter of 1795 draconian.

Whether or not Phillip agreed with the government's severe backlash is hard to ascertain. As his subsequent naval life showed, he clearly hated French Revolutionary ideas. During the planning stage for New South Wales, he had voiced a preference to run the colony according to martial law rather than civil law, which suggested a gut sympathy for anti-democratic systems.

Nevertheless, after being instructed in the end to install a 'truncated' civil law in the colony, Phillip had worked hard to do so.[38] He also knew from his own past that outright repression of deprived people rarely achieved the best outcomes. Through trial and error, he'd arrived at the position that 'resolved judgement' most liked a centralised authority, with just enough wriggle room to allow for discretionary flexibility.

In the shadow of the French Revolution, Phillip may have come to see that his exercise of power as a governor had been a sort of moderated authoritarianism. In order to create the most productive and least fractious outpost for his beloved Britain, he'd run a strong mini-state with a dose of toleration. He might also have mused that if Prime Minister Pitt ran the homeland with a touch more moderation he'd now be dealing with less need for naval impressment and sea fencibles.

Phillip's later roles in the counter-revolution gave him plenty of time to ponder this thesis further.

Bennelong's journey home

Bennelong's voyage from Berewal in 1795 took six months. Some vessels by this time could do the trip in two-thirds of that time. The delays he faced during the journey mirrored a whole year of postponements and tedious waiting. Before departing on HMS *Reliance* with the new governor John Hunter, Bennelong had been living on the ship with the crew in various ports around southern England for 214 days.[39]

The last leg of the voyage was the worst. It entailed three months of uninterrupted sailing between Rio de Janeiro and Sydney Cove. Normally, ships on this route stopped off halfway at Cape Town for revictualling. Hunter, though, calculated correctly that the Cape was too volatile at that time, as it had become a hotspot in the increasingly international French Revolutionary wars.[40] The shipbuilder on board, Daniel Paine, wrote a journal of this relentless passage, describing it over seven repetitive pages in grim little phrases: 'fresh gales . . . dull weather . . . squally . . . rainy'.[41] The only thing we know Bennelong did during this time was share with Paine some words of the Yiyura's language, Darug. Paine included at the end of his journal a vocabulary of more than seventy words. The ship's surgeon, George Bass, also later recorded twenty-odd words of Darug, which he too probably gathered from conversations with Bennelong on the *Reliance*.[42] Bennelong was by now fully conversant in English. Maybe, not yet fully disenchanted with the idea of engagement at this stage, he felt it was time the British advanced their own linguistic knowledge.

Paine and Bass were new faces for Bennelong but there were several men on board whom he'd known for a while. He was soon to learn that these familiars were as intricately linked to one another as any clan member back home. Hunter he'd met in Sydney Cove six years before. Unlike Phillip, Hunter was often away on supply missions, so the two really only became acquainted in Berewal. Bennelong clocked then that Hunter was about the same age as Phillip and was similarly reticent, determined and solemn. On board the *Reliance* Bennelong observed, too, that Hunter took special care of a junior lieutenant called William Kent, who turned out to be Hunter's nephew. Almost certainly Bennelong already knew Kent in another capacity – as a possible relative of Edward Kent, his host for several months in the English village of Eltham.[43]

Bennelong also knew the second-in-command of the *Reliance*, Henry Waterhouse. Even younger than Bennelong, he had been Phillip's teenaged aide during the colony's early years. Moreover, Waterhouse's father, William Waterhouse, had been Bennelong's other chief host while in Berewal, providing lodgings for him when he stayed in London. Much later, Bennelong may have heard on the colonial grapevine that Henry Waterhouse's sister eventually married George Bass, the ship's doctor. If Bennelong had found Berewal to be a densely populous place, he could yet sense that most people in the world nevertheless lived in small, interlinked circles like his own.

The reminders of Edward Kent and William Waterhouse were no doubt poignant. By 1795 these two hosts conjured not Bennelong's varied experiences in Eltham and London, but instead the Yiyura companion who had shared them with him, now dead and buried on British land. This was Yemmerrawanne, also from the Wangal clan, and thus an indirect relative of Bennelong's. He was about ten years Bennelong's junior – a mere twenty at the time of his death. Phillip had known Yemmerrawanne almost as well as he'd known Bennelong, seeing him at Government House on many occasions. Phillip had been pleased to include an even younger potential Yiyura diplomat among his party when he returned to Britain. Bennelong had just been pleased to have kin with him abroad.

Tragically, though, Yemmerrawanne had sickened within months of their arrival, suffering bouts of incapacity in both Waterhouse's London townhouse and Kent's Eltham cottage. He'd been especially ill through his last ghastly winter, with an unhealing leg sore and pneumonic lungs. Burying him amid so many strangers in the churchyard of Eltham in May 1794 had caused Bennelong to lose his last bit of interest in staying in Berewal. He'd found it hard to communicate the necessary protocols to his hosts. Hunter understood that Bennelong was fed up long before they managed to depart.[44]

At least during the four-week stopover at Rio de Janeiro, Bennelong could enjoy some distraction from thoughts of Yemmerrawanne. Rio offered dramatic natural beauty and, to Bennelong, an unusual mixture of people. In some ways the place seemed familiar. Situated inside a massive harbour, it boasted a protective narrow entrance, lovely small islets and sandy white beaches. Bennelong had also of course visited it briefly on the voyage out to Britain. In other ways, though, Rio was exotic. This harbour was vastly larger than the Yiyura's harbour. Hotter, too. The land rose more steeply out of the water. And the colonists were much, much more numerous.

In the 1790s, Rio was the capital of Portugal's gigantic Brazilian colony. With a long if patchy history of alliance with Britain, the city was a favoured port of call for British imperial ships throughout the eighteenth century. Hunter had stopped there to pick up cheap food, loads of rum and as many sacks of seed and seedlings as he could carry. When leading the first fleet in 1787, Phillip had done much the same thing.[45]

Even ship-hardened seamen like Daniel Paine admired the scenery at Rio. 'On the left hand is a peaked hill, from its shape called the Sugar-Loaf,' he wrote. '[Beyond is] most delightful country interspersed with villages and convents . . . [The scene is] more beautiful than language can describe, which is much heightened by contrasting it with the horizon-bounded scene from which the mariner has just emerged.' As a budding political radical, Paine noted that the Catholic administration ruled in an 'arbitrary' manner, demanded extortionist tributes to 'indolent' friars, and depended on a wretched system of imported slavery. On the other hand, as a soon-to-be colonist, Paine neglected to remark on how the bountiful crops he so admired, as well as the lucrative diamond mines, were the direct outcomes of Indigenous dispossession.[46]

Did Bennelong recognise the theft that had occurred here? It's hard to speculate. If no one had explained to him the history of Portugal's colonisation of eastern South America, some two centuries old by then, it would not have been easy to grasp from the faces he saw in Rio. Roughly three-quarters of the city's 100,000-plus people were black-skinned Africans. Bennelong might have assumed that it was their country, but for the fact that more than half of them appeared to be enslaved. They often wore chains, they did all the backbreaking work in the fields and down the mines, and they were frequently flogged – a practice that we know Yiyura people abhorred when they witnessed it among Britons.[47] Less than a quarter of Rio's residents were fair-skinned people descended from Portuguese Europeans, who to Bennelong may have looked rather similar to British Europeans.

What of the approximately one-in-ten inhabitants who seemed neither black nor white? Bennelong had lived with colonists long enough to know they could have been the offspring of black and white. Or he might have figured out that many in fact were Tupinambá – the original inhabitants of the land the Portuguese had seized and transformed. If Bennelong did understand this, such a spectre of what two hundred years of settler colonialism can do to First Nations would have been nothing short of terrifying.[48]

Hunter was unimpressed by the reception he received at Rio: he expected the viceroy there to make more time for him. In a huff, he stayed mostly on the *Reliance* in Rio's harbour. Perhaps Bennelong followed suit. But after so long cooped up in a ship cabin he probably took the liberty given supernumeraries to wander freely about the marketplaces, gardens, churches and famous stone aqueduct.[49]

Before Rio, there had been two months of sailing down the African west coast, including a brief stop at Tenerife. Whether Bennelong realised the horrific connection between African lands and South America in the form of the transatlantic slave trade is unclear. The extent of the hubris that enabled Europeans to wreak havoc on so many people across such vast distances would have taken time for any outsider to absorb.

The doctor George Bass reported that Bennelong's health improved on this first leg of the voyage.[50] Bennelong had fallen sick during the long wait for departure in English docks. Now, though, through Bass's dispensation of citrus fruits, and no doubt simply the prospect of finally seeing home, he perked up.

The Admiralty had arranged for Bennelong to return with Hunter in July 1794, but the final details were delayed by the chaos of also managing a war. By the end of the seven-month wait, Hunter was gravely worried about Bennelong's state of mind. 'So long a disappointment has much broken his spirit,' he wrote to the Home Affairs Office. 'I do all I can to keep him up, but am still doubtful of his living.'³¹ The delay was exacerbated by the coldest winter in living memory (some reported temperatures of −20° Celsius) and Bennelong's grief for Yemmerrawanne. All he wanted now was to return.

Phillip's earlier journeys

Phillip was not, of course, present on Bennelong's homeward voyage. On the topic of Rio, though, he would have had much to say. Phillip had visited Brazil so often that his combined time there amounted to four years – nearly as long as he'd lived in New South Wales.

During his transitional time back in Britain, Phillip wrote more notes about his future naval prospects than he did on his past colonial management. He asked the government to consider him for 'the Naval Board, the Colonel of Marines, or Greenwich Hospital'. When finally given a command, he wrote about potential improvements to his ship, his preparedness to take on landsmen, and his 'readiness to sail at a moment's notice'.⁵² Phillip's eagerness stemmed from a faith in his long naval experience in Germany, Minorca, India and Cuba, as well as Brazil. It was this last, though, that was undoubtedly the most important. In Brazil he had gained his deepest insights into how to defend an empire – an experience more pertinent in the 1790s than ever before.

Phillip's last visit to South America had been in 1793, on the voyage to England with Bennelong and Yemmerrawanne, although at that time the main focus had been on reaching their destination. A Portuguese gazette noted briefly that 'Arthur Filippe [the] celebrated officer' stopped at Rio during the month of February and that his ship carried 'two men from that new country . . . They were of a sweet nature, obliging [and] had great facility in pronouncing Portuguese.'⁵³ No British source survives to add further colour to this account.

A more memorable visit had been in 1787 on HMS *Sirius*, with the ten other ships of the first fleet bound for New South Wales. At Rio, Phillip had received a hero's welcome. Accompanying officers knew that foreign crews usually faced severe restrictions on their movements in Rio, due to viceregal efforts to curb smuggling – James Cook had grumbled about such treatment twenty years earlier. But Phillip was heralded with a thirteen-gun salute and an open invitation to all parts of the city. He enjoyed lavish entertainment and full rights to purchase whatever he wanted from the viceregal stores, which ended up including ten thousand musket balls.[54] Phillip wrote to Evan Nepean that 'tho' I desired much to be rec'd here as the capt. of the Sirius only, [the Viceroy] gave it out in orders that I rec'd the same honor as himself'.[55]

Portuguese colonists celebrated Phillip so well because they remembered his formal service to them over the previous two decades. On numerous occasions Phillip had sailed in South American waters as an allied or seconded captain to Portugal, helping them fend off Spanish threats to their colonial claims in Brazil.

The last of these occasions had occurred in 1783, when Britain was finalising the terms of its defeat in the American Revolution. This peace treaty involved negotiating agreements not only with thirteen of Britain's former American colonies, but also with one of the revolutionaries' key allies, Spain. The British government calculated, with some risk, that if it seized some of Spain's settlements in South America during the peace process it might end up with better prizes overall. Phillip was sent to Brazil as part of this dodgy initiative, which pleased the Portuguese colonists there no end, since they always felt threatened by their Spanish counterparts.[56]

As it turned out, the 1783 initiative failed, partly from poor weather, partly from poor intelligence, and partly from the fact that the American Revolution's peace treaty was concluded in the middle of it anyway.[57] Still, the Viceroy at Rio de Janeiro at the time understood that Phillip's mission would have benefited Brazil. He was gratified to know that British force might yet solve his problems in the future. He offered Phillip's crew then 'every possible mark of respect & attention'.[58]

This viceroy, Luís de Vasconcelos, may have first met Phillip in 1781 during an even dodgier expedition. There is less documentary evidence for it, but the historian Alan Frost makes a credible case that Phillip sailed 'under cover' at this time as part of an earlier campaign to unsettle Spanish claims in the southern Atlantic. What is certain is that the British sent a force to South America to survey the Spanish settlements near southern Brazil in March 1781 (in the middle of the American Revolution). The British force lurked around Brazil for about six weeks before joining a larger contingent sent to protect British interests in India.

Frost conjectures that Phillip was part of this cartographic exercise – admittedly a curious priority in the middle of a flailing war effort – so as to be ready to help a sudden secret strike on Spanish America. Frost's main prompt for his theory is a newspaper article published in 1787 which mused that 'about five years since, [Phillip had been employed] to carry out with him near 400 Criminals from Lisbon to the Brasils'.[59] If this operation indeed occurred, the Portuguese convicts were doubtless intended to be cannon fodder for the upcoming strike. Frost notes four facts: the Portuguese regularly sent convicts around the world at this time as soldiers in their colonial wars, the British navy promoted Phillip to the post of captain in November that year for unknown services, there are no documents extant for Phillip for the bulk of 1781, and Phillip was asked for his personal charts for this mission in January 1781, when he also wrote to the Admiralty of his expectation to be 'called forth' any day.[60] If Phillip was on this mission, here was another reason for the Brazilian viceroy's indebtedness to him, even though a British attack on their Spanish rivals never came to fruition.

Best known of Phillip's time in Brazil is his formal secondment to the Portuguese navy in the mid-1770s. The American Revolution had not yet broken out when he started this stint, which lasted three and a half years, but the storms were clearly brewing. Spain took the opportunity of American rumblings to make a grab for Portugal's lucrative settlements south of Rio de Janeiro, just when Portugal's firmest ally, Britain, seemed most distracted. Portugal asked for British assistance. A harried Admiralty said no, but they could rustle up one naval lieutenant, currently at a loose end, who, they said, was experienced, spoke good French, and actually wanted the position. Would he do? 'He is a lieutenant here but he deserves to have an order if your customs . . . permit promotion,' wrote Admiral Hervey to the Portuguese envoy. 'His name is Lieut. Phillips.'[61] The Portuguese happily accepted, and awarded Arthur Phillip his first captaincy.

Phillip arrived in Rio de Janeiro in April 1775. In all, he spent around half his secondment patrolling, defending, and at one point actively attacking the Spanish near the Portuguese settlements near Rio de la Plata. The other half of his time he spent in Rio de Janeiro, observing up close this microcosm of empire, and in particular the workings of Rio's diamond mines. Fragments of a report he wrote on these mines survive. They expose a dangerous, gruelling, and vastly inefficient system. Enslaved Africans did all the 'immense' labour of rock-splitting, he saw, but each African was overseen by a waged colonist who cracked his whip for any infringement. Mired in misery, the enslaved Africans invented elaborate ways of securing some diamonds for themselves, which in turn prompted the colonists to come up with ever more elaborate ways of circumventing them. Phillip realised that though the riches from colonial Brazil were great, they might have been greater still if procured more effectively.[62]

Needless to say, he refrained from sharing his views with his Brazilian bosses. By the end of his stint there he had established an excellent relationship with the then viceroy, the Marquess of Lavradio. This viceroy reported to his own government that 'Captain Arthur Phillips [is] one of the officers of the most distinct merit that the Queen [of Portugal] has in her service . . . I think that it will be a most important acquisition to secure that he should remain in the [Portuguese] Royal Service.' Lavradio went on to commend Phillip's maritime knowledge and his steady practice of reason, adding dryly that he avoids falling 'into those exaggerated and unbearable excesses of temper which the majority of his fellow country-men do'.[63]

If Phillip was ever offered a permanent position by the Portuguese government he did not take it. Around the time of Lavradio's letter, he learned that France had entered the American Revolution on the side of the revolutionaries (Spain would follow one year later). Phillip realised how significant this was for his beloved nation and hurried back home to see how he might help. He didn't want only to assist British allies but instead now to serve Britain directly.

Eighteen years on, as Britain once more faced existential threats from democratic revolutionaries, Phillip might have cast back to where he'd been during the last crisis. He perhaps saw that in Brazil he'd learned three critical lessons about empires. The first, and probably most relevant now, was the absolute necessity of crushing all rivals to your claims. He'd seen how the ever-menacing proximity of Spanish forces had made the colony of Brazil perpetually nervous. Nerves bred a paranoid atmosphere as well as a reliance on third parties for military aid. Phillip had witnessed Brazilian paranoia in the form of Rio's extreme protections against smuggling and had himself acted as a third party. He knew that quelling France's incipient revolutionary surge would be paramount if Britain's empire was to remain the boldest and least dependent on earth.

The second lesson, more pertinent to his governing days, was about slavery. Phillip saw in Brazil that enslaved labour was not as expedient as it seemed. Brazil's enslaved workers appeared cheap and plentiful, but they also gave rise to excessively fierce policing, elaborate controls against transgressions, and ultimately a group of people who had no hope of ever joining the economy as subjects. Phillip refused to import such an irrational system to New South Wales, though he'd always known that Britain continued to use it elsewhere in the world.

Third, Phillip came to appreciate in Brazil exactly why empires were worth defending. He knew that ordinary men like himself would never have risen to the level of celebrated viceregal guest without the opportunities afforded by aspirational colonies. Empires gave new chances to certain people – as long as they were white.

If to Bennelong Rio was a beautiful though opaque respite, to Phillip it remained forever his grand turning point, his most essential exemplar, and the truest confirmation of where his heart lay. Brazil had given Phillip his first captaincy, a crucial hurdle for anyone seeking lasting naval glory. It had also provided him with a model of empire in action, with compelling instances of what worked and what didn't. Finally, it had secured irrevocably his love for Britain over all other countries, and his determination to do all he could to ensure its supremacy survived.

The final meetings of Bennelong and Phillip

The last time Bennelong and Phillip were together was June or July 1794. The event is not recorded, but Bennelong's letter from Sydney said that he knew Isabella Phillip 'very well', and she only became Mrs Phillip in May 1794. Bennelong joined Hunter on the *Reliance* in August 1794, so this left only the intervening English summer months for the acquaintance with Isabella. The care that Bennelong suggested Isabella had provided to him during this time was most likely sympathy for his grief. Yemmerrawanne had died in Eltham on 18 May 1794. Bennelong spent the rest of the summer travelling between Eltham and London. The Phillips probably saw him when staying in London. It's possible, though, that they also went to Eltham to assist with the posthumous arrangements for Yemmerrawanne.

If he'd been back among the Yiyura, Bennelong would have led the sorry business for his young kinsman. As his own death would show twenty years later, this should have involved communal crying, feasting, wailing and dancing for several days. It should also have included a commitment to avoid uttering the deceased's name for a while. This is not even to contemplate the collective battle that should have been waged to avenge Yemmerrawanne's death. None of this, of course, occurred in Eltham in 1794.[64]

Instead, Bennelong's British hosts, including perhaps Phillip, organised a headstone for Yemmerrawanne's grave. The slab had the young man's name engraved indelibly upon it, no doubt too soon for Bennelong's liking and no doubt causing others to say the name too often. It read: 'In Memory of YEMERRAWANYEA a Native of NEW SOUTH WALES who died the 18th of May 1794 In the 19th Year of his AGE.' The Aboriginal taboo against speaking a deceased person's name was based on a worry that it might disrupt the spirit's smooth passage to the ancestral afterlife. Without such a clear transition, the dead threatened to remain entangled with the living. Deceased Ancestors may have animated everyday Yiyura life but they were resolutely of a different order and needed to stay distinguished from those who were still human.[65] Adding to his concerns about all that was lacking, Bennelong perhaps fretted over how Yemmerrawanne's spirit was going to conjoin with his Ancestors at all, given how far away he was from home.

Maybe, though, distance was never an issue. And maybe the absence of custom in this instance was secondary to Bennelong at least being there as a witness. But no Yiyura person had any prior experience of travelling across two oceans for this to be known either way.

Phillip had been present at many different types of funerals in his fifty-five years. He'd seen scores of burials at sea, the corpse weighted with wood or metal, sewn up inside sailcloth or a hammock and then pushed into the deep, as a captain or chaplain recited from a prayer book. He'd presided over officer funerals in New South Wales, where other officers formed a guard of honour beside a coffin. He'd witnessed Irish funerals with raucous wakes afterwards, 'suitable', as one of his colleagues noted, 'to the disposition and habit of the deceased'.[66] He'd even stood by during Yiyura funerals, acknowledging the mixed ritual of procession, conviviality and battle. Phillip knew more than most that different cultures commemorated the dead in different ways, and that for each mourner, caught in the first grip of bereavement, it was often the strict observance of tradition that brought the greatest comfort. Whether he tried to allow for more culturally specific practices to honour Yemmerrawanne is unknown. Possibly Phillip's lack of religiosity made such subjective acts seem trivial. Death was a fact of life, to the rationalist, and no particular ritual was going to change that.

In late May a few British newspapers repeated the same brief report about the death of Yemmerrawanne. 'One of the two natives of Botany Bay, who came over with Governor Phillip, is dead,' they declared; 'his Companion [Bennelong] pines much for his loss.'[67] By this stage Bennelong's emotions included more than just pining; they also involved a determination to leave Berewal as quickly as possible. Much later, John Hunter reflected that Bennelong had been 'fondly' looking forward to his departure ever since Yemmerrawanne's death.[68] Hunter had been appointed as Phillip's successor in February 1794, and so was officially responsible for Bennelong from that moment. It was probably Phillip, however, who got the *Reliance* on its way after the excessive delays. Hunter was almost as annoyed by the postponements as was Bennelong. Only Phillip, though, had the clout to make the case that the colony should not carry on any longer with an acting governor. In retrospect, the best gift Phillip could have given Bennelong in his sorrow was the assurance, at last, of a homeward berth.

It's unlikely the Phillips were present when Yemmerrawanne took his final breath in the middle of May. They were only ten days married at that point and the local papers made no mention of Phillip's presence at Yemmerrawanne's death. That said, the scholar Keith Smith suggests that Phillip might have been around very soon afterward. He observes that the Eltham parish registry which recorded the passing included a word that 'only two people in England, Bennelong and Phillip', would have known to use: 'Kebarrah', meaning a man who has undergone initiation by having his front tooth knocked out with a keba, or stone. The registry entry in full reads: 'May 21. Yemmurravonyea Kebarrah, a Native of New South Wales, died May 18th 1794, supposed to be aged 19 years, at the house of Mr Edward Kent.' Evidently someone wanted to have it recognised that the deceased, though young, had yet attained adulthood in the eyes of his own kin.[69]

A third person, however, may have learned this important word – the Yiyura men's periodic host Edward Kent, resident of Eltham, member of the parish, and owner of the cottage where Yemmerrawanne died. The exact connection between Edward Kent and New South Wales is uncertain. One historian speculates he was related to William Kent, the 34-year-old lieutenant on the *Reliance* and nephew of Hunter. The link would thus be naval. Another believes he was an aide to Lord Sydney, the cabinet minister who led the decision to create the colony and who now lived just outside Eltham. This would mean the link was bureaucratic. Both could have been true, exemplifying the entanglement of different sectors of public service at the time, all knitted together by nepotism and regional convenience. Bennelong and Yemmerrawanne had been visiting Kent at Eltham on and off for seven months. As Yemmerrawanne's illness had progressed, it became the preferred abode. Perhaps Kent himself was the drawcard, a man interested enough in the Yiyura to ensure that Yemmerrawanne's correct title was recorded for posterity.

At least two different medics came to see Yemmerrawanne as he lay dying.[70] None were to any avail. Yemmerrawanne passed from his worldly life on an English spring sabbath. It was the first cloudy day after a week of fine weather.[71]

LONDON

Journal of a Metropolitan Year, 1794–1793

Phillip marries for a second time while Bennelong prepares for an even bigger event • Earlier, they face trials and memories of the past • Phillip investigates his family history • Bennelong dresses for his portrait • Theatre and medicine in the men's lives • Taking in the sights and sounds of the city • Religion, sovereignty and arrival

Phillip and Isabella were married on 8 May 1794, in St Marylebone church near Regent's Park in London, not far from Phillip's temporary lodgings in Covent Garden. There are no personal testimonies of the day, but weather records indicate that it rained.[1] Perhaps Isabella's prosperous father, Richard Whitehead, was present, though he had only four months to live by then.

British weddings in the 1790s usually occurred in the morning, with either a breakfast beforehand or a luncheon afterwards for a select number of guests. Less typical, though just now coming into fashion, was the inclusion of a special wedding cake and the wearing of a white bridal gown.[2] There is too little in the archives on Isabella to guess at what she would have preferred. What we do know is that the Clandestine Marriages Act of 1753 required the couple to give three weeks' public notice of their intentions. It also mandated that neither could already be married. Despite Phillip's judicial separation from his first wife, Charlott, in 1769, the law forbade remarriage until one party died. Neatly for the new couple, Charlott had done so two years earlier.

Phillip seems to have met Isabella in Bath at the end of the previous summer. Both their names are entered as patrons of the Bath Circulating Library in August 1793.[3] These kinds of library, popular from the mid-eighteenth century, were private subscription services designed to provide both cheap reading and tailored social mixing. The Phillips' marriage was perhaps one ideal outcome of the libraries' mission. Unlike with his first marriage, Phillip did not sign any irregular legal settlement when he wed Isabella. This meant that when Richard Whitehead died in September of that year, his daughter's share of his considerable wealth went straight and solely to the new groom.

Bennelong and Yemmerrawanne did not attend Phillip's wedding. That week, they were caught up in an even bigger life event: preparation for Yemmerrawanne's last days as a young man on Earth. The two Wangal visitors took their final trip to Eltham on 7 May 1794, twenty-four hours before the St Marylebone nuptials. Most of the people involved with the men seemed to know then what lay ahead. Throughout the previous year, their London host William Waterhouse had invoiced the government for two sets of everything – two lodgings, two coats, two visits to the barber, and so on. But his bill for 1 May 1794 listed only a single chest 'for Mr Benalong' to take home certain gifts to New South Wales. No chest was ordered for Yemmerrawanne. It appeared he would not be needing it.[4]

Other sources reveal that London-based Waterhouse had a sincere regard for both men. It's doubtful, then, that he would have turfed his guests out in Yemmerrawanne's hour of need. More likely, the visitors themselves chose to spend this precious time in Eltham. They had stayed at Edward Kent's cottage twice before: for a fortnight over Christmas and for six weeks during autumn.

Eleven miles southeast of central London, Eltham was in the late eighteenth century a quiet village comprising around two hundred cottages.[5] Its once-famous medieval royal palace was now just a ruined hall, used as a barn for farm animals. The original patron of Phillip's colony, Lord Sydney, lived in a grand house one hour's walk away. But the main attraction of the village for the Wangal men was probably its simple rural difference from bustling London, if not also the personality of their host Edward Kent.

It took at least two hours by coach to travel to Eltham from Waterhouse's place in Mayfair. Once arrived, Bennelong and Yemmerrawanne could breathe cleaner air, see more trees, enjoy less noise. The environs were vastly different to their harbour homelands. The oak woods gave off no eucalyptus scent and no salty spray carried on the breeze. But at least nature felt closer here, as it had been for most of their lives back home. Yemmerrawanne could gaze out from his bedridden confinement at a green world and remember the enduring comforts of his own.

Most histories of Bennelong imply that Berewal was an intensely exotic experience for him, overwhelming in its difference and thus part of Bennelong's later supposed downfall. But to trace Bennelong's movements from the careful preparation for his kinsman's death back to the eager anticipation of arrival, rather than the other way around, changes the tone of the narrative. Instead of moving from adventure to death, we proceed more optimistically: from the sobering rituals of mourning to all the potential of foreign travel. The reversal nudges us to recognise what the previous chapter intimated: that Bennelong was not overcome by the events of travelling – or by cities, for that matter. He approached them on his own terms. He managed London with same degree of self-possession as he managed all other challenges in his life.

In similar fashion, most histories of Phillip assume that he lived out his post-governorship days in the fading glory of having founded New South Wales. To start an account of his return, though, with his new marriage reminds us that Phillip understood the moment rather as a chance to keep moving forward. He continued to act for his former colony in that first year back home, but, importantly, he began to make concerted plans for other quests too.

Like endings, time spent abroad or time spent immediately after a long absence tends to sharpen perceptions of a society's idiosyncrasies. Bennelong and Phillip's first year away from New South Wales shines further light on their respective cultures. Only cultural context gives meaning to an individual's actions.

April 1794

Bennelong and Yemmerrawanne spent twelve months in Berewal before the latter died. Phillip intersected with the pair on and off over this period. Stepping back through the single year – month by month, as if tracked in a journal – helps us see it in a new light.

The visitors' year can be pieced together from two equally partial types of evidence. Treasury records list their expenses but lack all editorial detail; newspaper reports describe their outings but often have too much editorial input, and also include some of the worst stereotypes of the era. Combined, though, these sources offer a semblance of the men's time in Britain's imperial centre.

Their primary outing in April 1794 was to the Houses of Parliament in London to attend a day's hearing at the trial of Warren Hastings.[6] It was to be Yemmerrawanne's last public appearance. This trial was one of the most scandalous legal events in British colonial history. Warren Hastings had been the leading political representative of the crown in British India through the 1770s and 1780s. In 1787, an oppositional faction of the British parliament, headed by the Whig politician Edmund Burke, charged Hastings with 'oppression and tyranny'. Seven long years later, his trial was still being heard.7

Burke's prosecution of Hastings was not the anti-imperial stance that some later took it to be. Burke was an advocate of empire his whole life. The loss of Britain's thirteen American colonies in the previous decade had appalled him; he believed they had been lost due to poor management. When Burke heard rumours of similar forms of mismanagement in British India, he leaped to curtail them, insisting that Hastings had 'sullied' and 'dishonoured' Britain's name. Burke was not criticising Britain's right to exercise its increasing control through Asia; rather, he wanted British representatives to exercise it more securely.8

Bennelong and Yemmerrawanne attended Hastings' trial at a particularly interesting stage. Just one week earlier, on 9 April 1794, Lord Cornwallis, Hastings's successor in India, had refuted in his testimony all of Burke's charges, not only defending Hastings, but also announcing that Britain's name was now beloved by Indians. Burke's case never really recovered. The House of Lords at length acquitted Hastings in favour of Prime Minister William Pitt's ruling faction.9

Although Hunter was now formally responsible for the Wangal visitors, Phillip seems to have been the driver behind their attendance at the trial. Phillip probably sided with the government's defence of Hastings; as we've seen, he showed deep loyalty to Pitt's increasingly reactionary government. Bennelong and Yemmerrawanne could have visited the trial at any point during the previous year but only now that it was turning in Pitt's favour did they do so. As earlier events will show, Phillip was keen to demonstrate to the Indigenous guests the operation of British power at its most decisive, irresistible, and legally rationalised.

What Bennelong and Yemmerrawanne made of either Burke's or Pitt's positions regarding a colonial governor's best practice is harder to gauge. A few newspapers carried reports of their attendance at the trial, but they were generally vehicles for satire of British politics rather than commentaries about the guests' reaction. For example, the Tory-leaning *World* newspaper published a sardonic imagining of the day, but targeted Burke for wasting so much public time and money with his obsession to prosecute Hastings. For the satire to work, Bennelong and Yemmerrawanne had to be characterised as naive buffoons. When told of the length and expense of the trial, the article stated, 'the Botany Bay men' were said to bow 'with due humility' and confess that their own 'savage' practices were not as sophisticated. What a 'proud day for England', the journalist could then quip. Whatever Bennelong and Yemmerrawanne were actually doing or saying was lost in the drive to the punchline.[10]

One sober report appeared in the *Oracle & Public Advertiser*. 'Two sooty natives of New South Wales brought over by Governor Phillips, [sic] attended the debates in parliament on Wednesday last, when they were introduced to several persons of consequence. They do not, by any means, correspond with the descriptions we at first received of our Antipodes; for, instead of vacuity of intellect [they display] much shrewdness and curiosity.' This article had no barrow to push about either Burke or Pitt. If accurate, it suggested that Bennelong and Yemmerrawanne gathered more about the grim implications for colonised people embedded in the trial than others realised. Did they ask pointed questions about who was standing for what in the debate, and then show scepticism about both sides? The article went on to note that the men spoke sufficient English to be understood and exhibited 'nothing of the character of savages'.[11]

March 1794

The month of March saw many medicines ordered for Yemmerrawanne while he was staying with Waterhouse at 125 Mount Street in Mayfair.

Still, he managed to make at least one public outing. This was listed in the treasury expenses as an 'Expedition' for him and Bennelong to see 'the Oratorio'. The *Gentleman's Magazine* records that on the designated day, during a month of lean offerings, the New Drury Lane Theatre presented G.F. Handel's famous oratorio, *Messiah*. The Wangal men may have been a bit disappointed by what they experienced that night: they had grown used to different sorts of performances while in Berewal.[12]

The performing arts were one of London's major attractions, and Bennelong seemed to take a particular interest. The bills of expenses demonstrate that he had been to several shows in the previous six months. Most of the operas and plays of the period accorded in some way with the Yiyura sense of good entertainment, combining as they did music, dance, costumes, elaborate stage sets, and significant interaction with the audience. They were also often dramatisations of well-known historical stories. Together, it all might have felt rather familiar. The finer meanings of what is covered by the Darug term 'garabara' (sometimes spelt 'corroboree') were and remain fuzzy to settlers, but it seems that garabaras in the eighteenth century similarly involved music, dance, ornate body decorations, and the narration of ancient and contemporary history. Perhaps they offered some balm to Bennelong, a glimpse of what awaited him when he managed to return.

If this was the case, the Wangal pair were to discover that London's performing-arts scene was much less exciting in March. This is because March fell during the forty-day period of Lent, a time in the Christian calendar of abstention from luxuries. The usual roster of shows in London's West End contracted noticeably – the only exception being oratorios. This form focused on music only, usually sacred over historical, and eschewed the dancing, props and added commotion of theatre. Bennelong and Yemmerrawanne may have been expecting the standard spectacle of acting, lights, jokes, tricks and audience uproar, but they would not have found it in a 1794 performance of Handel's *Messiah*.[13]

Probably neither Hunter nor Phillip arranged for the oratorio outing; they doubtless left the social excursions to the landlord William Waterhouse. The only exertion we know Phillip made in March was to pen a letter to the colony's quasi-patron, Joseph Banks, on the thirteenth of the month. Friends had been in touch: 'I cannot say that the letters I have recd from Sydney, are very satisfactory,' he began. 'For I am given to understand, that before I was clear of the land, *liquor* was sent up to Parramatta.' This liquor was being used to purchase livestock that Phillip had given to emancipated convicts by the very officers who were meant to curb liquor's spread.[14]

Phillip had established the settlement at Parramatta – as it was later named, after the Yiyura home of the Burramattagal – ten months after landing at Sydney Cove.[15] He'd meant it to be a breadbasket for the colony, just as Norfolk Island was meant to be its resource centre. This secondary settlement was fifteen miles inland, where fresh water and better farming soil could be found. Phillip's original vision was for Parramatta to be the chief locale of the public farms, worked by convicts who were driven equally by the fear of punishment and the love of social prosperity. Later, in theory, it was to be populated by industrious emancipated convicts. Under Acting Governor Grose, however, Parramatta was gradually parcelled out to officers as private land plots. These were now evidently being worked by convicts and stocked with the animals which had been designated for emancipists, all paid for in the ballooning currency of grog.[16]

Phillip's expression of shock over the presence of liquor in Parramatta was slightly disingenuous. As his own letter indicates, supplies had reached officers *before* he had departed in 1792. It was he therefore who had been the governor to order an especially large delivery of liquor that year.[17] Alcohol had always existed in New South

Wales, though Phillip had tried to limit its quantity and distribution in his five-year governorship. The reference to liquor in his letter to Banks signified more than the substance itself: it referred to the fact that under Grose its control was laxer; it was used as a dubious currency rather than a just reward; and its end was the privatisation of enterprises that were meant to be public.

Banks could do little about it, even if he wanted to. While he had a lot of power over what governors might do for him, he wielded less influence over the finer details of policy on the ground than Phillip knew. Phillip's annoyance with the reports coming out of New South Wales – and with London's response to them – was perhaps one reason why his interest in the colony cooled over the following two years.

February 1794

One of Phillip's efforts to embark on new endeavours occurred in February. On the sixth day of the month, Phillip paid a visit to the College of Arms in central London. The college's Waiting Book noted that the 'late governor of Botany Bay' called with questions about his lineage. Phillip produced for their inspection 'arms on a bend 3 camel heads'.[18] The College of Arms kept records of all the families in England, Wales and Ireland that had been awarded arms for 'heraldic achievement' since the fifteenth century. Phillip was evidently on a quest for a deeper understanding of his own history.

Phillip's father's origins have always been considered murky. During Phillip's life, a rushed concise biography stated merely that his father was 'Jacob Phillip, a native of Frankfort, in Germany, who having settled in England, maintained his family and educated his son by teaching the languages'.[19] After Phillip's death, scholars discovered that the school he'd attended in Greenwich listed his father's occupation as a naval steward rather than a languages tutor. No scholar, however, found any records of a Jacob Phillip in the city of Frankfurt. This led most later historians to declare him simply a 'mystery'.²⁰ In the twentieth century, some people added to the confusion by suggesting that Phillip descended from a Jewish family, but this turned out to be based only on flimsy interpretations of his image in portraits.²¹

Phillip's trip to the College of Arms leads us closer to the truth.²² The herald attending Phillip noted that further information about his family arms was 'not found'. Another hand, though, had added 'vid. [see or consult] Ferstens German Heraldry'. Heraldic researcher Richard d'Apice believes that Phillip's arms were not discovered among British records, but that something was unearthed instead in the College's volumes on armigerous families of German-speaking Europe. The 1706 edition of *Fürstsches Wappenbuch* (shorthanded to 'Furst's German Heraldry') indeed reveals that a coat of arms was created for a Philippe family in the seventeenth century, its rendition showing three animal heads on a bend. The animals in this volume are ambiguous: they could be horses, deer or camels. Importantly, though, a simplified version, linked to the same family, can be found on a 1667 print: here the beast is definitely camel.²³

The Philippe coat of arms was granted in 1646 to Claude-Ambroise Philippe, a member of the local parliament at Besançon, near today's Swiss–French border. Claude-Ambroise lived between 1614 and 1697.²⁴ For most of his life, the city of Besançon was a semi-autonomous state within the Habsburg-controlled Holy Roman Empire. It famously included many different cultures and faiths: French, German, Flemish, Catholic and Protestant. In 1678, however, Besançon was taken over by Catholic France, which soon afterwards revoked its century-long tolerance of Protestant worship. Most Protestants, known as Huguenots, consequently fled the town.

A contemporary local history indicates that Claude-Ambroise Philippe stayed on through the revocation period. He died in

Besançon more than a decade after the persecution of Huguenots began, suggesting either that he was already Catholic or that he converted.[25] Ambroise is a common Huguenot name, though, and many Huguenot Philippes turned up in German places as refugees from France from around the 1690s. If Claude-Ambroise's family was Huguenot, the patriarch may have somehow withstood the persecutions but his descendants perhaps could not. Biographer Lyn Fergusson has pursued this theory of the Philippe family being Huguenot and realised that while the city of Frankfurt received many Huguenot refugees, the smaller, lesser-known town of Frankfurt an der Oder near Potsdam received even more. The Edict of Potsdam in 1685 deliberately welcomed Huguenot people from intolerant France into the surrounding region. Some of these refugees were named a variant of Philippe.[26]

None of this speculation nails Arthur Phillip's ancestors as the progeny of Claude-Ambroise Philippe, a possibly suppressed Huguenot whose family fled to more Protestant-centred countries via a town called Frankfurt over the following three generations. But Phillip's claim to Claude-Ambroise's tri-camel crest suggests that Phillip at least believed they might be. As scholar Michael Flynn also muses, Phillip could have easily applied for his own coat of arms after serving as an inaugural governor.[27] He chose not to because he thought he already had one.

If Phillip was a descendant of Huguenot refugees it helps to explain much about the development of his personal loyalties. It accounts for his fierce attachment to the Protestant state that sheltered his family. And it throws light on why he held such a deep dislike of the French nation, which even for an eighteenth-century Englishman, as we shall further learn, was pointed and steadfast. Finding his arms in a German record book in 1794 may have confirmed many half-formed instincts for Phillip.

January 1794

The year started with unusually brutal weather in London. Temperatures barely rose above 1.5 degrees Celsius.[28] As a result, Bennelong and Yemmerrawanne spent most of January holed up in their Mayfair residence, hardly daring to venture onto the icy streets.

This month was tough in additional ways. The treasury bills itemise a 'schoolmaster for writing etc', suggesting some toil for the Wangal visitors, and also include 'two beds, coverings, and furniture (all rendered totally useless) and extra attendance, fires, and lights etc during Yemmerrawany's sickness'. Why these goods were 'rendered totally useless' is puzzling, but as historian Jack Brook has observed, it sounds like the verdict of an attending doctor who ordered the disposal 'of the room's contents to stop the spread of disease'.[29] The hardships of winter combined, then, with the dreariness of schooling and the wretchedness of ill health.

One positive distraction for the two men might have been found in sitting for their portraits. Around this time, their landlord William Waterhouse made a drawing of Bennelong in profile, sketched in pen and ink-wash on stiff scrap card and signed W.W. It measures roughly 5 centimetres by 5 centimetres. A similar profile of Yemmerrawanne also exists. Although unsigned, its materials and size suggest that 'W.W.' made this image too. Yemmerrawanne's portrait is a silhouette rather than a sketch, entirely solid, providing details only of his outline and short hair.

How did the men dress in Berewal? What did their clothing signify? Who managed their depiction in the sketches? And where did these images go afterwards? The bills for the men show that clothes were their greatest expense, after accommodation. Phillip set the standard by ordering apparel for them upon arrival worth nearly £40 – roughly £3000 in today's money. This included the basics of British gentlemanly attire: buckled shoes, silk stockings, buff breeches, cotton shirts, woollen coats and lined waistcoats. Later, Phillip added hats, gloves, cravats and underwear. Fashion historian Caroline Hamilton has noted the costliness of the total outlay, which compared starkly with the average £2 per year allocated to clothe each convict in Sydney. In January, Bennelong and Yemmerrawanne also acquired 'two great coats' in a valiant effort to resist the outside cold.[30]

Presumably the men had been wearing some version of British clothing since leaving Sydney in December 1792. The worldly sailors on board as well as their hosts in Rio de Janeiro probably wanted only some nod towards European styles. The locals in Britain, on the other hand, would have demanded full coverage to satisfy their codes of decorum. Doubtless Bennelong and Yemmerrawanne found the layers of silk, cotton and wool to be uncomfortable and restrictive.

This is not to say, though, that all the clothing was forced upon them or that every item was a defeat. We know that Bennelong had been choosing to don bits and pieces of British dress since his initial capture in late 1789, but, significantly, he rarely did so as the British intended. He had always worn his favoured jacket, for instance, over bare skin. As Grace Karskens has argued, his selective curation of British articles signalled to his own kin his status at that point as a critical negotiator for them.[31]

In Berewal, despite his greater conformity to British standards, Bennelong may have thought his attire signalled to locals that he, rather than Phillip, was the chief creditor in their relationship. Every day, after all, his outfits displayed the many gifts that the British had bestowed on him since arriving.

In Waterhouse's sketch, Bennelong wears the 'spotted quilting waistcoat' that Phillip purchased on 29 May 1793. He is also wearing what was probably the 'green cloth coat' purchased on 24 May and either a frilly shirt or a frilly cravat. His ensemble befits a gentleman of high rank in Britain, much grander than the garb of ordinary British people in this age. His hair is also shaped in a genteel British fashion, cleared of the decorative shells he usually tied into it. For various reasons, as became plain upon initial arrival, Phillip had arranged for this styling because he wanted the Yiyura men to present as people fit for royal court. That Bennelong pulled it off with such apparent aplomb cannot be overlooked. Straight of back, clear of eye, and pursed of lip, Bennelong's posture indicates a canny comprehension of British protocols, and a knowledge of how to play their game of influence through the display of status.

Waterhouse's portrait served as the basis of the image that colonists most associated with Bennelong for the next two hundred years. This was the ornate illustration by James Neagle, used to illustrate David Collins' popular *Account of the English Colony at New South Wales* (1798) as well as George Cooke's authoritative *Modern and Authentic System of Universal Geography* (1802). Neagle's rendition of W.W.'s sketch softened Bennelong's expression to the point of neutrality and added a vignette of supposed Yiyura artefacts, including clubs, shields and spears. The net effect was to divert attention away from Bennelong's resolute face and emphasise instead the clash between his clothing and his accoutrements. The juxtaposition of British attire with Yiyura implements invokes a sense of instability, possibly even ridiculousness: in Neagle's hands, Bennelong becomes less the master of his own imagery or destiny than a man caught between two worlds. This was the Bennelong that endured in settler memory.

The silhouette of Yemmerrawanne did not find a second life in later publication. This was partly because Yemmerrawanne was less significant for British audiences than Bennelong, especially after his premature death, and partly because in the eighteenth century, silhouettes were of low value – in fact the word silhouette was a synonym at the time for cheapness.[32]

Despite its lack of detail, the profile does suggest that Yemmerrawanne allowed his hair to be shaped like Bennelong's. This might mean that he followed Bennelong's example, too, in wearing full British attire while in Berewal. And, again, by doing this, he might have been trying to convey a certain level of canniness about his temporary environment. Whatever his thoughts on the business of portrayal, Yemmerrawanne turned out to be better served than Bennelong by not having his image disfigured by darkening imperial prejudices.

December 1793

Bennelong and Yemmerrawanne spent their only shared British Christmas with their Eltham host, Edward Kent. They stayed for twelve days, apparently without Phillip, who was in either Covent Garden or Bath. There was as yet no tradition of Christmas trees or gifts but there was a special meal on the day – probably goose, maybe plum pudding, enjoyed in a room decorated with holly and mistletoe. Bennelong and Yemmerrawanne may have especially liked the burning of a Yule log, which was meant to stay alight till the end of the year: controlled fire was often associated with festivity in Yiyura culture. Christmas would have been a pleasing lull before the winter truly set in.[33]

On 23 December, just prior to travelling to Eltham, Bennelong attended Covent Garden Theatre. Yemmerrawanne was too sick to go with him. The show that night was a double bill, a farcical play from fifty years earlier called *The Suspicious Husband* (a comedy of errors full of sexual innuendo and madcap misunderstandings), and an updated pantomime version of the Faust legend called *The Devil Will Have His Own*, in which Dr Faustus sells his soul for limitless knowledge to the accompaniment of dragons, real fire, claps of thunder, a balletic Harlequin, and even a character named Zany.[34] Few programs epitomised better the bawdy, action-packed, multi-genre essence of eighteenth-century British theatre.

It was the kind of entertainment that Bennelong evidently liked. He had first sampled this sort of show in August, at Sadler's Wells Theatre and, as noted, went on to see several similar productions before departing Berewal. All included boisterous content similar to that enjoyed now in December. The only exception – perhaps considered a mistake – was the Handel oratorio in March. As suggested, the correlation of the more typical version of London shows with public descriptions of contemporary Yiyura garabaras is worth contemplating.

Hunter once attended a garabara with Bennelong, and described the costuming, lighting, movements and music involved. The preparations were extensive, he wrote. Women painted the men with white pipe clay mixed with water: 'no fop preparing for an assembly was ever more desirous of making his person irresistibly beautiful'. Firelight was essential. It provided just the right combination of sparkle and shadow. The dancing was exceptionally complex. A chorus of two dozen performed difficult routines of wide-legged stomping, rapid knee trembling, pairs facing each other, pairs moving back to back, the company all sitting, then the company all leaping up. Hunter admitted the complexity was 'such as none of us could imitate'. The music entailed the beating of two sticks, a solo singer, and many children drumming their own bodies.[35]

Accounts by other officers agreed that Yiyura performances were elaborate, ritualised, and often went all night. Sometimes they were frightening, often they were joyful. Scholars today emphasise that what the Yiyura would have permitted outsiders to see was not what they would have put on for themselves alone. Even so, the same kinds of body paint, routines and instruments probably carried over. If the stories told in garabaras were not evident to eighteenth-century British observers, later Indigenous narrators assure that each carried 'multiple layers of meaning', communicating reflections on recent events and ideas on how to mediate them.[36]

We know that Bennelong participated in many garabaras around his Country. For a man so far from home, the energy and drama of British theatre presented the closest match to a beloved custom. He didn't need to understand every plot twist and innuendo. Going by the scripts of British performances at the time that survive, it's unlikely every local in the audience would have followed everything either. It was the celebratory if momentary immersion in a somewhat familiar artform that mattered.

There is less evidence to show that Phillip enjoyed theatrical shows. While he too attended the garabara that Hunter described, his own views are indiscernible. Colonial records indicate that in June 1789 Phillip presided over the first official performance of British theatre in New South Wales, when a makeshift convict company staged for the officers a well-known comedy called *The Recruiting Officer*. With a strong emphasis on slapstick, this play resembled *The Suspicious Husband*, but with an appropriately military overlay. Phillip's reaction, other than forbearance, is invisible.[37]

The critic Robert Jordan argues persuasively that convicts had put on non-official plays long before June 1789, starting on board the ships heading to Botany Bay. A marine's logbook recorded that just before arrival, some convicts 'made a play and sang many songs'. Jordan contends that the earliest theatre in the colony was convict-driven, not officer-created, but that these shows left few traces since 'what the convicts did in their spare time was of no interest to officialdom unless it involved breaking the law'.[38]

Although on his return Phillip moved between the two main centres of performance in Britain, London and Bath, he does not appear to have attended much if any theatre. Playacting was not high among the interests of a work-focused naval commander. He may have found it too entangled in the realm of irrational fantasy.

November 1793

Bennelong and Yemmerrawanne spent the entire month of November in Eltham. This was the stint that secured their fondness for the place, but it was a fondness born out of pain rather than joy. Yemmerrawanne was gripped throughout this stay by the illness that would eventually kill him.

Yemmerrawanne had already sampled a range of unspecified laxatives, bark brews, oil rubbings and blisterings. These treatments continued in Eltham, according to the treasury bills, but he now added Fothergill's Pills to the mix. Fothergill's Pills contained purgative plants, roots and herbs, as well as a dose of antinomy, helpful against parasites but later found to also cause significant heart problems.[39] Almost needless to say, nothing worked.

Scholars have tried to ascertain how a physician might diagnose Yemmerrawanne today. Most alight on pulmonary disease, though the patient also suffered from some sort of wound in his leg. The heavy reliance in eighteenth-century Britain on expelling bad humours from the body through bleeding would not, in this instance, have aided matters.[40]

If Bennelong was indeed a Garadyigan or healer, he would have looked upon Yemmerrawanne's trials with particular anxiety. Since he was always with his kinsman, he would have had plenty of opportunity to use his own methods. Many, interestingly, resembled British treatments. They often involved herbal drinks and pastes made of roots and stone. In addition, the Yiyura practised making cuts to the skin on the same principle of alleviation as British bleedings. One Yiyura healing that differed was the use of song and touch for sore parts.[41] Maybe Bennelong offered this to Yemmerrawanne. It would have given more soothing effects than the other remedies he tested.

Although Phillip did not visit Eltham in November, he could have empathised with Yemmerrawanne: Phillip had been plagued with poor health from youth. When only nineteen he had received one naval discharge that pronounced him 'unserviceable'. In the 1770s, a superior noted that his constitution was always 'delicate'. And throughout his years in New South Wales he complained of a debilitating pain in his side. The colony's surgeon once described Phillip's experience of this ailment as 'torture'. In a letter to Lord Sydney, Phillip guessed that his 'violent pain' came from his left kidney. It 'renders me at times unable to ride or walk'.[42]

Indeed, Phillip's bad health headlined his letter of resignation from the governorship, delivered formally in July 1793. 'It is, Sir, with the greatest regret, that I ask to resign a charge [due to] my complaint.'[43] He needed to focus on getting better, he explained, however much it distressed him to break a commitment to the state.

In the spa town of Bath, where Phillip went in search of treatment, his physician was Dr John Hutton Cooper. Cooper later married into the family of Phillip's friend Henry Chapman, but the Chapmans never took to Cooper, declaring him eventually a 'reprobate and fortune hunter'.[44] Sources do not reveal what kind of medicine he administered, but the Chapmans' opinion suggests it was not strongly tied to reputable research.

That said, it must be acknowledged that Phillip never again spoke of kidney pain after resigning his governorship. Either the Bath experience mostly worked for him, or his body just hadn't coped as well as his mind had with the stress of colonising others.

October 1793

The most remarkable outing for Bennelong and Yemmerrawanne in October was to the Parkinson Museum in London's Blackfriars Rotunda. The men crossed the Thames River for the purpose. Phillip probably accompanied them, knowing that Banks had deposited in the museum some of the things he'd been sending back from

New South Wales. He may have been anxious to see exactly which things they were.[45]

The Parkinson Museum had opened only five years earlier, though the bulk of its collection had been known to Londoners for two decades. Entrepreneur James Parkinson had acquired nearly thirty thousand items from Sir Ashton Lever, who was offloading his collection because he could no longer turn their display into a profit. Lever had been collecting nature specimens and ethnographic artefacts since the early 1770s, many from Captain Cook's first two Pacific voyages. His own museum in the West End never succeeded, principally because Londoners were not yet accustomed to the concept of museum-going.[46]

In October 1793 the purpose-built rotunda housed a kaleidoscope of objects. The grand round room at the centre had shelves running all the way up its dome, every inch packed with taxidermal animals, multicoloured rocks, glass-encased shells and dry-pressed flowers. Included were at least three stuffed kangaroos, and several specimens of coral, sea urchin, oyster shell and gum leaves from around the Yiyura's harbour. Running off the main chamber were a dozen or so other rooms crammed with human-made implements, from canoes to weapons to ceremonial dresses. Among these was one 'black club from N.S. Wales'.[47]

Bennelong's reaction to seeing these objects can be glimpsed in the writings of another museum patron that day, a teenaged medical student called Robert Jameson who happened to be visiting at the same time as Bennelong. He noted in his diary: 'I had the singular good fortune while there to see the two New Hollanders who arrived about 6 months ago . . . They seemed to affect a kind of chearfulness which was far from being real.'[48]

Was it the taxidermy that worried Bennelong? He had seen British officers pack off the skins of local fauna to Berewal for years, but only in salted form, not engorged with cotton and wire. It was one thing to see a stuffed deer's head in a British pub, but quite another to encounter an animal unique to his homeland petrified on a shelf in a dusty hallway.

Possibly it was the black club that disturbed. The Yiyura believed that some objects were imbued with special powers and could only belong to or be seen by certain people. Observing familiar objects in seriously unfamiliar places would have raised urgent questions around permission, means and effect. In this respect, of course, Bennelong's British hosts, if they'd been thinking comparatively, could have sympathised. Contemporary Britons would have been just as disconcerted to see, for example, a display of Captain Cook's clothing in Hawai'i or the curation of King George III's sceptre in the independent United States. All cultures have boundaries that only become clear when particular things cross them.

There is a third reason why Bennelong and Yemmerrawanne might have been distressed in the Parkinson. The eventual catalogue of sale indicates that the collection also contained human remains. It listed six human foetuses, two human hands, two human skulls, an arm, a tongue and an ear. Given the Yiyura's known aversion to the uncovered dead body, these items alone would have turned the visitors' stomachs. If Bennelong and Yemmerrawanne suspected that these remains came from their own people, they would have felt more than just wretched.

Phillip was possibly seeking in the Parkinson some certainty about precisely this question – whether or not there were Yiyura skulls on display. Researcher Matthew Fishburn has recently argued that Phillip brought at least three Aboriginal skulls to Britain on his voyage home that year. Banks had been harassing him for such items since 1790, and Phillip had twice put him off, writing tersely, 'you shall have heads when I can get any'.[49] But in August 1793, just before this visit to the museum, Banks wrote to two of his peers in Europe that he was relieved at long last to send to each of them a 'Cranium of a male native of New Holland'.[50] The only likely transporter of these skulls at this time was Phillip. Fishburn is convinced that a third skull went to the London-based anatomist John Hunter, whose personal collection cites one cranium from 'New South Wales' gained right before Hunter's death, which occurred around the time of this museum visit.[51]

Were there more skulls on that voyage from Yiyura Country to Berewal? If so, they would also have gone to Banks, that powerful adviser to government who so often got his way. In turn, he may have deposited them in the Parkinson Museum for the public's so-called edification. It's plain that Parkinson didn't have any compunction about displaying human remains.

The silence on this question is one of the more aggravating in the story of Bennelong and Phillip. All we know for sure is that the British practice of collecting human heads was not, even at the time, uncontroversial. Banks and Parkinson were on one end of an ethical spectrum: both had heard contemporaries tell them directly that the practice was in fact 'the greatest of crimes'.[52] Phillip's terseness on the topic suggests he stood a bit further apart from them on the spectrum. His reserve lines up, in an oblique way, with a preference for public-centred colonies over privatised ones, and for William Pitt's clearer imperial methods over Edmund Burke's more cynical ones. Each inclination in Phillip was a sign of an older approach to empire – monopolistic and subjugating to be sure, but not as individualistic, or arguably as macabre, as some of the attitudes that were now emerging.

If Phillip didn't yet have the language to discern this subtle shift in imperial sensibility, he may have rationalised his compliance with Banks's wishes as the cost of empire's reliance on an intensely nepotistic system of patronage.

Engraving of the rotunda in the Parkinson Museum, 1790s

September 1793

Phillip's personal aide while in New South Wales, Henry Waterhouse, had left the colony on naval orders two years before his boss. He missed reuniting with Phillip in 1793 because he was by then in Europe fighting the French Revolution. Henry was not present, therefore, to introduce Phillip to his father or to offer William's services as Bennelong's landlord. Probably Phillip already knew William Waterhouse via their shared naval networks, but if not he quickly made the acquaintance. Either Phillip or someone else in Home Affairs arranged for William's house in convenient Mayfair to be the primary lodging for the Wangal visitors.

William Waterhouse and Phillip were roughly the same age, though William came from a more genteel family. For nearly two decades he had enjoyed the position of musician to the king's brother,

Prince Henry Frederick.[53] William appears to have named his son after the prince, who in turn agreed to be Henry's godfather. At the time of the first fleet's departure to New South Wales, Prince Henry was also a rear admiral. He had evidently arranged for the appointment of his godson as Phillip's aide on the voyage.[54] The nepotistic system of patronage indeed ran deep.

Henry Waterhouse proved a major success in his role of aide, keeping up a relationship with Phillip for the rest of his life. It's difficult to tell who felt more indebted to whom in 1793: William to Phillip for launching his boy's career, or Phillip to William for providing him with a well-bred and loyal assistant.

Phillip and William Waterhouse must have met numerous times while Phillip acted as the Wangal men's official chaperone and Waterhouse their designated landlord. We can only speculate if they were together on the night in September 1793 when Bennelong and Yemmerrawanne took the initiative to perform a song at the Mayfair residence. The only evidence we have of this recital is a single sheet of music recording the notes and words of the men's song. They were written down by the Welsh folklorist Edward Jones, who lived directly across from Waterhouse.

Jones was also a musician in a royal household. He was the harpist for the king's son, the Prince of Wales. The two neighbours and semi-colleagues in royal service were likely friends. Waterhouse knew that Jones had a particular fascination for hearing and preserving folk music of all descriptions. Jones had recently published the well-received *Musical and Poetical Relicks of the Welsh Bards*, in which he asserted that a people's music was central to their liberty. Despite his professional position with royalty, Jones was something of a critic of empire. He was convinced that the English had managed to colonise the Welsh because they had suppressed Welsh music. He was interested in any attempt to 'save from oblivion' the music of other people now vulnerable to takeover.[55]

Jones's sheet is titled *'A SONG of the NATIVES of NEW SOUTH WALES'*. It claims to record 'the Singing of BENELONG, and YAM-ROWENY'. It goes on: 'when they Sang, it seem'd indispensable to them to have two sticks, one in each hand to beat time with the Tune; one end of the left hand stick rested on the ground, while the other in the right hand was used to beat against it, according to the time of the notes'.

We know this particular song was popular among the Yiyura because, remarkably, its lyrics were recorded in a similar way by at least two officers at New South Wales. In 1793 in London, Jones heard the men's lyrics as: 'Barrabula barrama manginewey enguna'. Two years earlier in Sydney, the linguist William Dawes heard from some other singers: 'Parabula Parama Manginiwa Yenbongi'. And at the same time, the judge-advocate David Collins heard: 'barriboolah, barremah . . . mangennywau yengonah'.[56]

Jones would have been delighted to learn that a couple of centuries later his efforts partly paid off. In 2010 a pair of Aboriginal musicians re-enacted the recital on Yiyura Country using Jones's sheet. Bundjalung man Clarence Slockee and Muruwari man Matthew Doyle donned Georgian garb and performed a beautiful version of 'Barabula' while standing on Bennelong Point in Sydney. Slockee commented that he found the experience served 'as a link to ancestors'.[57] It could not erase eight generations of colonisation, but someone like Jones would have argued that the performance yet stood for an essential liberty – indeed, an irreducible sovereignty – that had survived nonetheless.

August 1793

Before sickness hit Yemmerrawanne and before the weather turned cold, the Wangal visitors made the most of the outdoors. The late summer involved boating on the Thames, excursions to some iconic London sites and leisure rides around the countryside.

The boating occurred on 10 August. The bills state that a boat was needed 'for the natives bathing'. Colonists had reported Bennelong frequently swimming in Sydney Harbour in earlier years. At a time when few British people could swim at all, the sight of two men enjoying the waters of London's main river would have been rare, compelling and, given the condition of the Thames, not a little disturbing.

They also went to city spas, urban parks, and the armoury and zoo at the Tower of London. The latter, which housed animals gifted to the royal family from the thirteenth century on, included lions, tigers, eagles, jackals, bears, ostriches, and recently, two kangaroos.[58] The exotic nature of the animals matched the magnitude of the arsenal also housed in the Tower: to British people, both were interlinked symbols of their empire's reach and power.

Earlier in the summer, the *True Briton* newspaper reported that Bennelong and Yemmerrawanne 'have been at several of the Country Seats of the Nobility'.[59] It's not clear what all the places outside London the men visited were, but they included the camps of soldiers scattered on the city's outskirts. The *Morning Post* on 1 August commented that 'the Two Natives of Botany Bay . . . are now on a visit to the different encampments, for the purpose, as the Duke of Richmond shrewdly observes, of impressing them with a just idea of the *military genius of the country!*'

The Duke of Richmond, then in charge of military infrastructure in Britain, put his finger on the key intent behind these outings. They were not mere diversions or time-fillers. As with their visit to the Hastings trial, and even to the theatres and museums of London, Bennelong and Yemmerrawanne were expected to be dazzled by what they saw. Military strength and cultural luxuries were equal signs of a formidable nation: one showed that Britain could get its way on the world's stage, the other indicated the riches that victory brought or created. Each was, apparently, an important message for anyone associated with the empire to absorb.

Phillip was the guiding intelligence behind the men's jaunts. Like the Duke of Richmond, he was a diligent student of Britain's history of interaction with Indigenous peoples and knew that since the 1600s colonial officials had been bringing Indigenous envoys from elsewhere to Britain in order to woo them into national partnerships. His predecessors had escorted Native Americans and Pacific Islanders to Britain for the same reason, with a similar itinerary to that orchestrated for the Yiyura men. In all cases, the aim was to forge formal alliances with peoples who might otherwise side with Britain's imperial competitors, such as France.[60]

Phillip's observance of this practice is poignant because it suggests that he thought Bennelong might serve one day, too, as a negotiator for a treaty. The question was by no means resolved for Phillip in 1793, despite many then and later thinking that it was. Phillip knew from Britain's prior experiences that treaties had to be offered to peoples who showed signs of land cultivation, or of permanent construction, or of sustained social reason.[61] The fact that he sought to bring two Yiyura people to Britain implies that he had not yet ruled out these qualities among the Aboriginal population. To do so would have gone against a long and unbroken tradition – even if he knew that some of his direct bosses, in their minds, already had. Phillip hadn't yet figured out that in the absence of European competition for New South Wales, those same bosses would now never be challenged on the issue.

As to what Bennelong and Yemmerrawanne made of their excursions, so early in their stay, the records are dismally reticent. Red-coated soldiers may not have carried quite the punch that the Duke of Richmond assumed; many of the colonists back home looked like them, and few had thus far impressed the Yiyura as embodiments of 'military genius'. Likewise, the exoticism of the menageries and urban edifices may not have symbolised reach and power if no one bothered to explain them as such. Bennelong and Yemmerrawanne already came from a place of exceptional beauty and fauna: Britain's gardens and animals were conceivably less astonishing than imagined.

July 1793

On 15 July 1793, Phillip arranged for Bennelong to visit St Paul's Cathedral, one of London's most awe-inspiring constructions. It was by far the largest building in London; its massive dome dominated the city skyline throughout the eighteenth century, its ornate stonework conjured other empires of the past.

Phillip, whatever his family background, was baptised a member of the Protestant Church of England, or the Anglican Church, to which the vast majority of Britons then also belonged. As with most Anglicans at the time, religion featured only indirectly in his everyday life. Protestant Christianity ordered Phillip's yearly and weekly calendar, his activities on public holidays, and his basic understanding of right and wrong, but few mentions of his faith appear in any document by or about him.

The British monarch was and still is the head of the Church of England. As the representative of the crown while in New South Wales, Phillip had thus been obliged to establish a scaffold of Anglican conventions. His official instructions were to ensure 'a due observance of Religion and Good Order among all the inhabitants'. During his five-year governorship, this did not extend far. He allowed the colony's first clergyman, Richard Johnson, to distribute Christian reading materials and to hold open-air services, but he never got around to building a church anywhere in the settlements before he departed. In late 1791, Phillip issued a decree that 'every person will regularly attend public worship', yet he failed to define 'regularly' and did not himself appear at services every week.[62]

Anglicanism in the eighteenth century roughly entailed belief in one god who was the figurative if not literal creator of the world. This god existed in an ascendant position to the world and communicated his teachings via the Bible as well as through direct relationships in faith. Chief among these teachings was that God stood for love and charity while God's demonic foes encouraged evil and avarice.[63]

Such a theology differed starkly to Yiyura beliefs in this era. Although the evidence is much scarcer, the Yiyura do not seem to have held either to the idea of a single deity or to any sharp split between the sacred and the secular. Nor did they have just one repository of teachings, or a simple match of values to Christian understandings of virtue and sin.

Bennelong's cosmology instead teemed with many spiritual beings who were indivisible from nature. Indigenous educator Dennis Foley has described it as a 'totemic landscape' which recognised both how Ancestors made Country and how Country embodied Ancestors. Yawuru scholar Shino Konishi adds that each clan also had multiple stories of this process, 'of how the land was traversed and marked by the Ancestral Beings who created landforms, people, animals, plants, and celestial stars'. Humans accessed spiritual laws through their totem, which also served as a link to kin. Compared to Protestant Christianity, Yiyura morality seemed to focus on generational relations more than on, say, sexual relations; they emphasised respect for Elders more than rules about intercourse. It also seemed more worried about disloyalty and dishonour than about anger or envy.[64]

When Bennelong returned to his home, the colonist Collins quizzed him about his religious beliefs. 'I asked him where the black men (or Eora) came from?' Bennelong apparently hesitated. Collins prompted, 'did they come from any island? His answer was, that he knew of none: they came from the clouds . . . and when they died, they returned to the clouds.' Collins went on to say that Bennelong 'wished to make me understand that they ascended in the shape of little children, first hovering in the tops and in the branches of trees; and mentioned something about their eating, in that state, their favourite food, little fishes'.[65]

Collins was contemptuous of what he heard. His point in recounting Bennelong's words in his *Account* was to show that the Yiyura man's beliefs were similar to those of some evangelical Protestants, who, Collins thought, simplified Christianity to babyish tenets. Too busy belittling evangelicals, Collins did not stop to wonder if Bennelong was in fact telling him what Bennelong thought Collins wanted to hear – or, as is more likely the case, what Bennelong hoped would deter Collins from delving any further into Yiyura knowledge.

Bennelong's answers were doubtless cribbed from what he'd picked up in Britain. In places like St Paul's, he'd learned about a god who resided above the world and yet apparently created all of it; a god who was often depicted surrounded by cherubim and frequently symbolised by the image of pisces. Clouds and fish-eating children feature in no other references to Yiyura cosmology from this period, few as those references admittedly are. Bennelong may have been interested to listen to details about Phillip's religion but he was reluctant to divulge much about his own.

June 1793

The first full month of Bennelong's stay in Britain was a hectic time of shopping for clothes, discovering theatres, memorising landmarks, and moving into Waterhouse's Mayfair residence. For Phillip, the chief focus was on arranging for the Yiyura visitors to meet with King George III. In this mission, however, he did not succeed.

The high cost of the clothes Phillip ordered for Bennelong and Yemmerrawanne is the first clue that the governor assumed, as had so many governors before him, that he'd be presenting the men as envoys at court. All previous significant Indigenous visitors for the previous eighty years had met with the sovereign, among them the Ra'iatean Mai in 1774, the Cherokee Ostenaco in 1762, a delegation of Creek in 1734, and the four supposed Iroquois in 1710. Each of these arrivals had attended court either to broach the idea of a formal agreement or to confirm one recently made. Not all were ultimately successful but all were seen as sufficiently important to be granted an audience with the British sovereign.[66]

The second clue as to Phillip's expectations is the itinerary: all the previous delegations had also visited St Paul's Cathedral, soldier encampments, the Tower of London, palaces, gardens, theatres, shops, and the Houses of Parliament. Phillip understood this was the time-tested way that Britain got Indigenous people to be so overawed they would hand over the lands it wanted. He thought that Bennelong and Yemmerrawanne were to be the latest subjects of the practice.

And the third clue is the tutor Phillip hired to help the Wangal men refine their English language skills. He realised that communication would be critical in any future talks about Britain's long-term viability in Aboriginal lands. As early as 1791, Phillip had written home from New South Wales: 'I think that my old acquaintance Bennillon will accompany me when ever I return to England & from him when he understands English, much information may be attained, for he is very intelligent.'[67] A year and half later, Bennelong had become partially proficient. His time in Britain made him even more fluent.

In the end, though, the information that colonists wrought from Bennelong was not diplomatic. Bennelong never did meet King George III. Without strong backing from the Home Affairs Office that administered the colonies, Phillip failed to secure the meeting he'd always assumed would happen. The failure may have felt minor at the time, especially for a governor who was clearly moving on from his colonial experience. But this new attitude towards Bennelong encapsulated a momentous shift in British imperial policy. Where every earlier push into so-called New Worlds had generated a treaty, Britain's advance into New South Wales did not. The government now calculated that without direct threats from fellow Europeans – and also with a fresh determination to regain all that had been lost in the American Revolution – it could set a new legal precedent regarding prior occupants of the lands it desired.[68]

Twice that summer, Phillip visited St James's Palace. On 2 June 1793 *Woodfall's Register* wrote that 'the presentations to the Queen [included] Governor Phillip, on his arrival from Botany Bay'. Nine days earlier, *The Times* had written that he attended the king himself. On neither occasion did Phillip appear to take along his Yiyura guests. *The Oxford Journal* claimed that in between these royal visits the 'Natives of New South Wales' were observed watching the king's coach enter the palace.[69] Given the attention the press gave to king-watching then, the newspapers would have remarked if the Yiyura men had ever entered the palace too.

In one perverse sense, the fact that the Yiyura men did not appear at court may have been a blessing, at least for Phillip. Unlike many earlier Indigenous envoys, Bennelong had studied British colonists in intimate proximity for several years before arriving in their metropolis. His English may have already been good enough to understand a trap when he heard one. If the king's court had offered him comprehensible terms for a treaty, Bennelong would perhaps have rejected them out of hand, embarrassing Phillip profoundly.

Collins later received a letter composed during this month of June about how the Yiyura men were faring in London. He learned that 'Bennillong and Yemmerrawannie were well, but not sufficiently divested of the genuine, natural love for liberty and their native country, to prefer [Britain] to the woods of New South Wales.'[70] Such a deep attachment to their own land, and such indifference to other people's, might have made the men dismiss any hint of an unfair deal. Certainly, there is no trace of discontent on Bennelong's part that he missed meeting the British sovereign. He always knew that his task in Berewal was to gather knowledge about the foreign culture, not necessarily to make any compromises on behalf of his own.

May 1793

Phillip, Bennelong and Yemmerrawanne first arrived in London on 21 May. Most of their initial days were spent in temporary accommodation at the boarding house of a Mr E. Howson.[71] After six months on a cramped ship, they could finally have some space, quietude and fresh food.

The journey to London from the port in Falmouth took a solid two days. This meant they must have stepped from ship to coach almost immediately; they only docked in Falmouth on 19 May. The *General Evening Post* described their arrival at length: 'Governor Phillip has brought home with him two of the natives of New Holland, a man and a boy. The Atlantick has also on board four kangaroos, lively and healthy, and some other animals peculiar to that country . . . Specimens of their fishing-tackle, spears, and shields, are likewise brought home in the Atlantick.'[72] The *Post* went on to make many disparaging comments about the Yiyura men's supposedly low level of civilisation and high level of cruelty.

The next twelve months would raise questions about which society was the more sophisticated and kindly. The trying experiences of British medicine, weather, and certain Christian protocols would leave much for the Yiyura visitors to desire. The deeper meanings of both the Hastings trial and the Parkinson collection, meanwhile, were to prove almost too repulsive to grasp at all.

Some things, of course, would be positive. The meeting with Jones, Waterhouse and Kent. The British theatre and countryside. The leisure activities and holidays. If for Bennelong the whole trip was a fact-finding mission, it would deliver beyond his wildest expectations.

Whether his experiences were good or bad, Bennelong was notably never a pawn of his hosts. He dealt with everything London threw at him on his own terms.

For Phillip, that first year back in Britain would be equally divided between lows and highs. He would be disappointed not to conclude his governorship with a clearer sense of legal agreement with the Yiyura in New South Wales. He would be hassled by Banks to participate in a traffic that shocked many of his own peers. And he would be frustrated by the haphazard news that filtered in regarding the Sydney colony. On the upside, he would embark on a new marriage and discover a new interest in his family heritage. These endeavours perhaps confirmed for him that it would be better from now on to look forward to new horizons than to spend too long thinking about the past.

The *Atlantic*'s arrival in Falmouth was the start of a new chapter for everyone on board.

DÉTENTE

Forging Order, 1793–1790

Phillip and Bennelong depart for England • Earlier, in the colony, they approach food and land in different ways • Three examples of diplomacy between Bennelong and Phillip • Bennelong's relations with his womenfolk • Phillip's notion of separate gender spheres • Phillip builds Bennelong a hut

The passage across the Pacific Ocean in early 1793 entailed the usual mixture of 'brease', 'clowd', 'haz' and 'squarl' – or so wrote the British marine John Easty in his journal of the voyage.[1] The transport vessel *Atlantic* was carrying home Governor Arthur Phillip after nearly five years in New South Wales, along with Bennelong and Yemmerrawanne.

The *Atlantic* left Sydney Harbour on 11 December 1792. By mid-morning the ship was clear of the imposing sandstone headlands. As he sailed into open water, Phillip could look back and catch the summer sunlight shining on the harbour's surface. Beyond, he could see the blueish-green lands that he now knew held much greater complexities than he'd once assumed. The land itself had been hard to understand, both rich and unyielding. Managing its products and its distribution among members of the colony had proved even harder. This is not even to mention the problem of recognising the Indigenous people who claimed original sovereignty.

The early passage through the harbour had been slow. It had been accompanied by smaller British boatloads of officers bidding their final farewells, along with several watercraft of Yiyura fisherwomen going about their daily routines. If Bennelong had turned towards the southern coastline at this point, he would have gazed directly upon the buildings, pathways, docks and fences now constructed around it. He would have identified them as monuments to the foreign invasion, but at the same time seen in them reminders of how his people had yet curtailed, resisted, modified or otherwise survived it.

The ship had left its dock at dawn. David Collins, the judge-advocate who remained behind, observed that Bennelong's wife was greatly distressed by her husband's departure.[2] This was Kurubarabula, who had married Bennelong two years earlier. His marriage to Boorong was still some way into the future while his relationship with Barangaroo had ended tragically about thirteen months before. Kurubarabula's affection would not last, but it was heartfelt on the day she saw Bennelong leave his homelands.

There was no woman to cry over Phillip's departure. Between Charlott and Isabella, Phillip had no significant female partners. Women featured less often and less powerfully in Phillip's life than in Bennelong's. That said, Phillip had been charged over his five years as governor with disciplining up to 830 convict women, protecting around eighty free women, and preserving the integrity of the women of the Yiyura. He had tried to do so with as much detachment as possible.

Phillip's and Bennelong's leave-taking came at the end of two years of relative stability. It had not been a time of outright peace: skirmishes and disappointments had persisted throughout. But compared to the ambushes, kidnappings, and devastating disease outbreaks of the initial three years of the colony, this period had felt calmer. It was a period that might be labelled détente – an easing of troubles between peoples during which a kind of order is forged. Loosely, this order operated in New South Wales in three main ways: in how the peoples of the harbour managed land, in how they managed conflict, and in how they managed relations between the sexes.

Phillip and Bennelong had played leading roles in the creation of the détente. Indeed, these are the roles most often associated with them in modern memory. But the men did not always fulfil them in the manner most commonly assumed today. Phillip's role was not that of a nation-founding paternalist who controlled events through humanitarian beneficence; rather, he helped to forge orderliness (when he wasn't outright condoning violence) through a combination of inadvertent avoidance and rational compromise. His wider imperial priorities led him away from exacerbating tensions with the Yiyura, but when faced with direct differences he usually calculated a middle path between settlers' and Indigenous desires. Likewise, Bennelong's role was neither that of gullible ally nor treacherous sell-out; he too was a pragmatic negotiator. Importantly, at times he exercised what might be called a subtle politics of refusal. Bennelong led efforts in de-escalating relations between the two major groups in the harbour purely to protect the Yiyura from what he'd so far seen of the colonists' behaviour and its effects.

We know this détente was short-lived. Phillip's successors increasingly favoured settler wants over Indigenous rights, and these at length intruded into the Yiyura spaces and customs that Phillip had left untouched. Unlike the governor, Bennelong had to keep living with the colonists after their brief moment of understanding. Witnessing the erosion of the fragile stability he had helped achieve, Bennelong eventually disengaged from all colonial business. He may have reflected during this latter period that the work he had done in the early 1790s was at least a gutsy attempt at conciliation. It had slowed down the rate of destruction. And it served as an example of one way to defend community.

Food and land

Phillip's final year in the colony was his first year of a reliable supply of European foodstuffs. From June 1792, ships from both Britain and British Calcutta arrived carrying generous replenishments of flour, rice, beef and pork. These vessels also brought the first substantial numbers of livestock that did not either expire or escape immediately upon release. Earlier that year, too, the colony had finally managed a decent crop of wheat, barley and turnips. By October 1792 the surveyor Charles Grimes believed that the 'worst is over in the colony, [though] I make no doubt about it, they have been dreadfully in want'. Now, in fact, Grimes felt 'better and fatter than when I left England'.[3]

The dreadful 'want' of the previous four years was probably Phillip's biggest problem as governor. Certainly it was his most persistent. He could never get away from the stricken faces of officers and convicts alike, who recorded their fears of starvation more regularly than any other issue. 'Famine besides was approaching with gigantic strides,' wailed the marine Watkin Tench in 1790. Some, like the surgeon John Harris, believed this was due to the lack of ships from Britain, causing him to give up all hope of seeing home again, 'not from sickness but from starvation'. Others, like the felon Thomas Watling, thought that the potential of famine was due to the impossibility of growing anything. 'The face of the country is deceitful,' he complained, 'having every appearance of fertility [it is] yet productive of no one article in itself fit for the support of mankind.'[4]

It's true that promised deliveries of naval supply were chronically delayed, and that the harbour's shores seemed initially to reject most seeds, saplings and cloven hoofs. The news in 1790 of not one but two supply ships sinking to the bottom of the ocean was a particular blow. It came on top of the discovery that the general environment, celebrated by James Cook and Joseph Banks for being open and luxuriant, was instead dense with iron-like trees and rooted in unpredictable soil.

DÉTENTE

But this well-worn story of the colony's so-called hungry years needs some amendment.[5] As several scholars have recently pointed out, the colony never did get to the point of famine. Overall, the death rate was remarkably low compared to that in Britain, and the fertility rate was remarkably high, both of which are impossible to achieve under starvation conditions. Records show too that rations ranged between two thousand and three thousand calories per day, which is roughly within modern estimates of adequacy.[6]

How, then, to account for the discrepancy between narratives of deprivation and this evidence of sufficiency? Most recent revisionist scholars have been too eager to flip the usual explanation on its head. Instead of pointing to a neglectful metropolitan government and a colonial prejudice against Indigenous foods, they have posited a watchful metropole and a refreshing openness to local fare.[7] This reversal, however, is as dubious as the original thesis. Sending seven hundred and fifty convicts to an unknown overseas gaol is not indicative of a nurturing government. Equally, there is little proof in this inaugural period of any Briton exclaiming about the wonders of the colony's natural produce. The paradox is better explained by pointing to the conditions of a prison in exile and by the colonists' obsession with the familiar over the new.

What was essentially lacking in Phillip's penal settlement was freedom and enough of the known comforts of home. The restrictions on liberty bred negative feelings, as they always do, which in turn made the settlers take a poor view of any reduction in European commodities. They often equated less with nothing. This helped conjure the *idea* of imminent famine even when the reality was not as severe. Phillip had a vested interest in fostering a preference for European commodities over Antipodean ones because they were among the few things he could control in a prison without walls. As food historian Jacqui Newling reminds us, the distribution of food in such places served the requirements of discipline as much as it served the sustenance of inmates.[8]

The colony at Sydney in fact abounded with viable calories. Various British commentaries of the era revealed that the wild greens 'grew in abundance about the settlement'. They noted that fish were at times so plentiful that 'one haul of the sein [could] serve the ships company, hospital, battalion & a great part of the convicts'. They saw the 'oysters, cockles & muscles [that] are to be got for little trouble'. And they constantly remarked on the kangaroos, bats, reptiles and birds everywhere.[9] Phillip, however, limited the extent to which colonists could gather these Antipodean foods and always discouraged (or neglected to promote) a sense that they were equal to familiar foods.

Tench once outlined Phillip's method in this regard, as well as his own belief that local substitutions were inferior. He described how in 1790, when European rations had become unfeasibly low after two years of settlement, Phillip finally did 'employ all the boats ... in procuring fish' and order 'the best marksmen' to hunt for kangaroos. These measures worked, yet left Tench unsatisfied. The colonists recovered from the spectre of famine with local fish and game, but Tench wondered if a 'full allowance ... can be called so ... without pease, oatmeal, spirits, butter, or cheese?'[10]

How far Phillip himself subscribed to the idea of dearth is hard to say. Probably, Phillip was as subject to the spectre of famine as anyone else. The point is that he acted to make the most of the colonists' fears, keeping the vast majority of his charges just outside the margin of satisfaction.

Phillip's approach was rational in terms of controlling a small penal outpost but it was not necessarily so in terms of building a prosperous future state. Later monuments and countless commentators have anachronistically insisted that Phillip's 'vision and wisdom' forged the 'success' of modern 'Australia'.[11] In fact, his actions here served only the needs of the colony as an imperial prison. They worked actively against the growth of the colony into a thriving, healthy, independent nation.

In hindsight, it is possible to see that another effect of Phillip's food policies was to minimise, for a while, the colonial threat to Yiyura resources. During Phillip's era, the Yiyura did feel an increased pressure on their food supply, especially on fish through the winter months, but most seemed to maintain tolerable sustenance during those five years. Living around a colony that preferred its own shipped goods and its own desperately tended crops, the Yiyura could enjoy enough of their local greens and fauna until at least the mid-1790s. Only after 1795 do the sources report an uptick in Yiyura people entering the colony for the explicit purpose of acquiring sustenance.[12] By then, which was well into Hunter's era, the British population had grown to such an extent that they made a significant incursion into the Yiyura's natural economy.

A similarly inadvertent restraint on colonial wreckage resulted from Phillip's land-granting schemes. His explicit instructions from the crown were to make surveys of the land as soon as possible and then to emancipate all those convicts who displayed 'good conduct' in order to work it. 'When that shall be done,' the instructions went on, '[it is our will] that you do pass grants thereof with all convenient speed to any of the said convicts.' Thirty acres were to go to freed single men, fifty acres to married men, and an extra ten acres were added for every child a family produced. The allotments were to be free of taxes for at least ten years, as long as they remained under constant cultivation.[13]

None of this occurred, however, until February 1792. The only grants Phillip gave before that – just two hundred acres in all – were to officers, settlers, and felons who had come to the end of their sentences. Historian Alan Atkinson has written that Phillip thus 'ignored' his directives.[14] But as Atkinson himself explains, this was less an act of defiance on Phillip's part than an exceptionally tight interpretation of 'good conduct'. Phillip was never persuaded that any convicts under his charge deserved to be released early. He preferred to see them repay in full their transgressions against the British state, even if it meant forestalling the capacity of the colony. As with his attitude to food distribution, then, Phillip's land policies were rational, but only in an imperial vein. A truly nation-building sense of 'vision and wisdom' would have placed the colony's long-term sustainability ahead of the crown's pursuit of punishment. It would have put more land under European cultivation sooner, and thus lessened the settler anxiety over provisions.

The one group who benefited, again unwittingly, from the slow capture of land was the Yiyura. If Phillip had followed the spirit of his instructions, the Yiyura would have seen more attempts on their homelands much earlier. Or, to put it differently, they would have been fighting off more encroachments than they already were. It is an often overlooked feature of settler histories that a colony's prosperity is at the direct expense of Indigenous wellbeing.

Thinking about Bennelong's position in relation to the colonial struggles for land and food conjures the fundamentally different ways in which Yiyura people understood both environment and sustenance. There could be no equivalent to British notions of freehold land, alienable from sovereign owners, because the Yiyura didn't believe that land could be alienated. They saw themselves as custodians of land. As already discussed, land was both made and embodied by a clan's Ancestors.

Particular totemic territories gave clans their identity and shaped their principal dietary customs, but they did not necessarily signify the only places where clans resided. As several writers have explained, eighteenth-century Yiyura people were relatively mobile over a number of specific clan areas due to changes in seasonal sustenance and the needs of inter-clan relationships. Bennelong himself exemplified how Yiyura individuals did not marry within their own clans. Families thus always included connections to other clans, which gave offspring a hierarchy of rights to other (though not limitless) nearby territories. Family units travelled regular pathways through their primary and associated territories in order to attend to kinship obligations as well as to gather food as it appeared in Country.[15]

The lack of long-lasting shelters in clan territories confused the early colonists, who thought only in terms of landed peoples (like themselves, who built permanent structures) or of nomads (as they perceived certain groups elsewhere to be, who supposedly built nothing). By 1790 Phillip understood that Sydney Harbour was made up of clan parcels, such as Bennelong's Wangal Country, and that the Yiyura had forged specific tracks from one end of the region to another. But because no clan appeared to construct enduring buildings, he still sometimes referred to the Yiyura as random 'wanderers' who did not satisfy European notions of territorial possession.[16] The Yiyura economy was confusing to Phillip because it didn't square with European expectations: if land was divided and tracked then why wasn't it also claimed via construction?

The key problem was that Phillip, like all colonists, presupposed environments of inadequate resources. People either had to roam to acquire food in this kind of land or they had to stay put in order to make it. He could not see that in regions such as that of the Yiyura, communities could be relatively free of either dictate. So long as the Yiyura travelled certain distances along kin-sanctified routes, there was no need to build powerfully extractive infrastructure over their ancestral inheritance. In early Sydney it was only the colonists who had a deep history of inadequate resources. Their predecessors had periodically faced insufficiency back in Europe, which had pushed them into concentrated farming on a massive scale.[17]

To be fair, Bennelong was no doubt as confused by Phillip's approach to land and food as Phillip was by his. During the early 1790s, Bennelong saw the colonists often send parties to the further reaches of the harbour hinterland, but they always returned so quickly and never with anything very useful to show for the effort. He saw them go to extraordinary lengths to grow their own plants, only to find them despair at the frequent failures, even while there was edible foliage all around. And he saw that the colonists devoted the majority of their labours to cutting down with metal axes huge eucalypts, but these intriguing implements were no match for the region's bloodwoods and red gums. The colonists seemed unaware of any use for fire beyond heating and cooking: they did not deploy it, as the Yiyura did, to flush out game or to help clear otherwise intractable trees.[18] And finally, the newcomers put a worrying amount of energy into hacking up sand, mud and shell middens to make dwellings, Phillip's house among them. To the Yiyura's way of thinking, this last activity suggested an unusual expectation that land should bend towards living people, rather than the other way round.

There is no direct evidence of Bennelong reacting to colonial impacts on Yiyura Country. Most British sources are too preoccupied with recounting his mannerisms and foibles, but some observations by John Hunter are worth pondering. Hunter noted that from mid-1790 Bennelong encouraged Phillip to go on short visits to Burramatta Country up the harbour, where Phillip had established a secondary settlement (which he later called Parramatta). Yet whenever Bennelong accompanied Phillip there, he showed signs of discomfort and wanted to be gone again immediately. Hunter had no full explanation for this behaviour, which he saw as oddly contrary, other than to remark that Bennelong evidently 'disliked' Burramatta, 'probably because fish is seldom procured there'.[19]

Bennelong had strong ties to the Burramattagal, who were named after the eels that were plentiful in their waters; he therefore had no natural aversion to either the Country or its food supply. His split reaction might better be seen as a two-stage response. First, he was urging Phillip to lessen his impact on the region by moving around to various sites, as the Yiyura did, so as not to completely ruin the Sydney site. But then, second, he was recoiling from the sight of the wreckage that the colonists had already inflicted at Burramatta. In 1791 Hunter remarked that 'Parramatta' showed 'great improvements', with buildings erected, roads cut, trees axed, and the ground 'grubbed up'. The same scene, though, made Bennelong 'press' Phillip to take him away and it made Bennelong's wife want to cry.[20]

Before 1790, rather than inducing the colonists to disperse, Bennelong may have used a different tactic. In 1789 Collins had worked out that the Yiyura attacks on colonists at Sydney Cove were attempts to 'prevent us from moving beyond the settlement'.[21] They were efforts at containment. By the time Bennelong got to know Phillip, he had perhaps decided that for the sake of land preservation he'd rather see the colonists employ a limited mobility similar to that of his own people. He realised the British were not going to depart anytime soon, and so a new approach to their impact was needed. He did not foresee that this switch in colonial approach would double the damage rather than halve it.

Bennelong's later total rejection of the colonists points to a third attitude to their environmental ravaging. Collins was the officer who came closest to understanding this eventual conclusion. While the Yiyura 'entertained the idea of our having dispossessed them', he reflected in his 1798 *Account*, 'they must always consider us as enemies'.[22]

If Bennelong passed through a number of stances regarding the colonial footprint on Yiyura Country, his attitude towards colonial food-gathering was more uniform. It might best be described as one of silent refusal. Bennelong was present during many of the moments of greatest colonial panic about food supply yet he never contributed any advice, sympathy or counterbalance. He resided in Phillip's house when Tench declared imminent famine and Phillip himself implemented the first reduction in European rations. He watched the colonists scramble now to add more local fish and kangaroos to their diet but offered no suggestions about better sites or methods. (Granted, the colonists never asked.) There is no chance Bennelong could have missed the new focus among the British during this crisis: Tench remarked how 'all our labour and attention were turned on one object – the procuring of food'. Bennelong simply refrained from involving himself in it.[23]

When the colonists discovered that the Yiyura gained nourishment from certain roots, they tried eating them as well, but without the necessary preparation. Soon they were bent double with 'violent spasms, cramps in the bowels, and sickness at the stomach'. They realised that the Yiyura must have 'some method of preparing these roots', but Bennelong for one never chose to explain what that was.

And when the colonists believed that winter saw all the fish 'desert' the harbour or become 'too shy' of humans, they yet witnessed Bennelong 'kill more than twenty fish' with his spear in just an afternoon. Again the colonists marvelled, yet Bennelong did not deign to teach them his skills.[24]

Partly because it is hard to read for absences in historical records, and partly because Phillip's colonists did not see Bennelong as having useful expertise on certain matters, no later observer has understood Bennelong to be exercising a politics of refusal here. Yet his intimate knowledge of colonial wants and fears makes his muteness on them seem deliberate. Such muteness is arguably a version of what Mohawk scholar Audra Simpson has called 'ethnographic refusal'. When

Indigenous people give faulty or skewed information, or none at all, Simpson argues, it is likely less an act of ignorance than a pointed protest against the terms of data exchange.[25] Just because Phillip rarely asked for help with his food issues doesn't mean that Bennelong was not also, through his silence, actively undermining the colony's growth.

In sum, Phillip's approach to land and food suited his immediate objectives, which were to manage a prison for the wider empire. His dogged commitment to London's dictates, however, had the ironic effect of checking colonial prosperity. What served London did not always serve the confidence or supposed entitlements of settlers. Less intentionally, Phillip's approach also curbed, for a time, the extent of the British encroachment into Indigenous worlds.

For his part, Bennelong attempted subtly to mould colonial impacts on Country and to stand somewhat aloof on the issue of British food supply. His actions worked similarly to soften the force of the invasion and thus soften the force of Aboriginal backlash. Neither his behaviour nor Phillip's is a traditional example of peacemaking, but each contributed to the détente between colonists and Yiyura all the same.

Managing conflict

When it came to direct conflict, Phillip and Bennelong practised more familiar forms of diplomacy. The pair gradually learned to negotiate with each other on behalf of their people. Phillip was motivated to negotiate because he'd seen how a lack of connection generally worsened violence. Violence, he knew, if it was uncontrolled, proved counterproductive to creating order. Phillip also had it in mind that Britain would need a negotiator if it was ever to sign a treaty for New South Wales.

Bennelong was equally motivated to negotiate because he believed, through the early 1790s, that some interaction with the newcomers would be safer for the Yiyura than total separation. The initial couple of years of colonial presence had not gone well.

Negotiation now meant that Phillip could maintain his authority among his charges and keep the lines of communication open with at least one Yiyura individual. It meant that Bennelong could help quell the bloodshed he'd witnessed so far and help prevent future problems from escalating.

Three incidents stand out as exemplary of their diplomacy. One, which concluded in December 1791, involved the burial of Bennelong's young Burramattagal friend Baludarri in Phillip's garden at Government House. How Baludarri ended up in the governor's garden is a convoluted story, but it reflected the way that Phillip and Bennelong worked together.

Baludarri was an older brother of Boorong's, around six or seven years younger than Bennelong and named for the local leatherjacket fish.[26] Probably because of his friendship with Bennelong, Baludarri was a frequent and welcome face in the colony by early 1791. Phillip liked Baludarri so much he even mused about inviting him, along with Bennelong, to travel to England when he left (in the role of youthful extra subsequently taken by Yemmerrawanne).

In mid-1791, however, Phillip's regard cooled when Baludarri appeared at his door in a rage. Baludarri explained that some convicts had destroyed his prized canoe, or nuwi, and that he was going to seek bloody revenge, not just on the six known culprits but 'upon all white people'. Phillip did not arrest Baludarri for these grave threats but neither did he appreciate what he regarded as an undue escalation of feelings. The governor ordered his officers to apprehend the accused convicts and made sure Baludarri witnessed their flogging. He went on to give Baludarri some trinkets in recompense for the wrecked nuwi, and even told him that one of the convicts had been hanged as punishment, though this was not true. Phillip confidently assumed that his actions had sufficiently repaid Baludarri and also taught his fellow settlers a lesson in swift colonial justice.[27]

When Baludarri took it upon himself a few weeks later to administer his revenge anyway by spearing a random convict, Phillip was furious. Baludarri's actions made a mockery of the governor's authority in front of other colonists. Phillip said now that he wanted Baludarri's head for 'wounding a white man'.[28]

At this point Bennelong entered the fray. He was with Phillip one day in August when some officers ran up to say they'd seen Baludarri boating in Sydney Cove. Phillip ordered the young man's seizure but Bennelong rushed to warn his friend and Baludarri escaped. It was a delicate moment for the two leaders. Phillip could not risk his charges seeing his edicts thwarted, but at the same time he did not want to inflame an Aboriginal counterattack. Bennelong could not allow an attack on his friend Baludarri but he nonetheless knew that undermining Phillip's leadership risked provoking some truly terrible reprisals.

The two men had been here before. They resolved this time to let some gentle back-and-forth between them erode the dilemma. Bennelong repeatedly asked Phillip to forgive Baludarri. Phillip, as Bennelong probably anticipated, refused to do so, yet nor did he issue any orders against Baludarri. A few months later, when Baludarri fell ill unexpectedly, Bennelong asked Phillip to send medical help to his friend. Phillip agreed and dispatched his surgeon (though sadly Baludarri died nevertheless, aged only around twenty). Now Bennelong applied to Phillip for Baludarri to be buried in the governor's front yard, arguably as a way of reclaiming a spot of Yiyura Country for a Burramattagal Ancestor. Phillip consented, doubting that the colonists would see this as an act of restitution or surrender. Both men gained something with this burial, Bennelong a version of recompense, Phillip an aura of benevolence among settlers.

Moreover, it was a neat way of ending the impasse between two groups of people.

The funeral of Baludarri in December 1791 went on to serve as the key demonstration to colonists of Yiyura deathways. Collins wrote about the event extensively, dwelling on the mournful procession that accompanied the body, the women's extreme lamentations and the men's martial preparedness.[29] But the burial also served to illustrate in microcosm the way that Bennelong and Phillip made their diplomatic efforts serve multiple agendas. They understood each other very well by this time and knew what to do to maintain harbour-wide order while they could.

A year earlier, Bennelong and Phillip had engaged in another negotiation. It proved to be a critical learning experience for their subsequent handling of the Baludarri incident.

In December 1790 a convict caught three Yiyura men attempting to dig up some potatoes he'd planted. When he tried to drive the men away, one of them, called Bangai, threw a fishing spear in retaliation and wounded him. Phillip heard of the attack and responded by sending no fewer than seven armed colonists to bring Bangai to him. Instead of grabbing Bangai the colonists shot him with a musket. Bangai managed to escape but left a trail of blood from garden to seashore.[30]

Bennelong identified with Bangai, though whether this was due to a close kinship tie or simply because he was a fellow Yiyura man is unclear. When he learned of the excessive colonial response to Bangai's action, he immediately sought payback by confiscating a catch of fish from two nearby colonists.

Six days later, Phillip and Bennelong learned that Bangai had died from the gunshot wound. Bennelong went to see Phillip, who instead of expressing regret over the death only scolded Bennelong for stealing the fish. Bennelong lost his temper.

Tench and Hunter give slightly contradictory reports of what happened next but it seems that Bennelong started shouting at Phillip and demanding to know who killed Bangai. Phillip called for armed assistance, knowing that if Bennelong attacked him at this point it might destroy their hard-earned détente across the whole region. Hunter's version explained that 'it was much feared [Bennelong] would do some violent act, that would oblige Governor Phillip to order him to be put to death . . . they wished to bring him to reason without proceeding to force'. Bennelong's reply to Phillip's threat of arms was to stomp off unmollified. He made sure to snatch a hatchet from the wheelwright's nearby shop as he went.

Both Bennelong and Phillip realised how stuck the other was in terms of their obligations and ambitions. But where a year later they quite quickly figured a way out of the situation with Baludarri, here it took them some weeks to reach a solution. In those weeks, Bennelong often went to Phillip's house to start the process of healing. Phillip gave him food and entrance to his yard but refused access to his house or hearth. Bennelong was affronted by the limitations. It looked like the understanding between the two leaders was stalling. While the Yiyura and the British did not immediately engage in violent recriminations with each other, neither did they advance much in communication during this month without their respective negotiators being on good terms.

In February 1791, however, Bennelong found a way back from the brink. He happened to be standing by when a British cutter capsized. The boat had been carrying a convict crew and four Yiyura people, who were catching a ride in it. The Yiyura – a mother and three youths – swam safely to shore, but Bennelong knew that the convicts could not swim. Along with some other Yiyura men, he helped save the lives of everyone in the water. He then undressed the convicts, built them a fire, dried their clothes, gave them something to eat, and accompanied them back to their settlement. Even Hunter agreed that without Bennelong's assistance, 'in all probability, one of the crew would have been drowned'.

The rescue was a huge favour to the colony, and Phillip saw it as such. The governor decided to think of Bennelong's actions as 'an atonement for his past offences' and admitted him back into his house. Bennelong, for his part, signalled to other Yiyura that Phillip had finally come to regard the confiscation of the fish and the hatchet as a fair reaction to Bangai's death. The leaders showed their respective peoples that justice had now been served, even if each party, perhaps knowingly, interpreted it in different ways. 'In consequence of this reconciliation,' Hunter wrote after the Bangai incident, 'the number of visitors greatly increased.' The Yiyura recommenced their collective return to the colony and their gradual attempts to domesticate the pale usurpers.

The first real test of Phillip and Bennelong's détente had occurred in late 1790, just two months after Bennelong decided to connect with Phillip as a free man. It revolved around the notorious killing of Phillip's convict gamekeeper John McEntire by the Bidjigal man Pemulwuy. This event has featured repeatedly in accounts of early Australian history, though rarely with regards to Phillip and Bennelong's relationship. Approaching the killing from such a view reveals a much rougher practice of negotiation than the two men later achieved. It was a foretaste of how their diplomacy would eventually work.

Pemulwuy was around Bennelong's age, a highly respected man of a clan located far away from Bennelong's Wangal. Pemulwuy and Bennelong were not closely affiliated; some even thought them adversaries. However, it appears that in November 1790 Pemulwuy resided for two weeks in the brick hut that Phillip had built for Bennelong. Phillip found it 'mysterious' that the man Bennelong called 'his enemy . . . had for more than a fortnight slept at his hut'.[31] While there, Pemulwuy took advantage of the blades found only in the colony and had his chin and head shaved. Adversaries or not, historian Keith Smith wonders if the two Yiyura men decided during this interlude to hatch a plan of attack on some member of the colony to show their displeasure at its continued occupation.[32] At the least, Bennelong might have listened to Pemulwuy's grand proposal and decided, carefully, not to derail it.

That the gamekeeper was chosen as the victim is unsurprising. Both Yiyura men knew McEntire. Bennelong had long made it clear that he detested him. Some months earlier he had shown signs of 'horror', 'resentment' and 'abhorrence' towards the man.[33] Pemulwuy never stated his exact objections, though the colonists were aware that many Yiyura suspected McEntire of killing several of their number.[34] McEntire was possibly the most disliked figure in all the harbour.

The gamekeeper met his fate on 9 December 1790 during a hunting expedition around Botany Bay (Kamay). A party of mixed Yiyura clans ambushed him in the forest. Pemulwuy was the one who plunged a stone-barbed spear (a ganadyul) into his lungs. At first the colonists did not know the attacker's name, only that he was the person who showed he 'had been lately among us' because he sported a shaven face and head.[35] Upon the spear's impact, McEntire knew his life was over. He managed to struggle back to Sydney Cove some eleven miles away but asked immediately for the clergyman and confessed he'd been a 'bad man'.[36]

McEntire did not in fact die for another six weeks but Phillip acted straightaway as if he had been murdered. He asked Bennelong for the name and location of the attacker. Bennelong answered that the man was called 'Pemullaway' and came from a clan around Botany Bay. Within days, Phillip ordered a gigantic party of nearly fifty armed colonists to march to Botany Bay and snatch two random hostages, as well as the decapitated heads of ten other local men. For the latter task he expressly provided hatchets and bags.[37]

Both Phillip and Bennelong committed significant mistakes in this incident, mistakes from which they would learn greater adeptness in the future. Phillip's mistake, most obviously, was to react with such disproportionate outrage. Settler historians across the generations have tried to explain his extreme harshness in this moment. W.E.H. Stanner believed it showed, finally, Phillip's true colours. Inga Clendinnen countered that it was more a performance of terror than anything genuinely felt. Most have opted for the contingency option, regarding it as 'uncharacteristic' of Phillip's personality. Grace Karskens has come nearest to a contextual reading by arguing that Phillip's abject cruelty here was the flipside of his measured toleration at other times: both were effects of eighteenth-century Enlightenment thinking in colonial situations.[38] That is, they were rational twinned responses to the unstable circumstance of British usurpation. Phillip sought to be neither mean nor kind, but rather to secure his authority as efficiently as possible in a place of yet dubious legal status.

What has been missing from the contextual reading is how it developed over time. Phillip continued to deploy a mixture of aggression and mediation into the 1790s, but through his relationship with Bennelong he learned gradually to lean more frequently on mediation.

Bennelong's mistake in the aftermath of McEntire's spearing was to misdirect Phillip in his search for Pemulwuy. He gave the governor the correct name but the wrong clan. Bidjigal Country circled the western edges of the Yiyura's harbour; it ended at Botany Bay, but it was not centred there. Bennelong knew that colonists assumed the 'Botany Bay clans' were either Gweagal or Kamaygal. He may have been pleased to see the colonial party set off with false information on 14 December, but if, like Clendinnen, Bennelong believed that Phillip's party would in reality be 'loath to shoot', he was sorely wrong.[39] The party, led by Tench, did fire shots. The chief casualty was a Gweagal man called Warungin, with whom Bennelong had a strong kin tie. Warungin was the brother of his third wife, Kurubarabula. Moreover, Warungin was deeply entangled with Bennelong's sometime ally, the Gadigal man Colebee. Warungin was in fact known to the colonists as 'Botany Bay Colebee'.[40]

Bennelong was irate about Warungin's unprovoked injury. A well-known portrait of him by an unnamed colonist dating from this time refers to Bennelong 'when angry after Botany Bay Colebee was wounded'. Along with anger at Phillip for his misdirected zealous reaction, he may also have been angry with himself, for being partially to blame for it. In protecting his casual associate Pemulwuy from colonial wrath, he had unwittingly exposed to harm someone much closer to him. It was an error in the handling of colonial politics that Bennelong would not repeat.

Other than Warungin's wounding, Phillip's avenging party to Botany Bay achieved remarkably little; the rest of the Yiyura people there eluded attack. Phillip sent another party the following week but this too was ineffectual. When McEntire actually died in late January, Phillip realised that the incident was best left to simmer rather than being reignited.

Unlike in subsequent moments of conflict, however, neither Bennelong nor Phillip apparently communicated well enough to their people that this one was over. Bennelong never explained sufficiently, or otherwise suffered adequately, for the attack on Warungin. As a result, the Gweagal remained hostile to Bennelong until the end of his life, and Colebee withheld his full trust. Phillip, in his turn, never formally retracted the bounty he'd placed on Pemulwuy. Eleven years later, Phillip's most ardent disciple, Philip Gidley King, when serving as the colony's third governor, outlawed Pemulwuy, which inspired a settler in 1802 to shoot him dead.[41]

Men and women

Bennelong's passionate marriage to Barangaroo had ended with her death in late 1791, around the same time as Baludarri's death. When she died, Bennelong was left with a two-month-old infant daughter called Dilboong. He still had his other wife, the Gweagal woman Kurubarabula, whom he'd married one year earlier. Throughout the era of détente, Bennelong associated often as well with two of his sisters, Karangarang and Wariwear.[42] Bennelong's world may have been patrilineal but it was nonetheless crowded with girls and women as much as with boys and men. In general, Yiyura women occupied the same spaces as men; they worked alongside men, if in different roles; and they exercised a similar right to be heard and understood. Bennelong's diplomatic endeavours with Phillip were carried out amid and around the girls and women in his life.

Phillip's experience of male-descended society was quite different. Like the Yiyura, the British assigned different roles to men and women. But British mores took the differentiation between the genders one step further by often physically separating male from female. Certainly Phillip himself spent the majority of his adult years completely removed from any close female presence. By 1790 he'd spent over half his life in male-only naval environments, and six years in an unusual marriage where he seemed to be more farm manager than conventional husband. British devotion to separate gender spaces often rendered those in the less valued space mere embodiments of ideas, rather than full subjects of society. The ideas most often imposed upon women in eighteenth-century Britain were maternal devotion, familial care and domesticity, all of which were associated in British custom with the private realm.[43]

The different gender conventions of Bennelong's and Phillip's worlds coloured the way the détente played out. The Yiyura's mostly intermixed world meant that all the connections Bennelong forged with the British in these years were enacted with or at least beside Indigenous women. Conversely, Britain's custom of separate gender spheres meant that when Phillip attempted to engage with the Yiyura he was surrounded almost entirely by men. True, there were fewer women in Phillip's colony than men – averaging overall around 20 per cent – but none of them exercised much power compared to men, so featured even less than might be expected in the history of Yiyura–British conciliation.

Bennelong's behaviour around Barangaroo's death exemplifies the way he interacted with colonists while mostly immersed in a mixed-gender society. David Collins observed many of the events related to her death as Bennelong's invited guest. The final event was the ceremonial battle to avenge Barangaroo's passing. Bennelong deliberately made it coincide with a whale feast occurring on a southern harbour shore. A beached whale had brought 'a large number of natives together', reported Collins, including many from Barangaroo's clan, the Gammeraygal. The men directed spears at each other, and from what we know of similar battles, the womenfolk hovered behind in tears of grief.[44]

Earlier, Bennelong had decided not to bury his wife, as was the common custom, but instead to cremate her – an honour sometimes awarded to more senior people.[45] He invited Phillip and the surgeon John White, as well as Collins, to witness the occasion. Collins noted that Bennelong's sister Karangarang was present, 'and one or two other women'. These probably included his other sister Wariwear;

Charlott Phillip, by George James, 1764

Boorong, painted by 'Port Jackson Painter', c. 1791

A View of Sydney Cove, engraving by Francis Jukes, c. 1804; this is the print found in Phillip's Bath attic in 1890

Rio in the 1790s: *Maritime procession in front of Hospital dos Lázaros*, by Leandro Joaquim

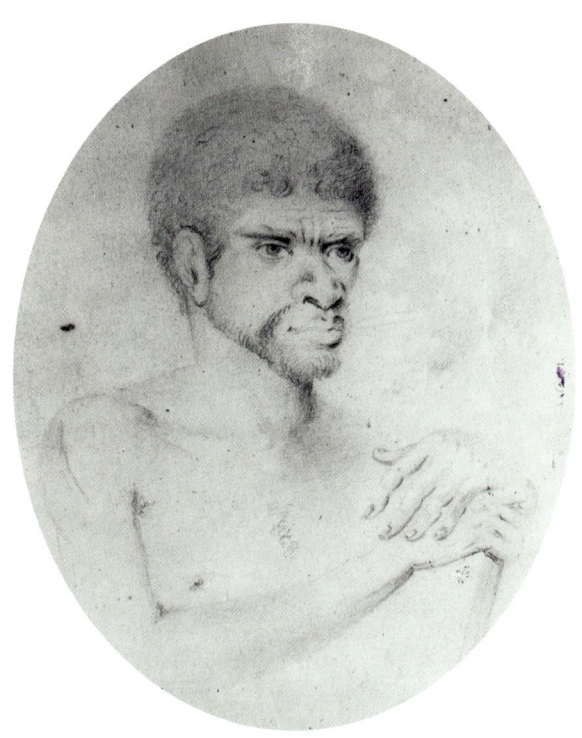

Colebee, from a sketch by Thomas Watling, 1790s

Claude-Ambroise Philippe, engraving, 1667,
with coat of arms in bottom left corner

Bennelong, pen and wash on light board, by 'W.W.', 1793

Silhouette of Yemmerrawanne, unsigned,
pen and wash on light board, 1793

Phillip's Government House, 1790

Bennelong (front nuwi) meeting Phillip, October 1790

Pencil sketch showing Bennelong's hut on the Sydney Cove promontory, with Phillip's Government House about midway, 1790

Native name Ben-nel-long, as painted when angry after Botany Bay Colebee was wounded, watercolour, c. December 1790

Captain Arthur Phillip, oil painting by Francis Wheatley, 1786

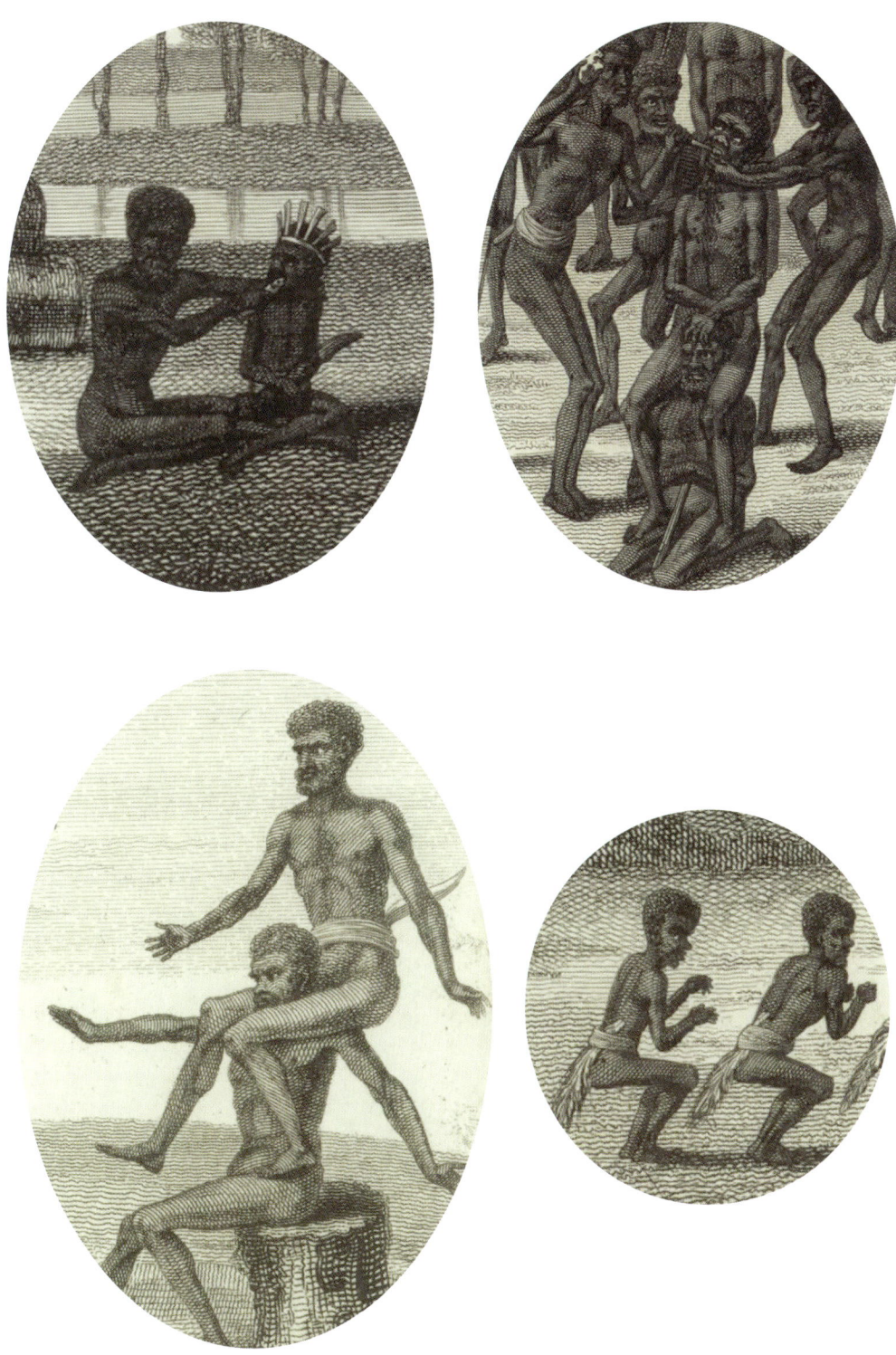

Scenes from a yulang yirabadjang, engravings by James Neagle, 1790s

Tupaia's sketch of three Indigenous fishermen at Kamay, 1770

Lieut. Arthur Phillip, by George James, 1764

Collins noted the presence of Wariwear's husband Gnunga Gnunga, who did much of the preparatory work.

Gnunga Gnunga dug a shallow hole and then formed a three-foot funeral pyre. Others carried Barangaroo's corpse – wrapped in a British blanket, probably donated by Phillip himself – onto the pyre. Barangaroo's most cherished material possessions, chiefly her fishing gear, were placed by her side. Then Bennelong placed some final dry wood on top and set the whole on fire.

The next day, the same three prominent colonists were brought back to the pyre to watch Bennelong rake Barangaroo's ashes together. Bennelong clearly wanted them to learn something about the Yiyura through this ritual, perhaps compassion. And Collins, for one, was indeed moved by the ceremony, describing how Bennelong 'preceded us in a sort of solemn silence, speaking to no one until he had paid Ba-rang-a-roo the last duties of a husband'. Bennelong raked with great care:

> laying the earth round, smoothing every little unevenness, and paying a scrupulous attention to the exact proportion of its form ... When all was done he asked us 'if it was good', and appeared pleased when we assured him that it was. His deportment on this occasion was solemn and manly; an expressive silence marked his conduct throughout the scene ... He did not suffer any thing to divert him from the business he had in hand, nor did he seem to be in the least desirous to have it quickly dispatched, but paid this last rite with an attention that did honour to his feelings as a man, as it seemed the result of an heartfelt affection for the object of it.

The most pressing problem for Bennelong now was how to manage his baby girl, Dilboong. The infant was still nursing. Bennelong raised the problem directly with Phillip, suggesting that he find a wetnurse for her among the convict women.⁴⁶ No doubt Bennelong could have found one among the Yiyura, which makes his act of reaching across the racial barrier significant. Another colonist, Daniel Southwell, remarked at this time that Phillip did sometimes oversee such an arrangement for Yiyura babies, perhaps as a result of Bennelong's request here.⁴⁷

We don't know if Phillip secured a wetnurse for Dilboong. What we know more conclusively is that Phillip agreed to be the Yiyura equivalent of a British godfather to Dilboong. Bennelong asked him to be her biyunga, which most colonists understood to mean simply father.⁴⁸ Collins, however, explained that it was also a word used by children for men who had no offspring of their own and who stepped in to care for them should a natural parent die. With his motherless daughter, Bennelong attempted to cement even further the non-violent connections between peoples at the harbour.

But before year's end, Dilboong, the little girl, or gurung, named after a small endemic 'ringing' bird, was dead. She had lived for less than five months. Once more the colonists were invited to bear witness at the customary farewell: the Yiyura men threw their spears, 'while the females began their usual lamentations'.⁴⁹

Dilboong's birth in August 1791 had been yet another occasion for Bennelong to connect with the colonists in ways that involved women. When Barangaroo was nearly due to deliver, Bennelong walked her up to Phillip in Sydney Cove and said that his wife 'intended doing him the honour of being brought to bed in his house'.⁵⁰ Bennelong did indeed think this would be an honour for Phillip. He also evidently thought it would serve as a way both of linking his offspring to the Gadigal Country on which Government House stood and of entangling Phillip in a web of local obligations.

On this auspicious day, Phillip noticed that Barangaroo wore two nets around her neck. He asked to see one. She took off the net, extracted some paperbark sheaths to be used for the birth, and then gifted it to him. In return, Bennelong asked for a British blanket as extra wrapping for the imminent baby, as well as a replacement net of British manufacture. Phillip provided both.

Despite these bonding exchanges, Phillip demurred at allowing Barangaroo to give birth in his house. To do so would have breached his sense of what was properly male space. He suggested the colonial hospital instead. Barangaroo refused – she was never as convinced as Bennelong of the benefits of mixing her personal business with that of the British.

No man was present at the eventual birth. On this score, the Yiyura shared British notions about gender separation. Barangaroo was probably surrounded only by Indigenous women when her time arrived, though she may have allowed some white women to observe. Wariwear had allowed a few female colonists to be present at her 'borning' some months earlier.[51] They reported that Wariwear's woman friends offered comfort throughout the labour and then helped deal with the umbilical cord after the baby emerged. Barangaroo's delivery apparently went well: Collins was astonished to see her walking about her campfire just a few hours later. 'The infant,' he wrote, 'whose skin appeared to have a reddish cast, was lying in a piece of soft bark on the ground.'[52]

Bennelong did thus not attend his daughter's birth. Around the same time, Collins witnessed him enjoying a happy afternoon with the rest of his womenfolk. This occurred at Bennelong's colonist-built brick hut near Dubuwagulya (later named Bennelong Point). Collins saw Wariwear and Bennelong's younger wife, Kurubarabula, steer their nuwi towards the hut. The women pulled their paddles in time and sang a harmonious song. Bennelong and his brother-in-law, Gnunga Gnunga, were waiting on the peninsula's edge, with one of Wariwear's older children sitting on Bennelong's shoulders. The men took the women's catch of fish and prepared it for eating while Wariwear and Kurubarabula joined Bennelong's other sister, Karangarang, who was readying some rock oysters. Collins found the idyllic scene one of 'unaffected simplicity . . . I remained with them till the whole party fell asleep.'[53]

Such a happy vignette jars with the colonists' accounts of how Bennelong came to acquire Kurubarabula as his other wife. This occurred in November 1790, just one month after Bennelong moved into his brick hut near the colony. He had recently returned from a trip to the Gweagal at Botany Bay. Phillip saw that he had hurt Barangaroo on her head during the adventure and scolded him for it. Bennelong, angry at being scolded, rebuked Phillip in return for his interference, and also threatened to hurt 'a woman' now arrived from Botany Bay.[54] Neither man had yet found a way to negotiate well with the other.

Alarmed at the threats, Phillip followed Bennelong to his hut and tried to take away all potential weapons, but was too late to stop Bennelong snatching up a wooden sword and striking an unfamiliar young woman.[55] This woman turned out to be Kurubarabula, then aged in her late teens. Phillip's men lunged for her and swept her off to the presumed safety of one of their ships. Phillip expected the other Yiyura milling about to applaud this chivalrous act and to reprimand Bennelong, but instead he was puzzled to find them only press him to return Bennelong's weapons. He couldn't understand why these Yiyura seemed not to show 'the least concern at the girl's fate'.[56]

Tench wasn't present at this moment but later articulated the colonists' bewilderment. Bennelong, he wrote, seemed 'unintimidated' by Phillip's actions 'and boldly demanded his prisoner, whose life, he told the governor, he was determined to sacrifice . . . Everyone was eager to know what could be the cause of such inveterate inhumanity.'[57]

In fact, Bennelong told the colonists directly what was the cause of his behaviour. He explained that Kurubarabula's father was his implacable enemy. In a recent battle, both Kurubarabula and her father had struck him. According to Yiyura customs, Bennelong now sought vengeance.[58]

Tench remained always incredulous about Bennelong's treatment of Kurubarabula, but Phillip perhaps did come round to viewing the altercation not through his own lens of separate gender spheres but rather through Bennelong's norm of integrating women into all politics. Two days later, Phillip released Kurubarabula to Bennelong, even while 'the general opinion' among the other officers 'was that the girl would be sacrificed'. The colonists were amazed to see that 'the girl herself appeared desirous of going ... she ran towards Bannelong's hut, without waiting for those who were going with her.'[59]

In the end, Kurubarabula was spared any more physical blows; resolution came instead in the form of marriage. The union of Kurubarabula and Bennelong was always secondary to that of Barangaroo and Bennelong. Barangaroo was initially annoyed by her rival, but it became clear that Kurubarabula would spend a great deal of time living with her Gweagal kin at Botany Bay and that she would never bear Bennelong any offspring. The marriage was rather an attempt at solving a problem between Bennelong's kin and the Gweagal. Sacrificing Kurubarabula would have been one way. Marrying her was another.

For a while, Phillip's personal beliefs about the proper role and place of women risked derailing his rapport with Bennelong. And Bennelong, with no understanding of women as passive ideals sequestered away in private domains, was probably as baffled by Phillip's reaction to the treatment of Kurubarabula as Phillip was by him. As Clendinnen has dryly pointed out, Bennelong had been present that year at no fewer than four hangings ordered by Phillip of male convicts who had broken colonial laws.[60] The governor clearly did not mind public admonishments. For someone who didn't share the same gender conventions as the British, it would have been hard to grasp Phillip's objections to the prosecution of Kurubarabula.

One other observation to be made of this incident is how little Phillip ever voiced a fear that Yiyura men like Bennelong might one day turn a similar rage onto white women. It's true that Phillip did not rate convict women's sanctity very highly – in many ways, he saw it as far below that of Yiyura women – but he was still in charge of some fifty to eighty free women. He also knew that convict men would riot uncontrollably if they thought the authorities condoned Indigenous assaults on their female counterparts. Yet the sources reveal no particular anxiety around this issue. In 1790 Phillip assured his superiors in Britain that there was no reason to suspect a Yiyura attack on either colonial buildings or colonial men. He didn't even bother mentioning his fears for colonial women, since an attack on them was apparently inconceivable.[61]

Possibly Phillip saw that one effect of Yiyura men like Bennelong being so intricately bound up with Yiyura women was an indifference to meddling with the sexual relations of other societies. Even if he didn't understand it this way, Phillip must have appreciated that the lack of Indigenous attacks on white women made his governing task much easier.

Finding traces of influential white women in any sources of the colony's first five years is difficult. In the eyes of the officers who left journals – none of whom was allowed to bring a wife from home – women are mostly subsumed into the unsexed categories of 'convicts', 'soldiers' or 'emancipists'. On the first fleet, women made up around two hundred of the nearly eight hundred convicts, and around fifty of the roughly five hundred non-convicts. By the end of Phillip's term, their numbers had risen to include an additional five hundred and thirty or so convict women, and thirty-plus non-convict women. The non-Indigenous sex ratio did not even out in New South Wales until the twentieth century.

While the percentage of women in Phillip's colony was low, it was still better than what was first planned. In 1786 Lord Sydney had envisaged even fewer women travelling from Britain. He thought that importing women from 'neighbouring' Pacific Islands would be a better answer to the question of reproduction.[62] Before sailing, though, Phillip managed to increase the number of British women, rightly guessing that procuring Islander women might create more problems than solutions.[63] But he also laid out a very firm schema for how convict women should be managed. He wanted some naval ships to arrive in New South Wales before the transports so as to organise separate accommodation. He wanted their clothing and cleanliness to be improved in order to distinguish them from harlots. And he wanted to assign living quarters according to each woman's 'degree of virtue'.[64] Phillip's understanding of gender was nothing if not segregationist and shaped by rigid ideals.

In reality, Phillip's agenda for women didn't transpire quite as desired. The ships in the first fleet arrived together, rather than in staggered fashion. The women convicts were not notably better clad or washed than the men, which is to say they were not well dressed or clean at all. And while Phillip at first succeeded in separating the women's accommodation from that of the men's (with the most virtuous women nearest to his own headquarters), very quickly the system devolved into heterosexual couples sharing the same huts.[65]

Despite the plan going awry, Phillip managed ultimately to achieve his greater ambitions for colonial women. It was in fact in the very rapid heterosexual partnering that occurred upon arrival that Phillip found a way to instantiate his vision of separate gender spheres. Notwithstanding the many popular narratives by twentieth-century historians about the anarchic debauchery of early Sydney, Phillip oversaw a comparatively staid sexual world.[66] Fifty-two weddings occurred in the first year alone. Phillip was also more than happy to condone de facto relationships.[67] In his world, male and female coupling meant that women stayed in the shared home, tending invisibly to domestic needs. This put them out of public labouring, out of public discussions and often out of public view.[68] Thus, ironically, such attitudes in practice obtained the same level of gender division as did literal segregation.

If convict women did not move in with a male partner, they were increasingly made to do jobs like sew clothes, raise orphans, or, from August 1789, serve as maids in freemen's homes.[69] The private sphere, then, and the practice of subservient familial assistance eventually described the experience of all female convicts in Phillip's colony.

It's worth noting that Phillip's gender ideology worked a bit like his views on food supply and land capture: it was more important to him to keep women in the private realm, performing only auxiliary functions, than it was to make the colony grow into a greater common wealth. One historian goes so far as to say it was 'almost perverse of him to insist on the sanctity of womanhood' over the maximisation of resources.[70] As with his commitment to empire, Phillip's attachment to British gender conventions triumphed over any sense of building an independent society.

All this helps to explain why Phillip usually interacted with Bennelong far away from the company of colonial women. In this regard, the British difference from the Yiyura was stark. The Pemulwuy affair involved Kurubarabula to a degree, though no white women featured in it at all. Similarly the Bangai incident had a Yiyura mother play a role by being inside the British cutter when it capsized, but no convict mother matched this part. And while Baludarri was always inseparable from his sister Boorong in Bennelong's mind, the connection didn't even register with Phillip. For the governor, conciliation with the Indigenous people of the harbour was an exclusively masculine enterprise.

On the question of colonial sexual assaults on Indigenous women, Phillip's strenuous commitment to separate gender spheres may have effected a better outcome than might be expected. The drastically skewed sex ratio of the British, together with the tendency to view women as idealised objects rather than full human subjects, pointed hypothetically to some very inhumane behaviours. And, given the general levels of violence apparent in the earliest years these almost certainly did happen. But compared to the evidence from the late 1790s, it's notable how few signs there are of the colonial rape of Yiyura women in Phillip's era. Colonists were not particularly concerned to cover up those signs when they did appear, from around 1796, in the form of venereal disease and pale-skinned babies.[71] They frankly admitted to them into the 1800s.[72] So it seems that the fewer allusions to colonial rape of Indigenous women in the initial era reflected literally fewer incidences of it.

Why? Phillip's encouragement of heterosexual couplings may have made many men simply too accountable to, or too preoccupied with, their new partners to find the opportunity.[73] And because of his insistence on the private realm for women, their public defilement was for him an especially heinous offence: he warned that it carried the risk of a death penalty, which worked as some deterrent.[74] Furthermore, Phillip tended to think of Yiyura women as even more defined by the qualities of femininity than were British women. He spoke about them as timid, weak, obedient, defenceless and distractable.[75] In consequence, he simply forbade most of the sailors and all of the convicts to mingle with them. Though this stricture was hard to police, everyone knew that the governor believed any 'abuse' of Indigenous women would 'disgust' the Indigenous men he so needed for his success.[76] With such high stakes, and such potentially severe repercussions, Phillip's reign managed to curb flagrant racialised rape.

Thus did the gender values of both Bennelong and Phillip play greater roles in the temporary stability between British and Yiyura than has been obvious. Bennelong's insistence on always including Indigenous women, as per his custom, reassured the Yiyura of some continuity and protection. Phillip's keenness for separate gender spheres among the British unwittingly aided the Yiyura; though, to his credit, it could be tempered when it came to respecting Indigenous ways.

The détente begins

The détente between Phillip and Bennelong truly kicked off in October 1790. This was the month that Phillip ordered convicts to build a brick hut for Bennelong's personal use. It measured twelve feet by twelve feet, the size of a tiny modern garage.

Apparently Bennelong requested the hut's siting on the far eastern tip of Sydney Cove, known to the Yiyura as Dubuwagulya. He knew this was Gadigal Country, not connected to him ancestrally. Possibly he saw that no Gadigal could or would challenge him for it now: it was too close to the colonists, and it might have been considered either already abandoned or already ruined.[77] For a Wangal man, the tiny peninsula offered proximity to the foreign people he'd by now committed to understand, but also some sense of distance. And for a good swimmer and canoeist, as Bennelong was, it gave assurance of escape as well as generous viewpoints on colonial activities and on more than a handful of different Yiyura territories.

Bennelong did not live in the Dubuwagulya hut all the time. As sailor George Thompson commented, he seemed to use it more as a casual shelter than a permanent base. Yiyura people 'cannot bear to be confined to a hut or tent', wrote Thompson; neither Bennelong 'nor his family will live in it; they will sometimes stay at the place for a day, then make a fire on the outside of it'.[78] Other colonists noted how Bennelong spent weeks at a time elsewhere in the harbour, maintaining relations with clans to the north, south and west.

Even so, Bennelong's claim to the hut did signal the beginning of the détente between Indigenous people and the newcomers. Hunter saw that whenever Bennelong used it, other Yiyura visited him there, which started to increase the general traffic to the colony, which in turn sparked the notion that cross-cultural communication was feasible.[79] Bennelong's fellow Yiyura evidently trusted his judgement and his ability to safeguard them. Tench agreed with Hunter, noting that only when Bennelong accepted the hut did the locals begin coming into 'the camp every night'.[80]

Bennelong's acceptance of the hut was triggered by the critical events of September 1790. That was the true watershed moment for Phillip and Bennelong, the moment when both men got to redraw the terms of relations between them.

GAYAMAY

Drama at Manly Cove, 1790–1789

Phillip is speared at Gayamay • What happened that spring • A winter of estrangement • Bennelong's escape • The autumn of captivity • Getting to know one another • Summer kidnapping

7 September 1790

Phillip lay faint in the boat, blood pouring from his right shoulder. Tending to him in a mad panic were his assistant Henry Waterhouse and the judge-advocate David Collins. The point of a long thin spear was still sticking out of his back.

The governor had made it to safety with only seconds to spare. His coxswain fired a shot to ward off the dozen or so Yiyura pelting him with a variety of weapons. The attack started when one of the Yiyura, a man unfamiliar to Phillip, launched a spear into the governor's shoulder. Phillip was completely unprepared.[1]

Waterhouse wrote that Bennelong was present at the spearing but soon afterwards was nowhere to be found. Bennelong therefore did not see Waterhouse fumbling desperately to break the shaft of the spear protruding from the front of Phillip's body. Only on the third attempt did he succeed. This was when Waterhouse himself was hit by a spear, which took 'the skin off between the thumb and forefinger of my right hand' and pumped him so full of adrenalin that he snapped Phillip's spear fully in half. In Bennelong's retreat from the scene, he perhaps only heard the governor roaring to Waterhouse, 'For God's sake... haul the spear out!'

What Bennelong did witness was a whirlwind of action, violence and political theatre. He called the place of this scene not Manly Cove, but Gayamay. The attack was dramatic. Garigal man Willemering had snatched up from the ground a particularly fine spear that Bennelong had laid down only moments before. Phillip foresaw its consequences and attempted to intervene by crying out 'weree, weree [bad, bad]'. But he was too late; he missed the original trigger for the strike, which had been his own outstretched hand to greet Willemering. Bennelong had just introduced this man to Phillip.

Before that, Phillip and Bennelong had engaged in some casual talk about spears in general, with Bennelong placing his 'remarkable fine spear' out of Phillip's reach and proffering him instead a shorter spear and a club. This was perhaps in exchange for Phillip giving him some wine and 'a jacket or two'. Or maybe it was a message to Phillip that he would soon be needing to defend himself.

By this time, Collins and Waterhouse had joined Bennelong on the beach. Neither had seen him for over four months. Waterhouse thought he heard some Yiyura calling out Bennelong's name during those minutes. They all noted that the Gadigal man Colebee was present as well, miming a joke about how Bennelong had escaped Phillip's house. Back in November 1789, Bennelong and Colebee had been grabbed together by Phillip's men from this very place, Gayamay.

When it was just Phillip and Bennelong on the beach, the pair had drunk wine and Bennelong donned both the jackets that Phillip brought him. Bennelong also took this time to re-enact some of the experiences he'd had while living with Phillip at Government House. He did so seemingly for laughs. Phillip claimed that he approached Bennelong, after so long an estrangement, with 'arms extended, to show that [I] was unarmed'. However, he kept his pistol on him throughout.

Phillip, Waterhouse and Collins had all arrived at Manly Cove around noon on that fateful spring day. In the morning, they'd been on an expedition to the harbour's South Head. On their journey back to Sydney, they were summoned by a boat sent from another group of colonists exploring the northern shores. The coxswain of the summoning boat explained to Phillip that his long-lost captive Bennelong was at Manly Cove and asking to see the governor. Bennelong sent a large piece of whale meat as a gift, and promised to go back to Sydney with Phillip if the governor met him at Gayamay.

For his part, Bennelong had been on the beach for some time. Over two hundred Yiyura were gathered there to take part in a whale feast. Bennelong had been surprised to see a bunch of colonists exploring there one morning. He realised that the group did not include his old captor Phillip but did include the Gadigal boy Nanbarree, who'd also lived with Bennelong in the colony. Perhaps it was the sight of Nanbarree that inspired Bennelong to ask these colonists to bring Phillip to him. He may also have been prompted to do so by the presence of Nanbarree's uncle, Colebee. The boy and his uncle together evoked Bennelong's own initial encounter with Phillip. It was a trauma still not resolved.

The dry

Phillip's spearing in September 1790 is one of the most often-told events of early colonial Australian history (though it is not usually told in reverse). Most histories of Sydney's foundation, or of Phillip alone, have followed the gist of the key colonial journals, depicting it as both an instance of random, isolated Aboriginal aggression and an example of Phillip's ultimately benign disposition. The governor famously issued no reprisals for the attack. These histories usually note that afterwards, Phillip was able to make progress on his explicit instructions from the crown to 'open an Intercourse with the Natives'.[2]

After nearly three years of effort at New South Wales, his great magnanimity yielded a breakthrough.

On the other hand, commentators on Bennelong – far fewer – entertain the idea that rather than a random act, the spearing was the outcome of a plan by Bennelong himself. They suggest that he orchestrated it as an elaborate payback, either for his own brutal kidnapping by Phillip in 1789 or for general incursions into Yiyura life over the three years prior. They go on to argue that this attack was why the détente could then proceed, because the slate had been wiped clean for Phillip and Bennelong.

In 2003 Inga Clendinnen implied that she was the first among settlers to come up with this more Indigenous-centred interpretation. She recognised the story that the British wanted to tell but argued rather that Bennelong had been pulling the levers of a necessary 'punitive ritual to settle grievances'.[3] But Keith Smith had published pretty much the same account in 2001. He placed more emphasis on Bennelong's determination to rebuke Phillip for his own 'abduction and capture' than on his will to avenge general infringements, but Smith's analysis of who was manipulating whom at Manly Cove, and with what effect, was similar to Clendinnen's.[4] Before Smith, too, both Isabel McBryde and William Stanner had raised the possibility of the Yiyura's complex control of that day, if not their exact leaders or intentions. In 1989 McBryde wondered if some 'significant power plays within local Aboriginal society' were at the heart of the spearing. Twenty years earlier, Stanner had thought that a random attack was 'improbable' and that the event was instead a 'public remonstrance' against 'major grievances'.[5]

Given the evidence we now have of Bennelong's total immersion in customary Yiyura payback culture, as well as his obvious leadership skills, it is plain that Phillip's spearing was no accident. Four factors point to Bennelong's orchestration. First, he had the time and the status to do it. Some scholars remain sceptical that Bennelong could have arranged an elaborate payback when no one knew that Phillip would be out that day.[6] However, payback rituals were a staple of Yiyura life, as we have seen, and so Bennelong only had to give the signal to surrounding locals for usual positions and actions to be assumed. He also had several hours in which to give these signals, knowing that the morning party had to get from the southern stretches of the harbour and back to Gayamay.

Many later historians, believing Bennelong wielded no power at the time, hold that he could not have commanded more than a dozen Yiyura to accede to his plan at short notice. But Bennelong's leaner and freshly wounded body that September was not a sign of having 'fallen on hard times', as has been surmised.[7] Instead, it was a sign of his elevation to a leading role in customary clan battles. Bennelong had heard frequently from others that Phillip desired a reunion; there were four long months of winter in which to tell his peers how they might act if opportunity arose.[8]

The second factor implicating Bennelong as the mastermind is his interaction with Phillip's party on the beach. His conversation may have seemed like casual chitchat to the colonists, but to Bennelong it was probably more like an important recounting of recent history. To get to this point, he had offered Phillip some whale meat as an invitation and Phillip had responded with his own treasured specialties – wine and jackets. Bennelong then reminded Phillip through mime, due to a chronic lack of shared language at that point, of his offence in capturing him. Colebee added his own reminder through charade that Bennelong had eventually escaped from Phillip.

Third, Bennelong employed some insights into Phillip's culture that he'd learned back in the autumn of that year. While a captive, he'd observed Phillip more closely than perhaps Phillip had observed him. Bennelong knew that Phillip would be interested in an unusual spear; collecting and weaponry combined so often in eighteenth-century British culture. He also knew that all the colonists put great store in the thrusting clasp of right hands. It meant they were about to shed one level of caution. He could have safely prepared Willemering beforehand with instructions about which spear to use and when exactly to strike.[9]

Finally, there is the question of Willemering himself and Bennelong's strange, immediate absence from the scene after the spearing. Bennelong claimed afterwards 'highly to disapprove' of Willemering's conduct, and also that he would 'execute vengeance upon him'.[10] Within a couple of months, however, Phillip learned that no such thing had happened, and that in fact Bennelong was on good terms with the man.[11] Willemering was from a northern clan, the Garigal, but known around the whole harbour because he was a Garadyigan or healer. Older than Bennelong, the two may have been friendly because they shared a similar role. At the time, Phillip explained Willemering's actions as those of someone who feared being abducted himself.[12] They were more likely those of an associate or near peer. As well, if Bennelong had been truly shocked at the spearing, he would no doubt have leaped to help Phillip, as he later did with the capsized British cutter in February 1791.[13]

The problem with the colonial version of Phillip's spearing is that it plays too easily into historical ideas about Aboriginal people having only impulses rather than politics. It also celebrates Phillip's magnanimity without, yet again, paying attention to what his so-called humanitarianism meant in context. Phillip's lack of reprisal was not an act of altruism or indulgence. Like Bennelong's conduct, it was calculated to achieve a specific outcome. As the following two years would reveal, neither an impulsive, apolitical Bennelong nor an indulgent, empathetic Phillip could have forged the kind of complicated détente that then occurred between their respective peoples. Order was only accomplished from mutually canny, if not always mutually understood, behaviour.

Resolution occurred that same month. The spring of 1790 was particularly dry, allowing for easy outdoor gatherings. After several open-air meetings between Bennelong and colonists in the weeks following the attack, Bennelong finally re-entered Government House. He visited with a handful of other Yiyura people. A throng of convicts and officers came hurrying to see him, eager to witness again the object of so much of their governor's energies. Watkin Tench worried that the crowd would alarm Bennelong, but the opposite seemed true: Bennelong 'marched on with boldness and unconcern'.

Once inside, he expressed 'honest joy'. He asked after Phillip's wound: it was healing faster than expected. Phillip asked after the whereabouts of Willemering: he was back with his Garigal people. Together they ate beef and bread, and Bennelong felt comfortable enough to go from room to room greeting the servants he remembered from his time in captivity. He talked loudly, in ways that he'd been told not to before, and explained some of the odder items in the house, such as candle snuffers, to his Yiyura entourage. At the first mention of the group's desire to return to their north shore camp, Phillip's men obliged. The governor was keen this time to 'banish all appearance of constraint'.[14]

By now, Phillip had met Bennelong's new wife, Barangaroo. All the colonists agreed she was a formidable force. Phillip had wanted her to visit Government House too, but she refused. When the party had arrived to pick up Bennelong for the formal rapprochement that day, Barangaroo had 'violently opposed' it. She cried and scolded, despaired and threatened, and even dashed one of Bennelong's fishing tools onto rocks to stop him. The colonists thought she was worried about another abduction, so they decided that Reverend Johnson and a then-teenaged Boorong would remain at the couple's camp. These individuals would serve as guarantors of Bennelong's return.[15] In reality, Barangaroo was perhaps worried about the whole idea of contact. For the rest of her life she remained critical of diplomatic conciliation with the colonists on Yiyura Country.

A few days prior, Phillip had met with Bennelong and Barangaroo on the north shores of Barangaroo's Country of Gammeray. And a few days before that he had shared a mini-picnic with the pair on Bennelong's harbour island of Memel. Phillip understood that winning over Barangaroo might be the last step in the long effort to secure Bennelong's confidence.

Barangaroo's company would come at a significant cost. It eventually meant the loss of young Boorong from the colony. The Burramatta girl had been with the colonists since early 1789, mostly lodging with Reverend Johnson and his wife. When Phillip's men first reconnected with Bennelong just after the spearing they had tried to use Boorong as their advocate to woo Barangaroo. She was 'instructed to take [Barangaroo] aside, and try if she could persuade her to comply with our wish', so Tench explained. The woman and the girl walked away to confer, 'but it was soon seen, that Barangaroo's arguments to induce [Boorong] to rejoin their society, were more powerful than those of the latter, to prevail upon her to come among us'. At the end of October, just as Barangaroo finally agreed to come to the colony, Boorong switched places with her and left the Johnsons for good.

Bennelong had opened negotiations for a détente one week after the fateful spearing. He sent up a fire signal from his temporary residence in Gammeray; several colonists hurried over there and learned that talks were on. Bennelong told them that Phillip was to meet him in Gammeray in two days' time, and was to bring with him the goods that colonists had recently stolen from the Yiyura – 'fish-gigs, spears, a sword, and many other articles'.[16]

Bennelong had one more move to play before embarking on his new role as intermediary. Phillip turned up at the appointed place and time, on 17 September. He brought with him the property requested – its theft freely admitted – only to discover that Bennelong and Barangaroo were off fishing in their nuwi in the middle of the harbour.[17] Having co-ordinated the physical punishment of Phillip for his capture, Bennelong was now exacting some mental retribution. He not only solicited shame for the colonial thefts by stipulating their return, he also claimed the upper hand by foiling the start of the talks. Bennelong was underscoring in the clearest way he knew how that he and Phillip would fashion a détente between their societies on an equal footing, or not at all.

The cold

Before their re-encounter at Gayamay, Phillip and Bennelong had been estranged for four months. For Phillip, his third Antipodean winter was by far the toughest, bringing difficult news and arrivals from home to add to the ongoing issues with New South Wales land, convicts and fellow officers. This is even aside from the failure – after Bennelong's departure in May – of attempts to establish a meaningful relationship with the Yiyura. Bennelong's experience during this cold season is harder to discern, due to his near-total absence from British eyes, but some clues can be found in his new associates and on the surface of his own body.

Phillip's winter was defined by the staggered appearance of the second fleet from Britain during the month of June. This was the first contact the colony had received from home since it began. Phillip had expected the fleet several months earlier, and with it a bounty of supplies. Instead, the ships arrived without the crucial *Guardian*, which carried most of the food, medicine and clothing. The governor learned now that the vessel had sunk off Cape Town in December 1789.

What did disembark were nearly four hundred female convicts, of whom Phillip 'did not reckon' much.[18] More than five hundred men also arrived, most of them in a horrendously poor state of health. And they were the lucky ones, having survived the criminally mismanaged, privately contracted voyage. Around one-quarter of the convicts on the final three ships of the fleet died en route. Of the convicts who made it, nearly half died soon after landing. Reverend Johnson best described the appalling revelations of the *Neptune*, the *Scarborough* and the *Surprize*:

> The landing of these people was truly affecting... When come on shore many were not able to walk, to stand, or to stir themselves in the least... The misery I saw amongst them is inexpressible; many... were covered over almost with their own nastiness... Scurvy was not the only nor the worst disease that prevailed amongst them (one man I visited this morning, I think, I may say safely had 10,000 lice upon his body and bed)... The usage they met with on board, according to their own story, was truly shocking; sometimes for days, nay, for a considerable time together, they have been to the middle in water chained together.[19]

Phillip, in his typical way, was more reserved in his reportage but even he was shaken. He also felt compelled to explain to the new Home Affairs Minister William Grenville that this was what happened when state-run empires contracted out their tasks to unscrupulous companies. 'I will not, sir, dwell on the scene of misery,' he wrote. 'But it would be a want of duty not to say that it was occasioned by the contractors having crowded too many on board those ships, and from their being too much confined during the passage.' He added that 'there are 488 under medical treatment; when the ships arrived we had not 50 people sick in the colony'.[20]

Not that Phillip was the biggest fan of even healthy convicts. Thus far he'd found them to be too lazy and too recalcitrant to build the kind of settler colony the government envisaged. Experience had taught him, he explained now to Grenville, 'how difficult it is to make men industrious who have passed their lives in habits of vice and indolence. In some cases it has been impossible; neither kindness nor severity have had the effect . . .; there are many who dread punishment less than they fear labour.' Among those recently arrived and not instantly expiring, Phillip still counted more than a hundred as being unfit for work: 'Amongst the females there is one who has lost the use of her limbs upwards of three years, and amongst the males two who are perfect idiots.'[21] To under-secretary Nepean he asked that in future he be sent only skilled prisoners.[22]

Even more earnestly, Phillip asked Nepean for better free settlers. He wanted 'intelligent and industrious' people, not those who, 'having nothing to lose . . . may become a burthen to the settlement'.[23] He repeated this plea to Grenville, begging forgiveness for saying again 'what I have mentioned [earlier] – that it is professional men who are wanted . . . we are much distressed for a good master carpenter, a sawyer, and a brick and tile maker, in whom confidence could be placed.'[24]

That winter, too, and for the first time, Phillip provoked a few officers and soldiers to voice frustration with his rule. The once-admiring officer Daniel Southwell wrote to his mother that 'our austere Govr's behaviour' was 'universally censur'd'.[25] The usually circumspect Reverend Johnson likewise felt moved to tell a correspondent that a recent published account of the settlement was 'much too flattering'. He went on to report that everyone wished they were 'back again in old England' and that the colony was 'never likely to answer the wishes & expectations of government'.[26] Finally, a just-arrived marine, William Hill, said what most of his rank-and-file peers were coming to think – that Phillip's regime felt like 'incompetency, injustice, or oppression'.[27]

The sour cherry on top of all this malaise was the news Phillip received from home. Not only had King George III suffered, if briefly, some incapacitating derangement, but the French monarchy seemed to be coming undone by a popular civil rebellion. Young and radical Watkin Tench was both easily comforted by the king's recovery and ideologically charmed by the French Revolution, but his governor would have been disturbed by each prospect.[28] Phillip's loyalist politics centred on a stable royal succession at home, and while he was no admirer of absolutist France, he never held that political change should rise up from below. As it had in most of the Protestant kingdoms he knew about, reform should rather occur organically, he felt, guided by aristocratic and military elites.

In Phillip's first letter home after the arrival of the second fleet's initial ship (but before the truly disastrous ships), he tried to be upbeat. To his old friend Nepean on 17 June 1790, he wrote that despite everything he had full confidence the colony could be self-supporting in a 'little less than two years'.[29] In similar vein, he spun his moribund relations with the Indigenous people as less worrying than might be assumed. 'There is little reason to think the natives will ever attack any building, and still less to suppose they will attack a number of armed men.' He admitted they might try to steal cattle or assail an escaping convict, but since there were hardly any cows left, and he loathed 'stragglers' too, this didn't concern him much either.

Phillip knew full well that opening an 'intercourse' with the Yiyura had little, really, to do with security; it was mostly about legality. His orders from the crown to 'conciliate their affections, enjoining all our subjects to live in amity and kindness with them' was a nod to the international legal tenet that Britain followed. In all other places the British had settled, they had performed at least a semblance of purchase, agreement or treaty-making with the original inhabitants. This had required at least one key go-between from the Indigenous people to provide consent. Britons believed that, unlike the marauding Spaniards, they never simply thieved what belonged to others, but instead acquired territory by lawful means.[30]

Phillip's truer feelings about his failure in this task were revealed a few weeks earlier in a letter to Banks. 'Our Native has left us', he brooded, referring to the departure of Bennelong from his house. This was 'unlucky for we have all the ceremony to go over again with another'. Later in the letter Phillip reflected with even greater despondency on the endeavour before him: 'I think that Mans [i.e., that man's] leaving us proves that nothing will make amends for the loss of their liberty.'[31]

Phillip's letter to Banks added one further snippet of information. He wrote that Boorong, who was still living in the colony with the Johnsons, reckoned Bennelong 'went after a Woman he had often mentioned and who I had as often told him to bring to live with him.' This woman was Barangaroo.

There are many signs that Bennelong had risen in status during his winter away from Phillip, but his relationship with Barangaroo was perhaps the greatest. She was not only an influential woman among her Gammeray clan; the Gammeraygal themselves wielded disproportionate power around the harbour. This meant that Bennelong had connected with one of the main people of one of the main groups in the vicinity. The fact that she was a good decade older than him in an age-revering culture adds further to the sense that he had achieved notable esteem.[32]

Bennelong had been in pursuit of Barangaroo since at least the summer of his captivity. Officer William Bradley noted that when Bennelong and Phillip were out in a boat one day, they saw some women at Banarung, a beach the colonists called Rose Bay. 'Among this party was a woman whom Benallon was very fond of,' Bradley noted. Her name was 'Barang-ooroo'. Bennelong and Barangaroo drew near enough to talk, though not as near as Bennelong would have liked, since his leg was then in a shackle.³³ There's a chance that he had been trying to seduce Barangaroo for even longer: it may explain why he was up on a northern shore, just to the east of Gammeray, when he was nabbed by Phillip's men.³⁴ Whenever the passion started, some sudden urgency regarding it in the autumn triggered Bennelong to dump his fledgling relationship with Phillip and leave Government House.

Barangaroo was certainly compelling. Phillip described her as 'very strait and exceeding well made'. She bore such an impregnable sense of self-possession that it appeared to colonists she was clothed even when she went 'entirely naked'.³⁵ To Bennelong there was even more than power and charisma about her; they shared an intimate grief. Both knew the experience of losing a partner in the epidemic that had torn through the harbour in early 1789. Bennelong lost his first wife. Barangaroo lost her husband and two children.³⁶

Another sign of Bennelong's accumulating esteem among his peers that winter was a change to his body. When the colonists saw him after the four-month absence they were taken aback by his appearance. Tench thought him 'greatly emaciated [and] disfigured by a long beard'. Phillip declared him 'so poor and miserable' that he was not at first sure it was the same man. But Bennelong himself was proud of his scars and harder physique. He took elaborate care upon first reconnecting with Phillip to show him all his various wounds. One proved that a spear had gone through his left arm. Another was still healing above his eye. 'These wounds,' Phillip recorded, 'were received at Botany Bay.'³⁷

To have gained such marks from clans located more than twenty miles to the south revealed not only that Bennelong was now considered important enough to withstand the first barrage of spears in customary vengeance battles. It also meant that his reputation for responsibility and bravery stretched nearly the full range of the coastal Yiyura groups. What is not clear is whether Bennelong's elevation was the result of his previous six months intermingling with the colonists or in spite of it.

Another experience for Bennelong that winter probably involved whales. The cold months often enticed whales into the harbour, much more frequently than they do today. Bennelong's association with whales has been overlooked by historians, but it's notable that at least two of the most significant moments of his midlife involved these massive sea mammals. Ostensibly the reason why Bennelong was at Gayamay on the fateful day of Phillip's spearing was to attend a whale feast. Just over a year later, stricken with heartache, Bennelong would use the occasion of another whale feast at another spot to commemorate the death of Barangaroo.

The closest any colonist ever got to ascertaining Bennelong's personal totem, or even his clan totem, was Collins's gleaning that 'his name was that of a large fish'. It's possible that Bennelong's particular ancestral conduit, or that of the Wangal in general, was the whale. It's highly likely that both were some kind of marine creature: the two nearest clans to the Wangal – the Burramattagal and the Wallumedegal – were associated with the eel and the snapper respectively.[38] If Bennelong was linked especially to whales, he would have been not merely participating in whale festivals, but also guiding the Yiyura's thanks for the whale's life and distributing the meat to guests. He would not have eaten any whale flesh himself.

On this topic of Bennelong as a whale there can only be the roughest of settler speculation. It could just be coincidence that two key moments for him involved whales. His relationship with whales, however, remains, as Claude Lévi-Strauss once said in a different context, 'good to think'.³⁹ It reminds us to contemplate his reconnection with Phillip from an Indigenous perspective: to think in terms of totemic explanation, deliberate strategy and local politics, rather than in terms of bizarre luck, random aggression and colonial benevolence.

The wet

Bennelong left Phillip's house in the damp night hours of 3 May 1790. Both Hunter and Collins remarked simply that he 'walked off' without the slightest warning. Tench, the most flowery writer among the colonial officers, described it in greater detail. 'There is reason to believe that he long meditated his escape,' Tench began. 'About two o'clock in the morning, he pretended illness, and awaking a servant who lay in the room with him, begged to go down stairs. The other attended him without suspicion of his design; and Baneelon no sooner found himself in a backyard, than he nimbly leaped over a slight paling, and bade us adieu.'⁴⁰

We know that Phillip was quietly desolate at Bennelong's departure. Others, feeling less responsible for making an overture work, were just baffled. Tench couldn't understand how the only person in the colony to get more than his fair ration was sometimes 'furious and often melancholy'. While he was staying at Government House, Bennelong received 'his allowance . . . like any other person', Tench noted, as well as any extra fish or corn available. Tench explained that this was not due to colonial egalitarianism, but was rather a means of preventing Bennelong guessing that the invaders were more vulnerable than they appeared.

Hunter and Collins were also surprised that Bennelong should have scarpered when he was 'treated with every indulgence', although they both eventually showed an awareness of what lay behind his actions. Hunter clearly disapproved of the way Bennelong had been brought into the colony. Years later he reflected that anyone who had experienced kidnapping 'in so treacherous a manner', and was kept from his family for so long a time, would naturally be suspicious.[41] Collins came to see 'how far before every other consideration [Bennelong] deemed the possession of his liberty'.[42]

Even before Bennelong left, Phillip was not in the best mood regarding colonial affairs. Three weeks earlier, he'd written a letter to the Home Affairs Office requesting some leave from duty. 'As the settlement is now fixed,' he began, 'whenever his Majesty's service permits, I shall be glad to return to England.' He didn't want leave 'at this moment', but since at least a year must pass before it could be granted, he felt compelled to ask now. That same day, Phillip wrote more revealingly to Nepean. 'To Lord Sydney I have exprest a wish to have leave ... Mrs Phillip [Charlott] was supposed to be dying when I left England, and whoever the estate goes to some steps should be taken to secure the payment of two annuities for which I gave security.' Phillip added a wry comment about the colony: 'dismal accounts will, I make no doubt, be sent to England, but we shall not starve, though seven-eighth of the colony deserves nothing better'.[43]

Prior to Bennelong's departure, a more pleasant event occurred for both captor and captive. On 9 April, the pair travelled by boat up the harbour to Burramatta Country. The colonists called the secondary farming settlement there Rose Hill, but on this journey Bennelong reminded Phillip that its real name was Burramatta, place of the eel.[44] The following year, Phillip formally changed the name to what he'd heard Bennelong say: Parramatta.

Phillip's friend Philip Gidley King joined the pair for this excursion and left an account. The journey took around four hours. The party dined at the governor's Rose Hill quarters and then walked the five or so miles to what the colonists called Prospect Hill. Along the way, Bennelong told King that the distance encompassed at least eight different meaningful Aboriginal sites. King thought it 'a very pleasant tract of country, which from ... the gentle Hills & dales & rising slopes covered with grass, appeared like a Vast park'.[45] As historian Bill Gammage explained more than two hundred years on, this was no natural landscape but one assiduously managed by Aboriginal fire regimes for millennia. The rainy La Niña conditions of that autumn also aided the impression of European parkland.[46]

King observed Bennelong closely. The lieutenant had been away for virtually the entire life of the colony, leading the satellite base at Norfolk Island. This was only his fourth day on the mainland and he had much to learn of Yiyura ways. King found Bennelong 'a stout well made man about five feet six inches high ... he is a very good natured fellow, & has a great deal of humour'. He went on: 'he is under no restraint ... he is perfectly satisfied with his situation & walk[s] about constantly with the governor'. King noted that Phillip always took off his small sword when with Bennelong 'to make him sensible of the confidence he places in him'.[47]

The appearance of comfort and mutual trust, however, was all entirely new. Up until only one week before the daytrip to Burramatta, Bennelong had been shackled in an iron leg cuff, the other end of which was attached to a convict minder. This state of affairs had been going on for more than four months, since the start of his captivity in late November 1789. Bennelong's iron cuff has featured too infrequently in historical accounts of early Sydney. It is a powerful disruptor of the usual story of Phillip's gentle temper and supposed denial of all forms of slavery. It is also one of the most perplexing objects in Bennelong's history: it makes his willingness to engage with the British even more astonishing than it was. The fact of the iron cuff does not negate stories of Bennelong's later, if temporary, diplomatic efforts. What it underscores, rather, is the deep power of ritual payback, such as strategic spearing, to forge new beginnings after terrible transgressions.

Another observer of Bennelong, this time in Government House, was Daniel Southwell, the naval officer so soon to write grumpy letters about Phillip's censurable style. As did King, Southwell found Bennelong entertaining. One day that wet April, he saw Bennelong perform a little mime for Phillip's guests. 'Benallon relates, with a deal of humour (chiefly by gestures and signs), the manner of his being caught.' Bennelong tells his audience that he was 'decoyed with a fish – and says "beial, beial" – very good, very good'.[48] The scholar Keith Smith corrects Southwell's understanding, and shows that this was no lighthearted commentary on the fish. What Southwell heard as 'beial, beial' was biyal, biyal, meaning *no, no*, not *good, good*.[49] Bennelong was protesting the way he had been lured by colonists.

The week beginning 5 April was tumultuous in the colony. That Monday, Phillip and Tench rowed out to South Head to see if the longed-for second fleet was anywhere in view. Rations of British foods were getting alarmingly low. A month earlier, Phillip had even sent his store ship *Sirius* to Canton to get more foreign produce. He'd directed the vessel to go via Norfolk Island so it could unload some two hundred convicts before heading on to China, in an effort to ease the burden on rations in Sydney. Phillip and Tench were stopped during their reconnaissance by a boat they knew came from Norfolk, but instead of news of an English fleet, the men on board informed them of a catastrophe. The *Sirius* had wrecked at Norfolk Island. No lives were lost, only the hope of a quick fix from China. 'Dismay was painted on every countenance,' as Tench put it.[50]

Collins, the lesser wordsmith, felt that the awful mood of despondency 'need not be described'. Instead, he launched into an account of how Phillip now rallied the colonists into a flurry of fishing and hunting to augment the low stores from home. Supervised convicts were directed to obtain more fish. The most skilled marines were ordered to shoot more kangaroo.[51] Neither activity reversed the sense of deprivation entirely, but as Phillip wrote to Nepean that month the colony was not going to starve. As we saw in the chapter 'Détente', Phillip had a strong interest in limiting any notion of bounty in the Sydney surrounds. He also knew that British ideas of what constituted proper sustenance were unlikely to turn around quickly. However plentiful New South Wales was in both fish and kangaroo, certain colonial behaviours meant that no settler in 1790 was going to feel wholly sated.

How much Bennelong understood of the colony's perception of dearth is hard to gauge. What did he think as he saw parties of shooters and fishers go off to claim animals about which he knew far more than they? It's plain he did not offer any advice on how best to procure local game – when it came to food, he maintained a practice of silence through the years. Did he laugh to see colonists sigh when forced to substitute fresh snapper (wulumay) for tough salted pig? If so, no one recorded it. What does shine through in the sources is Bennelong's determination to consume all that he could while in Government House. Officer Bradley noted his appetite was 'beyond every thing incredible'; he could eat more than twelve pounds of fish in one meal.[52] Southwell likewise found it 'extraordinary . . . 'tis certain he can manage the share of six men with great ease'.[53]

At no other time did any observer mention a gargantuan appetite in Bennelong. None of the many different records on him while he lived abroad cited it, and in no period other than this drizzly autumn was he described as anything but slim. It is almost as if he deliberately depleted what he realised was most cherished by his captors but which somehow could not be withheld from him. In a small but pointed way he could, through eating, bring about a fraction of the loss that the colonists had inflicted on him.

Bennelong's food consumption conjures the spectre of his alcohol consumption. An overindulgence in drink is the quality most often attributed to him in histories of the past two hundred years. Yiman and Bidjara scholar Marcia Langton long ago identified the way colonists plied Bennelong with alcohol, thus creating the first example of a long-enduring stereotype, the 'drunken Aborigine'.[54] Early settler stories of Bennelong's alcoholism certainly served as the bedrock of this image. But was Bennelong himself actually addicted? The first solid accusation came in 1805 from John Turnbull, that lowly sailor who could not believe anyone fortunate enough to be introduced to London's high society would throw all his privilege away. 'He is so addicted to drinking', Turnbull added to the list of Bennelong's other faults, 'that he would scarcely ever be sober could he obtain spirits ... [it] exhausts all patience.' Turnbull's diatribe was among the new wave of commentary from 1800 which sought to scold Bennelong for rejecting the colony. It informed the damning obituary of Bennelong that appeared in 1813, which in turn informed decades of assumptions.[55]

In early 1790, however, Bennelong's drinking did not appear uncontrolled. Tench wrote that Bennelong was fond of wine and would drink spirits, both 'with eager marks of delight and enjoyment'. King somewhat contradicted him by saying that Bennelong 'is fond of wine but cannot bear the smell of spirits'. Reports later that year, after Phillip's spearing, mention Bennelong frequently toasting George III in front of the governor. Historians have focused too much on the fact of this incessant toasting instead of the reasons for it. Rather than assume the toasting appealed to Bennelong as a chance to drink, it was more likely a way for this known political operator to confirm his truce with his former captor. He understood that Phillip represented a sovereign who lived elsewhere and who liked to be evoked through alcohol. Bennelong could take part in this obscure ritual – just as he took to wearing colonial clothes – in order to signal his understanding of Phillip's world and his own ambassadorial role in it.

There's no doubt that colonists used alcohol from the very beginning as an 'agent of seduction' in their dealings with First Nations people.[56] What's not so clear is whether Bennelong as an individual ever fully fell for it. Where he might have consumed colonial food in order to deprive his captors of what they most valued, he seems to have drunk their mood-altering liquids more as a means of securing political stability.

The hot

In early February 1790, Phillip and Bennelong took a boat together to the harbour's South Head. They had been on many such excursions with each other by now. This was the day they encountered Barangaroo at Banarung/Rose Bay, when Bennelong had 'much conversation' with her but could not get as near as he wanted due to his iron fetters.[57]

Phillip seemed not to notice the exchange between the pair, being preoccupied with the information Bennelong communicated to him about their surrounds. During the trip, Bennelong told Phillip the names of the places and clans around them. The governor learned that the northern shore was Gammeray, and so the people there were called Gammeraygal. He gathered that a clanswoman's description always had an additional suffix, so someone like Barangaroo would be called a Gammeraygalleon. Phillip discovered that the land his own settlement had colonised was called Gadi, peopled by the Gadigal. Bennelong himself was from a place just further west along the southern shore, called Wanne. This made him a Wangal.[58]

Bennelong's knowledge extended to the far-inland northern peoples of Gomerri and all the way south to the Gweagal of Botany Bay. The geography lesson made Phillip confident, as he told Lord

Sydney, that he would soon glean from Bennelong further critical information, such as the Yiyura's 'customs and manners'.⁵⁹

One particularly stark fact acquired that day was Bennelong's estimate of the local death toll from the smallpox epidemic of the previous year. 'Judging from the information of the native now living with us,' Phillip wrote to Lord Sydney, 'one-half of those who inhabit this part of the country died.' The governor did not qualify this number to his boss. From his own observations of the effects of the disease in 1789, the figure felt about right.⁶⁰

Bennelong himself bore evidence of having contracted smallpox. Many noted the telling pockmarks on his face. Other aspects of his appearance were keenly described by officers that summer. Tench thought him 'about twenty-six years old, of good stature [and] with a bold, intrepid countenance'. Hunter called him 'a very good looking fellow, of a pleasant, lively disposition'.⁶¹

Collins noted his missing front tooth. The colonists had learned long before meeting Bennelong that the Yiyura knocked out the front tooth, or dara, of boys when they were initiated into manhood. In the first few months of the first fleet's landing, Phillip had realised that his own coincidental lack of a front tooth won him some unexpected respect. When he bared his gums to a few locals in 1788 'it occasioned a general clamour' and gave him a 'little merit in their opinion'.⁶² Bennelong may have been confused to find that among colonial men only Phillip bore this feature, but he was perhaps relieved that at least the British leader had the potential to be his equal.

Despite the shackle that remained on Bennelong's ankle through the whole of that summer, the men's relationship had been steady since at least late December. The two had sat down together to share Christmas dinner. Phillip's cook had served them salt-preserved turtle, brought in from a colonial reconnaissance to Lord Howe Island some weeks earlier. Turtles were rare in Bennelong's harbour but not unknown. The colonists thought turtle meat a luxury and 'excellent' eating.[63] Bennelong, for his part, dug into his Christmas fare with clear enjoyment. 'No common councilman in Europe could do more justice than he did' to the dish, stated Tench.[64]

Interestingly, Tench noted Bennelong's gusto on this occasion because he had earlier seen another Yiyura man refuse to eat turtle. Tench had wondered then if there was a general local aversion to the delicacy. He didn't realise that turtle was probably the man's totem, and therefore forbidden food. Turtle was evidently not Bennelong's totem, so it was allowed as sustenance for him. In late 1789, the colonists still had much to learn of Yiyura society.

Before Christmas, Bennelong had been less easy with Phillip. For the first four weeks or so of his captivity he had kept his distance, or, as one officer put it, appeared 'very sullen & sulky'.[65] Most of the observing colonists believed the change in relations between Bennelong and Phillip around mid-December resulted from the sudden departure then of the man who had been kidnapped with Bennelong, the Gadigal man Colebee. The colonists soon appreciated that even though the pair had been standing together in the shallows that day in November 1789, it didn't mean they were especially close friends. 'The presence of Coalby seemed to be a check upon the chearful temper of Banalang,' observed Hunter. It made the officers think that Bennelong was some kind of subordinate or even enemy of Colebee's: 'he was always very silent in his company'.[66]

After nearly a month of captivity, with both men restrained by iron cuffs, Colebee managed to break the rope that tied his shackle to his minder and flee from the colony. Several assumed that Bennelong would have followed if his own minder had not discovered the problem just in time.[67] However, rather than being inspired to attempt an escape of his own, Bennelong from this point onwards appeared to relax. 'He was much more cheerful after Coalby's absence,' remarked Hunter.[68]

Bennelong's demeanour may well have been calmer after Colebee left, but the colonists' explanation for the change was not necessarily correct. It's true that Bennelong and Colebee had a complicated relationship; they were from rival clans and later had some bitter disagreements. But they were both Yiyura, and both concerned about the British invasion. It is possible that they decided together, in those first few awful weeks of captivity, to make the most of this chance disaster. One would try to go and one would stay. One would leave to warn their people what colonists were capable of, one would remain to gather crucial information about them. It made sense, too, that Colebee should be the one to go. Smallpox had wreaked more damage on his Gadigal clan than on any other group in the harbour: Colebee knew they had simply too few senior men to lose. The Wangal, a bit further away, had survived the epidemic better – they might be more able to spare one younger male for a while.

Some of the colonists' comments about Bennelong after Colebee escaped support this hypothesis of joint calculation. Tench noted that Bennelong clearly knew how to 'temporize'. From late December, the captive seemed to throw off all reserve and he 'pretended ... satisfaction in his new state'. From this moment, too, Tench saw that he 'acquired knowledge, both of our manners and language'. Likewise, Bradley remarked that within days of Colebee's escape Bennelong 'became quite composed, & seemed reconciled better to his situation than before'. The prisoner stopped being fearful and expressed much more interest in colonial gadgets and tools. Such behaviour fits a conjecture that Bennelong now had a mission to pursue for the duration of his ordeal.[69]

Those initial few weeks Bennelong and Colebee spent together in a locked room were surely miserable. Bradley reports that they had their faces shaved and their bodies clothed. Neither experience was familiar, let alone under physical bondage. Tench describes the atmosphere obliquely, saying it resonated with 'awkward wonder and impatient constraint'.[70]

The one silver lining was the discovery of two Yiyura children residing nearby. These were none other than Boorong, then aged around thirteen; and Nanbarree, who was about ten. They had come alone to Government House six months earlier, in April 1789, at the height of the smallpox epidemic, each nursing a dying relative. Nanbarree was found first, tending to his father on a beach. The bodies of his mother and sister lay nearby, already dead. When his father also died, the surgeon John White said Nanbarree could live with him. Boorong was found lying alongside her fading brother. At length, the clergyman Richard Johnson took her in to live with him and his wife Mary.[71]

Had Boorong and Nanbarree been a touch older, they might have satisfied Phillip's desire for a native interlocutor and Bennelong might never have been stolen. Their minds, so the colonists reasoned, would have been supple enough both to retain their own language and to learn English. They would have known enough Yiyura history to communicate it to the colonists, and would have been sufficiently powerful among kin to convey good news about the British. Moreover, all this would have come about without the need for violence (other than the violence wrought by smallpox).

As it was, Phillip felt the children were too young. 'I brought these people up with the hopes [that they] would be the means of reconciling them to live near us; but unfortunately [they do not] have weight with the natives.'[72] Hunter elaborated further, observing that even though Boorong and Nanbarree quickly learned English, 'the governor was desirous of having a man or two in our possession, to whom we might teach enough of our language without the danger of losing any part of their own, to render them useful to their countrymen'.⁷³

Records of how the children experienced their grief-stricken months in the colony are thin. They must have been bewildered by the rapid changes in their circumstances on top of the loss of their family. At least, they had each other, and perhaps understood that it was extraordinary to have survived the epidemic at all. Something of their great longing for community is revealed in their first sighting of Bennelong and Colebee. Collins described the children as being in 'raptures of joy' when the men were dragged into the settlement. Bradley went so far as to say they were 'frantic with joy'. It was from the children's exclamations that the colonists learned the men's names.⁷⁴

Collins and Bradley both believed that seeing the children so healthy and energetic would reassure Bennelong and Colebee about their imminent fates. Each was a little surprised when it didn't. Nothing in those first few weeks, it turned out, could remove what Bradley saw as 'the pang that they . . . felt at being torn away'.⁷⁵

Of course, neither Boorong nor Nanbarree were strangers to the captives. Boorong was a Burramatta girl, probably familiar to Bennelong's nearby Wangal kin from birth. Nanbarree was Gadigal, the son of Colebee's recently deceased sibling. However entangled their prior histories with the men, though, each would go on to have even deeper interconnections later. Boorong would eventually become Bennelong's fourth wife and she would bear him his longest-surviving child, Digidigi. Nanbarree would later be comforted by Colebee when he underwent initiation, and would fight alongside both Colebee and Bennelong in many ritual battles.

For Bennelong, especially, the ties to Boorong and Nanbarree survived even death. Within a decade of Bennelong's own burial, both these younger Yiyura joined his grave. Their experiences as the three

Aboriginal individuals most exposed to the colonists in this founding era bound them together forever.

25 November 1789

Despite their frantic struggles, Bennelong and Colebee found their legs snapped into iron cuffs which were then chained to the boat itself. They could hardly believe it. The past few minutes had been terrifying and chaotic. They could still hear their friends and relations crying and screaming from the shore, but the British boat had made a clean getaway and was speeding southwest towards the dreaded colony. Five pale-skinned captors were in the boat with them. Their leader – the man who did the most talking – looked like he was having almost as bad a time as the captives. Lieutenant Bradley later wrote that this dual kidnapping was 'really most distressing'.[76]

The seizure was not unopposed. Tench and Collins claimed that it was easily done, but others reported that spears rained down on the colonists as they shoved their boat out of the shallows. One spear went through the folded sail, another damaged the hull's stern, but the counterattack was not enough to stop the capture. The colonists had planned it for days. The different Yiyura clans fishing at Gayamay that day were taken completely by surprise.

Before throwing their spears at the retreating boat, the many families on the beach had yelled in horror at what they were seeing. The Yiyura did not understand abduction. They settled their differences through direct confrontation, not by disappearing their foes. Over the sound of the yelling came a blast of shots, opened on the protesting Yiyura by the colonists until their boat was clear of the cove.

The seizure involved deceit as well as force. Bennelong and Colebee had gone over to the British boat believing the colonists wanted to give them two large fish. To the Yiyura, gifts of food were customary forms of sociability, and Bennelong and Colebee just happened to be the ones who saw this sign of goodwill. They were among those senior enough to move away from the group and risk a meeting. They had waded towards the British unarmed, unaware of the cascading consequences of this chance moment.

The mixed Yiyura group on the beach that day were of a 'great number', according to Bradley, and came from a range of clans. Why so many different peoples would have been welcomed onto Gayamay Country then is unclear, but all seemed to be engaged in a special haul of fish. Hot weather always brought more edible sealife. Bennelong and Colebee were especially out of place: Colebee's Gadigal clan were based on the southwest side of the harbour, the closest to the colony; Bennelong's Wangal were from lands even further southwest, more than six miles away by water. They were evidently honoured guests to be included on that day, identified perhaps as important overseers of the catch, or as custodians of the fish, or just as special friends of some of those assembled. They were outsiders to the northern clans, but not so distinct that their kidnapping didn't arouse fury and anguish on their behalf.

The British boat was led by Bradley, experienced naval officer and fledgling coastal surveyor. He had four others with him to row the vessel and aid his task. He understood his orders. They came directly from Phillip. Since 'no endeavour to persuade them to come among us' has yet worked, the governor judged 'it necessary that a Native should be taken by force'.

Bradley was doubtful from the outset. He eventually saw the whole affair as 'the most unpleasant service I ever was order'd to execute'.

DECISIONS

Enduring History, 1789–1783

Smallpox devastates Yiyura Country • Phillip experiments with kidnapping • A second invasion by the French after a first invasion by the British • Officials debate the idea of a penal colony • Bennelong comes of age

In late 1789 Phillip could hardly have been surprised that he hadn't yet achieved a relationship with the Yiyura. When explaining his reasons for kidnapping Bennelong he mentioned that the Yiyura seemed still to have a 'hostile disposition in them towards us'.[1] The causes were plain. In the preceding two years, the colony had not only taken over a section of Yiyura Country and made a dent on local resources. In addition, they had shown a terrible ability to injure people with unfamiliar weapons. They had appeared to have enticed their own pale-skinned enemies to follow them here from the ends of the earth. And worst of all, they had unleashed upon the Yiyura population the deadliest disease that anyone in all the harbour could remember.

The smallpox epidemic, the rivalry with the French at Botany Bay, and the various armed disputes and land-snatches were in many ways the results of decisions made at other times and in other places. Phillip's arrival in New South Wales in January 1788 might be called an inaugural moment in retrospect, but it was more the result of long-running plans, dreams, grudges and practices.

The Yiyura were not passive victims of all this prior history. The way they responded to the British intrusion in the initial two years reflected some of their own earlier decisions. The way they made sense of the epidemic and French arrivals spoke of a specific cosmology of good and evil. The way they resisted colonial offences was evidence of a society with strong conventions about dealing with transgression.

Bennelong did not, as far as we know, interact directly with Phillip in these two years, but he surely knew of him and what he meant for the people of his harbour. News circulated quickly among Yiyura clans. He would have heard about the various encounters between the strangers and locals. Similarly, he'd have got wind of the conjunction of the two different sets of newcomers down south, at what he called Kamay. He did not need to hear stories about smallpox. Like the majority of Yiyura, Bennelong contracted it himself in the autumn of 1789. He was lucky to survive it; his first wife, whose name is unknown, did not.

Smallpox in Yiyura Country

The epidemic lasted about three months, before burning out in June 1789. This is in keeping with the behaviour of most newly introduced viruses – either they kill their hosts or survivors build relative immunity.

Historians have written far more words on the cause and nature of this epidemic than did the colonists. The scarcity of the remaining British observations has somehow prompted the overly large volume of later accounts; speculations and hypotheses have sprouted and bloomed among the gaps in the historical record. As yet, we have no firm means of establishing anything definitive. Debate has centred chiefly on whether or not the disease outbreak really was smallpox, and whether or not Phillip's fleet was the original carrier.

Although some continue to suggest that the disease might instead have been chicken pox or some 'native pox', most scholars now agree that it was caused by variola major, a virus endemic at that time in Europe, Asia, and Africa but not yet Australia.[2] Commentators agree less on the means of introduction. The three possibilities are Phillip's British fleet of January 1788; a French fleet that arrived in Botany Bay soon afterwards; or fishermen from Makassar, in today's Indonesia, infecting Indigenous traders in northern Australia, who then infected other Indigenous people southwards until the disease reached Sydney Cove.[3]

The reason it's impossible to say yet exactly how smallpox arrived in Sydney is the number of curve-balls in its history. There's the fact that all through 1788 no colonist seemed to manifest it.[4] The virus ideally needs living human hosts to carry it from one to another, and it can usually only infect the next person within a few weeks of infecting the previous person or it will die out.[5] How did it survive for fourteen months with no symptomatic human host? Phillip himself was stumped on this question: 'it never appeared on board any of the ships in our passage', he wrote home to Lord Sydney, 'nor in the settlement'. He went on to confirm that he saw the first living case of it in the colony on 2 May 1789, and evidence of smallpox death among the Indigenous population just a few weeks before that.[6]

The Makassan fisherman theory is compelling but incomplete. There is no evidence of smallpox appearing in Makassar in late 1788, which would have been necessary for it to reach Sydney, many thousands of miles south, by early 1789. This absence is quite glaring in the detailed records of the Dutch East India Company, which was stationed in Makassar in the period. Nor is there evidence of smallpox marks on any Indigenous people encountered by later colonists in the stretch of land between the northern Australian coast and Sydney – a puzzling lack as around half of sufferers did typically survive. Furthermore, the coincidence of Makassan smallpox reaching Sydney just as the first colonists arrived is, as Worimi historian John Maynard says, a bit incredible: 'It's hard to believe,' Maynard states, 'that after hundreds of years of trade with the Makassans, [smallpox] suddenly travelled down from northern Australia to arrive in Sydney at that exact moment.'[7]

The conjecture that the French introduced the disease involves the same problem as the British theory – the time lapse between first arrival in early 1788 and first outbreak in March 1789 is just too great.

The only thing different about the British arrival is that we know Phillip's fleet also brought vials of smallpox matter to use for inoculation, should smallpox ever appear. Tench confirmed this key point, but somehow dismissed it as a source: 'It is true, that our surgeons had brought out variolous matter in bottles; but to infer that it was produced from this cause were a supposition so wild as to be unworthy of consideration.'[8]

It is not so wild. Viruses have escaped from controlled containers throughout modern history. Some scholars have doubted that the matter in the vials could have withstood the high temperatures in parts of the ships' passage and in Sydney's summer, but others remain confident that it was technically possible.[9] Of the colonial journalists of the time, Collins certainly believed the disease had come from his own people. He admitted it was an undesirable effect of their arrival, but hoped that other gifts from the British would cancel out the 'evil impressions' that smallpox had made upon the Yiyura.[10]

Even if historians could agree on a British transmission via bottled variola, one final conundrum remains – that of the means of its escape. Commentators have by turns suggested deliberate release by Phillip; deliberate release by senior officers other than Phillip; deliberate release by convicts or rogue marines; or accidental release.[11] All the deliberate-release scenarios lean on the fact that the British had decided to use smallpox as a weapon in North American campaigns in the 1760s.[12] They clearly knew how to do this, and several in the first fleet had the experience to repeat the decision now.

Without doubt, the accidental-release theory aligns most neatly with apologist versions of colonial foundation, which this book has tried to unpick and re-analyse. However, given what we now know about Phillip, it does also seem the likeliest. Deliberate release would have gone against the complex efforts Phillip subsequently undertook to forge a diplomatic understanding with the Yiyura. He was not in the middle of a battle with an Indigenous population at some remove, as the British had been during Pontiac's War in North America. He was instead committing to live in their own homeland, and to execute his crown orders to start a relationship with them.

More obviously, weaponising smallpox in Sydney would have been astoundingly risky, and thus quite out of accord with Phillip's rationalist mindset. He had no way of knowing that a smallpox epidemic would not also take out his own people – many colonists reported surprise that none of them contracted it when signs first emerged. Most Britons of this era would have been familiar with the basic principles of immunity and would have known that if they had ever had smallpox themselves, or had ever undergone inoculation, they would fare better than the unexposed.[13] Yet no one in Sydney believed that this described every settler among them, and as Collins pointed out, by 1789 there were at least forty children who did not enjoy immunity. Any outbreak of smallpox, as everyone then knew, put everyone present in some degree of danger.

The idea that Phillip's subordinates or even the convicts could have stolen the vials and let pox-matter loose suggests a level of indiscipline that similarly counters everything we know about Phillip. The governor easily if randomly sent men to the gallows for theft of rations. He would have been sure to hunt down any culprit who put a significant part of his mission in the colony in jeopardy. The records, however, are silent on him ever investigating such a colossal crime.

The smallpox outbreak of 1789 lives on in contested commentary because the effect of it was so staggering. As we have read, Bennelong later told Phillip that he estimated around half of all Yiyura people to have died in the three-month brushfire of the epidemic. Those closest to the colony were hit the hardest; Colebee's Gadigal were reduced to near oblivion. The unfathomable toll makes sense of a lot of later behaviour. It helps explain why someone like Bennelong thought it so necessary to make a peaceful link with the newcomers in order to understand and ideally to tame them – at least for a while. Equally, it sheds light on why others, such as Barangaroo, never came to terms with the British and tried mostly to get as far away from the colony as possible.

The snippets of observation left to us from this period are heartbreaking. John Hunter reflected that 'it was truly shocking' to see complete families lie together as corpses: 'I have seen myself, a [dead] woman sitting on the ground, with her knees drawn up to her shoulders, and her face resting on the sand between her feet.' Earlier, William Bradley saw the virus had made 'dreadful havoc'. He relayed that Yiyura bodies had been found scattered around the whole harbour: 'Some have been found with a child laying dead close to them and some, who have apparently used their utmost exertions to get at water, having been found laying dead between a cave and a run of water.'[14]

The colonists learned the Yiyura's word for the disease, galgala, which led some to assume it was a well-known local malady.[15] Today, Indigenous people translate this term as devil-devil, which fits the pattern of any group of people naming a new phenomenon with the word for a known evil. When smallpox hit the Cherokees in North America in the 1730s, for example, they called it *Oonatàquára*, a term associated with punitive upper-world spirits: it was their way of incorporating a novel phenomenon into old systems of understanding.[16]

Likewise, when SARS-CoV-2 hit the world in 2019, many in the west reached for the easily understood term of 'the pox'.

The first British kidnapping in Yiyura Country

Bennelong was among those who survived the encounter with smallpox. One of the first things the colonists noticed about him were the tell-tale pockmarks on his skin.[17] The disease did, however, kill his first wife. Few colonists gleaned this fact but Philip Gidley King, during his close if brief study of Bennelong in 1790, gathered that she had died a short while before Bennelong's capture. 'He sometimes mentions this circumstance,' King noted, 'and it occasions a momentary gloom.' He added that Bennelong would always sing when asked, 'but in general his songs are in a mournful strain'.[18]

During the emergency, Phillip did not of course yet know Bennelong. The Yiyura case that most troubled him then was that of a Gayamaygal man called Arabanoo. This man was the first victim of British decisions to kidnap a local Yiyura person. His death from smallpox meant that Bennelong became the second.

Arabanoo died in Government House on 18 May 1789, after contracting smallpox only eight days earlier. The colonists had plied him with their medicines with no success. Most of them seemed deeply pained by this death, a mixture of sorrow that such a 'gentle and placable' man should be lost and regret that once again the colony had no potential adult link to the Yiyura.[19]

Arabanoo had lived with Phillip for nearly six months. At first the colonists called him Manly, after the place where he'd been taken. Phillip had named this place himself, after the impression he had of the men of the northern beach. The colonists learned Arabanoo's real name after he had been with them some weeks, by which time he appeared partially resigned to his circumstances. He was no longer shackled in irons but remained with his captors, tolerating parts of their diet and attempting in a half-hearted way to learn their language.[20]

One reason why Arabanoo chose to stay with Phillip by April 1789 might have been because two Yiyura children were then also living in Government House. Perhaps he felt obliged to stay on as their guardians. These two children were, of course, Boorong and Nanbarree who featured in the last chapter. The children had also suffered from smallpox but had recovered. Arabanoo was the primary carer for both. He was said to treat Nanbarree with the kindest of attention and Boorong with sympathetic affection. He encouraged them to be brave.[21]

From the descriptions by Tench, the children reacted to their calamitous losses in different but understandable ways. Nanbarree appeared numb and dissociative for a time, while Boorong was overcome with tearful emotion. Both drew confidence in their situation from the example of Arabanoo. Tragically, it was through his provision of care to the children that Arabanoo himself contracted the virus. He died a few weeks after Boorong and Nanbarree finally got well.[22]

Earlier, Arabanoo had expressed his devastation at the damage that smallpox had wrought. When taken to the shores to search for old friends, his look of agony, Collins acknowledged, was unforgettable. 'All dead! All dead!' Arabanoo exclaimed, and hung his head in silence.[23]

Arabanoo had been captured on the last day of 1788, a seizure as violent as Bennelong's eleven months later. It followed the protocols established by British imperialists elsewhere who always sought out potential Indigenous interlocutors to secure later, hopefully advantageous treaties. Two lieutenants took two boats up to Gayamay, and approached a pair of men on the shore, pretending to communicate pleasantries. They then lassoed the men around their necks, though one broke free and fled. Arabanoo was dragged into a boat to the screams of his countrymen standing on the beach. The horrified Yiyura threw spears at the colonists but could not halt the abduction. The colonists realised that Arabanoo thought he was about to be murdered. They read his relief at only being manacled as some kind of acceptance of his fate.[24]

Phillip was prompted to order the capture of Arabanoo because the Yiyura had been escalating their guerrilla attacks over the previous ten months. Far from getting any closer to conciliation, Phillip believed by December 1788 that it was slipping further and further away. 'The natives now avoid us more than they did when we first landed,' he sighed in a letter home. He despaired at the number of vengeful strikes made on his men. Notably, he did not represent these strikes as unjustified, though he preferred to blame them on convict robberies than on the colonial intrusion in general.[25] Eventually, he came to think that only a forced meeting would break the cycle of hostility and get him closer to acquiring a negotiator.

In November 1788, Officer Blackburn had admitted that the Yiyura's attacks were so 'troublesome to our fishing and foraging partys' that now all boats had to be well armed. The Yiyura were co-ordinating in groups of sixty or more to throw spears and stones at any colonial excursion. Tench called it 'unabated animosity', which bred 'endless uncertainty'. He reported one potential bloodbath at the brickfields on Gadigal Country, where over one hundred Yiyura warriors had assembled before a convict detachment scattered them by brandishing metal shovels.[26]

At least three attacks had occurred in October; a convict was speared in September; another was stripped and beaten in August. One Yiyura man sent a spear sailing clean over John Hunter's head while the captain was sitting in his docked cutter, rendering the normally perceptive Hunter dumbfounded. 'What reason they could have had for this treacherous kind of conduct,' he wrote, 'I am wholly at a loss to guess.'[27] Three more convicts were speared in July and four were outright murdered in May.

The attacks had also become harbour-wide. Several occurred in Botany Bay, the home of the Gweagal and Kamaygal. Many were carried out in the west by the Wangal and in the north by the Gayamaygal. Sailor Newton Fowell noted that attacks happened now 'at all parts of the Harbour'. It was becoming standard for the Yiyura to throw a spear at pretty much any colonial vessel that ventured up or down their waters. Nothing about that year seems to warrant historian Inga Clendinnen's characterisation of it as one of 'hope' and 'dancing'.[28]

There are no public records, retrospective or otherwise, about Bennelong's whereabouts during this period of mutual sabotage. In 1788 he was roughly twenty-four years of age, old enough to be an initiated man of his clan, young enough to follow the guidance of his Elders when it came to dealing with an unprecedented arrival of settlers. It's possible that Bennelong was in or associated with the Yiyura raid that occurred on 21 August 1788. This happened at the western end of the colony, near where the colonists were already building their first astronomical observatory. That day, five nuwis full of Yiyura people pulled up to the peninsula's edge, later called Dawes Point. Some of the party then distracted the colonists with small talk while others lunged to steal a goat. A sailor saw what was going on and tried to stop the theft but was quickly 'menaced' by spears. The Yiyura killed the goat and pitched it into a waiting nuwi. They sped off to the area that Phillip later learned was Bennelong's Wangal Country.[29]

On this occasion, Phillip was nearby and took it upon himself to follow the nuwis into Bennelong's clan land. Collins reported that the governor managed to get close to some of the party but failed to effect any talks or the recovery of the goat. If we presume that several among this party were Wangal, given their destination, then Bennelong might easily have been one of them. He may have had his first encounter with Phillip at this stage, long before Phillip was aware that he was having his first encounter with Bennelong. Further, it's provocative to wonder whether Bennelong glimpsed then, or at some other time that first year, a desire in Phillip to forge a relationship beyond violence. The goat incident caused Collins at least to articulate the growing frustration of the officers. 'It was much to be regretted', he wrote, that none of the Yiyura 'would place much confidence in and reside among us; as in such case, by an exchange of languages, they would have found that we had the most friendly intention towards them.'[30]

Any friendly intention was likely opaque throughout 1788. But Bennelong perhaps pondered what else these strangers sought so repeatedly from his fellow Yiyura. If not violence, then what were they offering and when, exactly, might they be expected to leave?

The French in Yiyura Country

At least since the winter of 1788 the Yiyura had only to contend with one set of invaders. For a while in the previous summer it looked like they might have to face two. Just one week after the British landed in Kamay (Botany Bay), a pair of ships from the French empire, commanded by Jean-François Lapérouse, also anchored. The Yiyura eventually learned that these two French ships were not attached to the eleven British ships, and in fact represented Britain's most detested foes. It almost looked like the British had lured their enemies to follow them here to Yiyura Country, and to bring with them old hatreds and resentments that belonged properly back in Europe.

The French sailed away on 11 March 1788, having stayed for just under seven weeks. The unlikely concurrence of both British and French imperial representatives arriving at Kamay, each for the first time, has been glossed over too quickly by historians. Scholars have dismissed the political significance of Lapérouse's presence by claiming that his voyage was 'only' scientific and thus no true challenge to Phillip. Similarly, they have minimised Phillip's anxiety about Lapérouse's ships by focusing on his 'unfailing' politeness to the French commander.[31]

As discussed in relation to Joseph Banks, however, science and politics were not as neatly severed in the late eighteenth century as modern readers sometimes assume. Saliha Belmessous describes all European ventures in the Southern Hemisphere at this time when she states that 'the French [explored] in the Pacific in order to map it and gather scientific data, which were necessary preludes to any attempt at colonising the region and controlling trade routes'.[32] Phillip was a dedicated student of Britain's three Cook voyages, which had yielded enough information to launch the colonial venture he was now heading, so he understood this truism better than most. He was also a veteran of two different British wars against the French empire. The cost to France of those wars had contributed hugely to its present desire to find fresh wealth in the Pacific region. There is no way Phillip could have missed the threat of competition that Lapérouse's arrival represented.

This is not to say, though, that Lapérouse and his two hundred men were about to engage in a direct contest for imperial sovereignty in 1788. In her 2021 book *Beating France to Botany Bay*, Margaret Cameron-Ash makes a welcome contribution by refocusing on the French threat. But it goes too far to assert that Phillip and Lapérouse raced to a 'photo finish' for Sydney Harbour, and that this convergence amounted to 'the most significant naval victory in the era of Anglo-French rivalry'.[33] Lapérouse carried neither the instructions nor the settlers needed to fight Phillip on the spot for the site. If Lapérouse had arrived one hour or one day earlier, it would not have changed how Phillip proceeded to unload his cargo of twelve hundred colonists.

Nevertheless, Phillip was well aware that, just as in North America during the whole of the previous century, the French arrival meant that nothing could be taken for granted. He knew that British colonists had in the past been forced to make formal alliances with Native Americans because fellow Europeans were observing their legal claims. They had needed to give meaningful concessions to Indigenous people because fellow Europeans could always make counter-offers. And they had felt compelled to add ever more arms and people to their colonies because fellow Europeans could otherwise pitch their own arms and people against them. The arrival of Lapérouse in Botany Bay reminded Phillip of the global context of his undertaking. It underscored how much the new penal colony was about securing Britain's place in the European drive for the Southern Hemisphere. Dumping convicts was at best a second-order priority. France may not have been in a position to fight Britain for New South Wales just at that moment, but Lapérouse's scouting mission of seven weeks in the exact same area where the British were trying to establish a foothold told Phillip that, one day, it might.

Phillip's concern about the French presence was charged additionally by his own personal antagonism towards France. Phillip had not only served in Britain's war against the French allies of the American revolutionaries in 1778–1782, and in Britain's seven-year global war against France in 1755–63, he had also spied officially for the British state in French ports in the mid-1780s (and probably earlier too, as discussed in the next chapter). If Phillip, as well, carried a sense of familial persecution by France as the descendant of Huguenot refugees, his Francophobia would have been among the most extreme of any in New South Wales. For a rationalist, an 'unfailing' stiff upper lip was the prefect expression of this sentiment.

Cameron-Ash is right to speculate that the two commanders probably met on 20 February 1788, although no source confirms it.

British surgeon Arthur Bowes Smyth records that Phillip had the day before sent over some horses to convey Lapérouse the nine or so miles by land from Botany Bay to Sydney Cove.[34] Others report that a party of four French officers duly came and stayed as guests of the governor for two nights.[35] French sources are scarce after mid-February and the British sources are cagey, but it makes sense that Phillip would have entertained Lapérouse at about this stage. The governor had just moved from his ship's cabin into his makeshift headquarters, a huge prefabricated tent of timber and cloth . By this third week of February, he had also made a formal proclamation of sovereignty over a gigantic swathe of land; sent Philip Gidley King to build a garrison at Norfolk Island; verified a freshwater source, and arranged for the officers to erect their tents on its eastern side and the convicts to set up on its western side; and undertaken a quick hydrographic survey of the harbour. Phillip was finally confident enough to confront the leader of the colony's potential rival.

Phillip had of course already received plenty of intelligence about Lapérouse's mission. Scholar Alec Protos counts eleven separate meetings between officers of both fleets during the layover.[36] Less concerned than Phillip with international politics, the other British officers relished their connection with any Europeans after eight months of sailing. The chief surgeon John White recorded that the French were 'most hospitable, polite, and friendly'. The astronomer William Dawes discussed observatory-building with his counterpart Joseph Dagelet. Hunter enjoyed a walk around Botany Bay with some French naturalists. Collins was charmed by Lapérouse's compliments about Captain Cook. And Tench noted how circumspect Lapérouse was regarding British qualms over 'security'.[37]

Amid all the show of goodwill, Phillip sent word to Lapérouse that he'd be willing to send on any of his papers to the French ambassador in London when the first British ship went back. It was just as well that

Lapérouse accepted this offer, handing over at least the journal of his earlier travels through the Pacific Ocean from Russia. These were the last documents to survive of Lapérouse's two-year voyage around the world. His ships wrecked in the Solomon Islands, soon after departing Botany Bay, annihilating all crew and everything on them.[38]

What the Yiyura made of the comings and goings between two supposedly separate but equally unprecedented sets of white people has barely registered in scholarship. In fleeting nods to this question, most histories have conceded that 'skirmishes' took place between the Yiyura and the French, if not directly yet between the Yiyura and the British.[39] Few have meditated upon the Yiyura's destruction of a grave that the French left behind in March 1788. Tench mentioned that the 'natives' pulled down the wooden monument on the grave 'and defaced everything around'.[40] With no further discussion of the incident, readers are left to assume that this is all Tench ever expected from an impetuous people. In the context of the guerrilla war then burgeoning, however, the Yiyura attack on the French grave was most likely a deliberate act of retribution.

The grave belonged to Père Laurent Receveur, priest and naturalist with the French expedition, who arrived in Kamay bearing scars from a battle with Samoans a month earlier. He died from his injuries on 17 February 1788. Whether the local Kamaygal sought vengeance on Receveur personally or whether they wrecked the grave simply because it represented invasion is unclear. We do know that the French had sometimes shot at Yiyura individuals. Tench learned that his counterparts had 'found it necessary ... to chastise ... the Indians [by] pointing a musket to them'. Bradley concurred that the French had been 'obliged ... to fire on them once or twice'. Lapérouse himself wrote hostile opinions about the Yiyura in his fateful journal: 'the

Indians of New Holland who, although very weak and not numerous, are, like all savages, very ill-natured and would set fire to our boats if they had the means of doing so'.[41]

A thought experiment

The mystery of the attack on the grave prompts an imagining of what each of the three groups involved made of the first month or so of their triple convergence. The Yiyura, although they had encountered James Cook's tall ship eighteen years earlier, had the least prior knowledge of what the British and French were seeking in their lands. What they saw on two different parts of their coast, narrated backwards, was the following:

One day, after being here nearly a full moon cycle, the crew of the eleven ships bearing the red flags of the British navy assembled at a cove called Warrane on Gadigal Country. They stood in their hundreds in line formation on ground from which they had already removed many trees. A tall, yellow-haired man recited a long speech. Another, shorter, older man recited another speech. Three incredibly loud explosions shot out of weapons. Then music, dancing and drinking took over. Had the Yiyura understood the content of the British speeches, they may have felt inclined to desecrate more than a grave memorial. Collins and Phillip had just proclaimed 'full power and authority' over half of the continental landmass.[42]

Earlier, the harbour-based Yiyura would have communicated to those in Kamay that small parties of the British had been seen rowing around the edges of their waters. Just as in Kamay, these parties resisted all invitations to being formally welcomed on separate clan countries. Twelve days earlier still, the full complement of eleven red-flag ships had arrived at Warrane, seemingly abandoning their original port down at Kamay. This day also witnessed great festivities among the disembarked, though no speeches were then made.

Before the day of festivities, only one ship had been at Warrane while the other ten red-flag ships stayed at Kamay. This solitary vessel went back and forth between Kamay and the harbour, evidently deciding which of the ports to choose. Some observing Yiyura might have reasonably assumed that the fleet's final choice of Warrane had something to do with the sudden arrival in Kamay of two white-flag bearing ships. Now there were thirteen vessels, but the red flags seemed to want to get as far away from the white flags as possible.

The arrival of the red-flag ships at Kamay had been shocking enough. First one ship turned up. Then three more the next day. Then seven more the day after that. Altogether they seemed to carry an extraordinarily large number of humans, but none of them seemed to seek the sanction of a formal welcome. Several Kamaygal and probably Gweagal met with the crew of these vessels. They puzzled over whether the pale-skinned people – so undecorated, so unscarred, so unbearded – were even men. At one point they had felt compelled to bring to shore one of their own women to indicate the question. A pale-skin then undressed to prove his sex, which produced at least a moment of mirth.[43] Altogether this influx of strangers was the most surprising thing to have happened in the region for years.

How the French experienced these same events was quite different. They no doubt heard of the self-regarding speech-making at Sydney Cove on 7 February right after it occurred. Unlike the Yiyura, they knew immediately what it indicated. They understood that Phillip's extraordinary claims to the mass of New Holland resonated with a previous key moment of European history-making – the Treaty of Tordesillas of 1494. Phillip's commission claimed all of the continent from the northern, southern and eastern coastal edges inland to 135

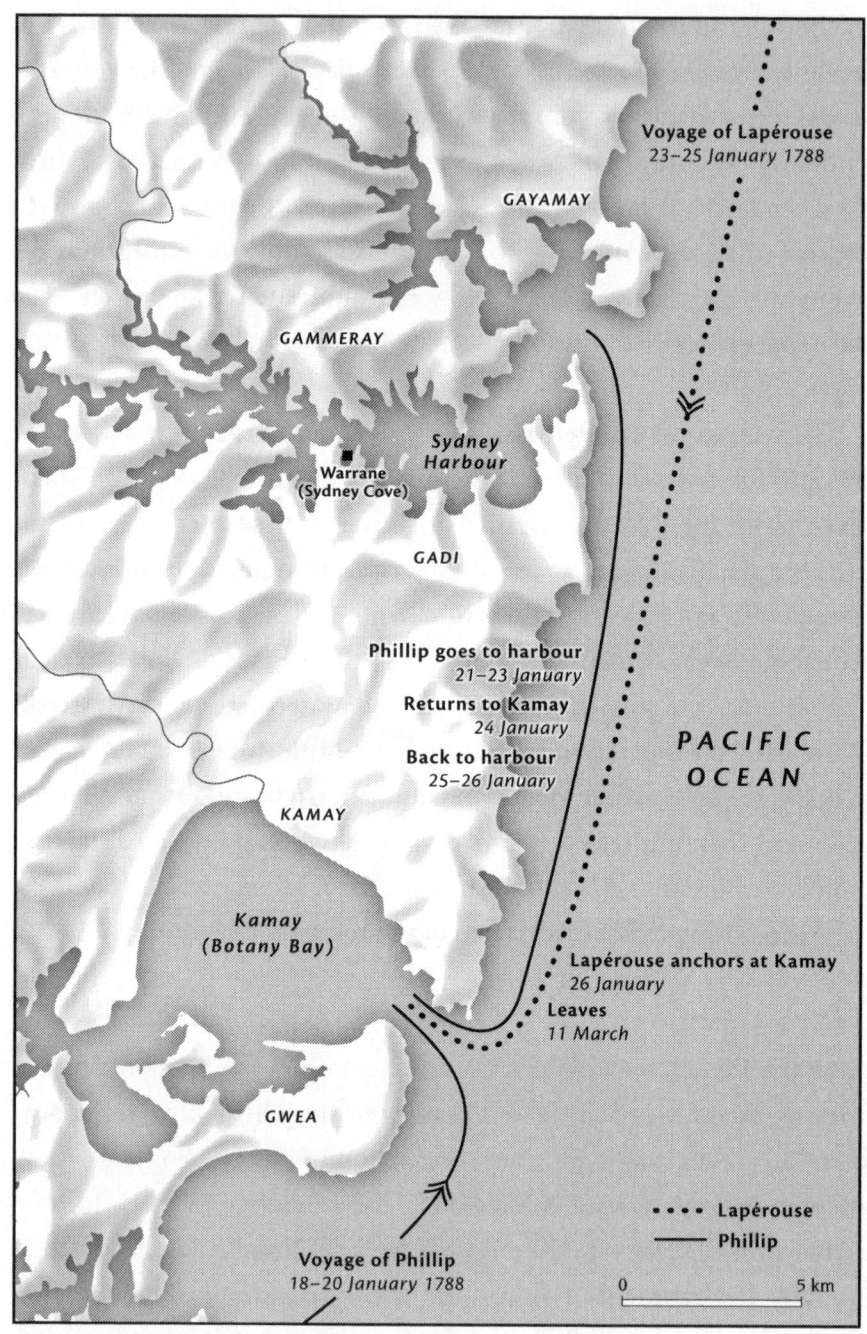

Movements of Phillip and Lapérouse, 1788

degrees longitude, amounting to more than half of today's Australia.⁴⁴ Lapérouse would have recognised that 135 degrees longitude is almost exactly opposite the longitudinal line drawn down the American continents in 1494. The Treaty of Tordesillas had divided the known New World between the two most avaricious empires of the day, Spain and Portugal. The British empire in the eighteenth century was deploying a more accurate sense of geography than the Spanish and Portuguese possessed, but in doing so it was conveying a similar sense of worldly command and entitlement.⁴⁵

Lapérouse, given his aristocratic education, understood as well that Britain did not intend to leave the unclaimed western half of the continent to France, as Portugal had left the western Americas to Spain in its day. In their gestural re-enactment of the Treaty of Tordesillas, the British meant the western half to be an offering to their friendlier rivals, the Dutch. Britain still competed with the Dutch for global power at this time, but viewed them as at least fellow Protestants. The British had not devoted quite so much energy to trying to block the Dutch over the previous century as they had to blocking Catholic France.⁴⁶ The French commander realised that no part of the southern continent was to be left to them at all.

If Lapérouse ever once wondered about the rights of the Indigenous peoples of the land now being carved up in an exclusively European enterprise, he did not leave a trace of it for later historians.

In late January, the French didn't see John Hunter organise a series of small boating reconnaissances around the harbour. They were, though, doing the same at Kamay, scouting for potential resources and mapping the region's natural defences.

It was on 26 January 1788 that Lapérouse figured out that Phillip was not, as rumoured, going to set up the British penal colony at Botany Bay (as he called it). Just as the French commander brought his two ships into the famed bay that morning, he saw ten British vessels retrieving their anchors in order to voyage out. Lapérouse was confused. He had received intelligence more than a year before about the British intention to start a colony at Botany Bay; now he saw them hurriedly sailing away. Within hours, however, Lapérouse met with the remaining ranking British officer, John Hunter, who explained in rather cryptic fashion that his commander had opted instead to settle a bit further north.

Phillip was in fact already there awaiting the rest of his fleet. 'The English lieutenant seemed to be creating a great deal of mystery,' Lapérouse was bemused to note. He decided not to press Hunter further, though soon gathered from more junior sources that Phillip's preferred spot had calmer waters and a more protected prospect than Botany Bay.[47]

If not for a monster storm on 25 January 1788 Lapérouse would have crossed paths with Phillip himself. The British commander had gone ahead in the *Supply*, determined to be in place in the harbour when his remaining ships appeared. But he had to battle 'almost a hurricane' in order to make it. Phillip's short journey of twenty nautical miles took nearly seven hours through thunder and lightning. The same storm caused Lapérouse, a less dogged man, to stay out at sea.[48] The French ships had by this stage voyaged all the way down the Atlantic Ocean and throughout the entire Pacific Ocean. They were in no tearing hurry.

The most startled group among the three peoples at Kamay that summer was, briefly, the British. The French, for their part, were the least surprised. They were only at Botany Bay because their government had told them to observe British operations there; they also knew from Cook's records that they would find an Indigenous population. The Yiyura, in their turn, were hardly expecting anyone, but many of them recalled the arrival of Cook's *Endeavour* eighteen summers before, so the presence of thirteen tall ships now was not completely unprecedented. The British, however, thought they'd be facing only Aboriginal people. They did not for one minute think they'd see the menacing white flags of the Bourbon monarchy fluttering at them in Botany Bay. 'We as soon expected to see St Paul coming through to the Bay as two strange ships,' wrote the marine Ralph Clark.[49]

Phillip was the first to get over his shock. While he hadn't suspected the French would be in New South Wales, he did realise that, like his own nation, France was searching for new opportunities in the Pacific. Straightaway, upon discovering the French ships, he issued orders that no one was to provide information about British experiences thus far to French crews.[50] It was this stricture that made Hunter speak in such an elliptical way to Lapérouse. It was also arguably what pushed Phillip to make the official proclamation of British dominion sound so formal and militaristic.

To most observing Britons, the extent of the claims read out on 7 February at Sydney Cove was another surprising element. Several noted the gargantuan nature of the orders, though most dwelled on the breadth of Phillip's powers over them rather than over the original inhabitants. 'I never herd of any one single person having so great a power vested in him as the governour has by his commission,' muttered Clark. 'It is a more unlimited one,' Bowes Smyth agreed, 'than was ever granted to any governor under the British crown.'[51]

The days before this proclamation had seen a flurry of activity. Phillip ordered Hunter to make his reconnaissances, directed convicts to fell trees, and told marines to pitch his enormous tent. He also decided to name this harbour site Sydney Cove, after his direct superior in England.

Nothing ever caused Phillip to regret his decision to switch the designated site for the colony from Botany Bay to Sydney Cove. How much he already knew about Sydney Harbour is a matter of some controversy today, but Cook had certainly sailed by its entrance back in 1770 and written in his journals: 'wherein there appear'd to be safe anchorage'.[52] Phillip made the definitive call on 23 January. He had been checking out the harbour for two days at this point, as part of a small surveying group from Botany Bay. This was before he knew that Lapérouse was on his tail, but his instinct to find a location more defensible against rivals was already in play. He reported to Lord Sydney that he thought it 'the finest harbour in the world, in which a thousand sail of the line may ride in the most perfect security'.[53]

The British fleet's initial arrival at Botany Bay had occurred over three days. Many officers recorded their first impressions of the Yiyura, which have since served as provocative ethnographic data for anthropologists. What historians of colonisation might rather note is that these early accounts all clocked how much more numerous and organised the Yiyura were compared to what Cook's officers had suggested. Hunter confessed his bewilderment at seeing so many Indigenous people and such a high degree of social sophistication. Collins recorded how the Yiyura shouted at them unwelcomingly and seemed far from being simple savages.[54] All these officers were well versed in British laws against seizing the lands of recognisable people without a treaty. They would have wondered how the legal takeover of New South Wales was going to transpire.

Planning a colony

Phillip's fleet had left Britain eight months earlier, in May 1787. The intricate planning for its departure had also taken around eight months, and involved multiple arms of the British government: the Navy Board regarding the ships, the Home Affairs Office regarding the settlement, and the Treasury regarding the finances. Phillip was involved in it all. By March 1787 almost everyone had come to agreement. There would be eleven ships to transport convicts and military personnel to a new colony in New South Wales. Practically all labour would go towards the 'common good' of said colony. There would be a slightly better ratio of women to men than first proposed. Phillip would administer a kind of abridged civil law, more liberal than the martial law initially favoured but also one without any mediating juries or governing council. He would uphold the Protestant religion. And he would take possession of a truly vast amount of territory.[55]

Discussions had started with Phillip's first memorandum to Lord Sydney in September 1786.[56] This document contained his immediate thoughts after accepting the offer of the governorship. It revealed straightaway his dislike of convicts, his distrust of them being anywhere near Indigenous people, and his request to have total control over their discipline. More conventionally, it also expressed Phillip's intention to run tight ships which carried enough supplies to insure against mishap and which followed the latest in public health protocols.

The memorandum also famously included Phillip's hopeful comments about the Indigenous inhabitants of New South Wales, as well as his scornful views about the possibility of imported slavery in the colony. These two points have always featured in the admiring accounts of Phillip, which are most of them. Given what we now know of their aftermath, however, each might be read here with some finer degree of nuance.

First, Phillip stated in this 1786 memorandum that he 'shall think it a great point gained if I can proceed in this business without any disputes with the natives, a few of which I shall endeavour to persuade to settler near us, and who I mean to furnish with everything that can tend to civilize them, and to give them a high opinion of the new guests'.

Many writers have seen these words as evidence that Phillip was 'philanthropic, characterised by Enlightenment benevolence'.[57] What they show more clearly is that he was fluent enough in British imperial history to know that Indigenous people usually disputed invasions. As we've seen, Phillip understood he'd need to make a proper connection with locals in order one day to turn invasion into legal settlement, as his predecessors had done in other new worlds. His use of the term civilise was not just a pejorative assumption that the Yiyura were unsophisticated – the civilising process here meant coming agreeably to British terms for cession.

Second, Phillip's memorandum added that Britain's laws will 'of course, be introduced in [New] South Wales, and there is one that I would wish to take place from the moment his Majesty's forces take possession of the country: That there can be no slavery in a free land, and consequently no slaves'.

Alan Frost argues that this pronouncement was Phillip's condemnation of Britain's haphazard deployment of liberty around the world, whereby slavery was banned in the British Isles but practised in some colonies.[58] But since Phillip was not given elsewhere to much philosophising about concepts like liberty, and since we know he already disapproved of slavery in Brazil on utilitarian grounds, it seems he was commenting rather on the inefficiency of such a system. It's also notable that he was referencing slavery only in terms of mass labour. In practice, he had no qualms about depriving individuals of their liberty, via iron shackles, when it came to forcing political connections.

The Home Affairs Office appointed Phillip governor on 3 September 1786. Interestingly, the Navy Board, Phillip's chief employer over the previous thirty years, was not the most enthusiastic force behind this decision. When informed of the choice, Admiral Lord Howe replied that he himself would not have selected 'Captain Philips ... for a service of this complicated nature', but if the Home Affairs minister was satisfied then this would suffice.[59] Lord Sydney, the Home Affairs minister, was indeed satisfied. He had known Phillip for at least two years, maybe four, and regarded him a proven servant of the state. More pertinently, his under-secretary, Evan Nepean, was a close colleague and friend of Phillip. It was probably Nepean who put Phillip's name under Sydney's nose. Sydney knew he wanted someone unquestioningly loyal, and this man fitted the bill.[60]

Sydney had been thinking through possible directions for the British empire since taking up the formal position of Secretary of State for Home Affairs four years earlier. Despite the wording of the job title, his new office was charged with overseeing Britain's colonies. No single subject could have been more topical in the early 1780s. This was when Britain realised it was definitely going to lose thirteen of its most prized colonies in North America. Even before signing the peace treaty that concluded the American Revolution, Sydney and other parliamentarians had begun pondering where the empire could make up the shortfall, and what needed to be done differently so as to ensure it never again faced colonial revolt.

A secondary problem arising from the American loss was the overflow of convicts in British gaols. Until the revolutionary disruption, the government had been able to send almost a thousand convicts a year to North America. Now it needed a new destination. Ideally, the government wanted to solve the question of imperial regeneration and the question of convict excess with one answer. It needed fresh outposts to replenish the resource wealth and global leverage lost through colonial independence, and it saw that it could use convicts as the initial means of doing so.

Throughout 1784, various officials debated the possibilities. Lord Sydney agreed with most of his colleagues that convicts could be appropriate seed colonists, but his instinct was to choose already-known areas to colonise and to be more flexible than tough in administrative approach. He favoured the west African coast, which was familiar via British slaving, and he proposed freeing the convicts upon their transportation. This, he believed, would avoid the risks involved with untested territories and forestall rebellion in a resentful colony later down the line.[61]

Too many of Sydney's fellow parliamentarians disagreed. An investigation into potential African bases declared that the land was too harsh and the diseases too bad for Britons to thrive there.[62] Likewise, they dismissed Sydney's idea of freed convicts building a colony out of pure love for their motherland; they felt that the American colonies had revolted because they enjoyed too many liberties from London, not too few. The opposers planned to exercise much tighter control over any new colony because leniency, in their estimation, had produced the worst kind of ingratitude.[63]

The upshot was to turn to the other key region under consideration – New South Wales – and to send unemancipated convict settlers along with more than half their number in military personnel. No European knew very much about this place, but the government did have some evidence from Cook's expedition of 1770. It concluded that the land seemed both resourceful and healthful. Moreover, New South Wales had several strategic benefits. It might provide a welcome stop for fresh trade routes forged through the Pacific, now that Atlantic trade was so tainted by the emergence of the United States. Or, it might serve one day as an additional community of consumers for Britain's Indian exports. Or, in the simplest sense, it might prevent other empires, such as the French, gaining a base in this unpoached zone of the world.

As part of its ambition to regroup after revolutionary loss, the British government decided additionally to increase rather than decrease its colonial regulations. It was not going to risk any chance of settler backlash. This is why Phillip's powers over Britons and Indigenous territory in New South Wales turned out to be so extensive.[64]

ENDURING HISTORY, 1789–1783

At length, Lord Sydney gave the green light to an operation that fulfilled his basic brief to address both imperial and penal issues. But it was also one which went against his personal preference for a nearby colony and a more liberal rule. At least he managed to appoint the man he felt would deliver this compromise in a reliable fashion.

The New South Wales option had been on the government's table since at least 1779, when Joseph Banks, the naturalist on Cook's *Endeavour*, urged cabinet to consider it. Britain was then still in the grips of the American Revolution, so did not have the space to consider the plan fully. It is significant, though, that officials took care to file away Banks's advice for a later time. Banks had assured parliament that the best place for a 'fertile' colony grown by 'convicted felons' would be Botany Bay. He was confident that the inhabitants of this coastal region would pose no practicable problem since they were negligible in every way. He suggested they had neither the numbers nor the nous to make any trouble over a treaty.[65]

Becoming a man

During these years of imperial decision-making that would go on to have such a huge impact on his life, Bennelong was moving into manhood. Around about the close of the American Revolution, Bennelong was in his late teens. Like all Yiyura men, he now faced adult initiation rituals. The main one was yulang yirabadjang, the removal of a front tooth.

The ceremony of tooth evulsion involved many elements that the Yiyura did not want settlers to witness. Collins had the honour of seeing a part of one such ceremony in 1795.[66] Aspects of that part are discussed here, respecting that other aspects are not appropriate for a historical narrative.

What Collins saw unfolded over several days. The ceremony was held on a special cleared site called a yulang. More than a hundred relatives of the initiates assembled at the site.[67] They were soon joined by Garadyigans, the healing men designated to perform the operation. Amid the Garadyigans's chants, a dozen or so initiates came forth and sat down cross-legged in the yulang. The boys clasped their hands over their bowed heads. Each Garadyigan then performed an elaborate rite that supposedly extracted a bone from his own body. Collins heard that the more the Garadyigans suffered in this rite, the less would be felt by the initiates.

Nothing more occurred that day. Each group slept at the yulang separately. At sunrise the Garadyigans started their performances again, with the boys once more in their seated positions. The first rites saw the Garadyigans act as dingos, which Collins thought gave the initiates 'power over the dog'. Next came various representations of kangaroos, which were thought to award permission to hunt these animals. Finally, the initiates presented themselves on the shoulders of kneeling relatives. A Garadyigan then lanced a boy's top gum using the bone he'd conjured earlier. He placed one end of a 'throwing-stick . . . high up on the tooth' and hit the other end with a keba, or stone.

After some strikes, the tooth came out. Friends could now dress the initiated in a laurel and a girdle, 'in which was stuck a wooden sword'. The blood from the procedure was left to run down and dry on the body. Each initiated man was called kebarrah, presumably after the stone used in the ceremony. This was the word used to describe Yemmerrawanne on his 1794 headstone – a nod to how recently he'd come of age.

In this 1795 yulang yirabadjang, Bennelong's young friend Nanbarree became a man and his uncle Colebee was the chief attending relative. Bennelong did not seem to be at this event, though he was recorded as attending an earlier ceremony. In the middle of the Pemulwuy scandal, Bennelong had disappeared from the colony for a few days. When he came back he told Phillip that he had not only been at a yulang yirabadjang but had also performed in the ceremony as a Garadyigan. Bennelong showed Phillip his personal throwing-stick to prove it.[68]

If Bennelong was a practising Garadyigan during Phillip's governorship, he certainly was not when just a teen. No colonist, of course, was yet present in Bennelong's Country to witness his initiation, though Hunter once recorded, 'I well recollect Bennillong, in the early period of our acquaintance with him and his language, telling us . . . that his own tooth was bour-bil pe-mul, buried in the earth.'[69] Presumably every man recalled his yulang yirabadjang; the pain associated with it was obvious to all. Only the recently initiated refused to acknowledge the temporary agony – their forbearance in the moment signalled their future courage in battle.

Around the same time that Bennelong lost his front tooth he would also have had his nasal septum pierced. This was not as painful, nor did all men continue to wear the bone or reed decoration in their nostril throughout adulthood.[70] No commentaries or images of Bennelong show that he liked to wear a nasal ornament. Perhaps for him, his dental gap was enough to demonstrate manliness.

On the cusp of manhood, Bennelong would not have been able to guess that his entire society was correspondingly on the cusp of upheaval. There's no way he could have looked out from Wangal Country towards forested Gadi, or towards the smoke arising to the south from Kamay, or towards the fresh sea spray coming in from Gayamay, and realised that everything was about to change.

BEGINNINGS

Saltwater People

Phillip as sailor and spy through the American Revolution and before • Bennelong at six, when Cook arrived at Kamay • Phillip as a farmer and, earlier, in the Seven Years' War • Bennelong's birth and parents • Phillip's youth and background • Saltwater worlds

Sailor and spy

The two main reasons why Lord Sydney appointed Phillip as inaugural governor were his proven skills as a naval officer and his past discretion as a government spy. Together, these experiences indicated a competent and trustworthy loyalist. Phillip's naval background is well known and frequently lauded in histories of him. His work as a spy is less often acknowledged and sometimes even denied. The official description of Phillip by the organisation that secured his memorial in Westminster Abbey admits he was a 'naval intelligence officer' but baulks at 'true spy'.[1] Whatever the label, it's clear that in the mid-1780s Phillip was paid to gather intelligence about the French for the British Home Affairs Office that the French did not know he was gathering.

Phillip spied in pre-revolutionary France on two separate occasions. In 1786 he was paid £160 to travel to the Mediterranean town of Hyères, close to the naval port of Toulon. This was a follow-up mission. A year earlier, he'd been paid £150 to travel directly to Toulon to investigate the state of French maritime rearmament. Both times, he was the employee of Evan Nepean, the under-secretary to Lord Sydney at Home Affairs.²

In this period, British espionage was run by the Admiralty, the Treasury, the Foreign Office, and the Home Affairs Office – continuing an ad hoc practice that had been operating for at least two centuries.³ Nepean went on to assemble elaborate spying networks for at least the next twenty years, but at the beginning of his intelligence-gathering career, he relied on pre-established connections. Most especially, he inherited the confidential service of an Anglophile Dutch outfit, headed somewhat remarkably by a woman, Marguerite Wolters.

This organisation had been selling the British government information about various political happenings around Europe since at least the 1730s. It had begun under Marguerite's husband, Richard, who built on the goodwill of the then formal Anglo–Dutch alliance. Marguerite had inherited the business upon Richard's death in 1771, not only maintaining it through the breakdown of the Anglo–Dutch alliance during the American Revolution, but even extending it to include agents in Dunkirk, Paris, Brest, Nantes, Rochefort and Toulon.⁴

In 1784 Marguerite Wolters sent word to Nepean that France seemed to be re-building its navy after sustaining significant losses during the American Revolution (where it had sided, of course, with Britain's foes, the colonial revolutionaries). The British took this to mean that France was planning to renege on its recent agreement to withhold additional military support from its imperial holdings in India.⁵ Who knew if it also meant France was rearming in order to take on brand new portions of the world, such as the South Pacific?

Ascertaining a rival's maritime capacity was crucial in a contest where control of saltwater realms meant everything. Nepean's bosses – Lord Sydney and the prime minister himself, William Pitt – needed to know exactly what they were dealing with. In October 1784, Nepean recorded in his *Secret Service Ledger* that he asked Phillip to go to 'Toulon & other ports of France for the purpose of ascertaining the Naval Force, and Stores in the Arsenals'. Since Phillip was at this time an officer in the navy, his assignment had to be endorsed. Admiralty records show that he was granted leave for twelve months to attend to 'private affairs'.[6]

Phillip evidently sent home numerous reports from France, though only two survive in British national archives. Both confirmed the rumour of French rearmament. 'The French certainly pay the greatest attention to their Navy,' he wrote. The Toulon dock was 'in very good order and very superior to what it was when I saw it before the [American Revolutionary] War'.[7]

No reports survive of Phillip's second mission, though again it was officially granted by the Admiralty for twelve months to address 'private affairs'.[8] We know this stint was cut short by the call – also from Nepean – to come home in order to consider the governorship of a new penal outpost for the empire.

Before these spying missions of the mid-1780s, Phillip worked diligently as a naval officer in some of the duller campaigns of the American Revolution. Like all the wars that Britain waged in the eighteenth century, this one had global dimensions. When France, Spain and the Dutch stepped in to support the revolutionaries against Britain, the war spread to all the maritime areas where these European powers competed: the Indian Ocean, the Caribbean Sea, the North Sea and the Mediterranean. Phillip's duties during the revolution included obtaining supplies from Madras for a potential British assault on Spanish colonies (which never happened); defending the English Channel against a possible French invasion (which also never happened); escorting a troop of German soldiers from Hanover to Britain to serve as cannon fodder in India; and overseeing repairs to other ships in the Thames that then went on to see action under different captains.[9]

In the five-odd years he spent making these rather unglamorous contributions to Britain's war effort, Phillip probably undertook his clandestine year in Brazil. As noted in the chapter 'Journeys', there are no records of Phillip's whereabouts for most of 1781 but there are several suggestions that he was lurking in South American waters during that year, waiting for an order to pounce on Spain's holdings. This eventuality also failed to transpire, but if the suggestions are true, his mission would have allowed Phillip to underscore his reputation for reliability.

The middle years of the 1770s were spent, as we also saw in 'Journeys', on official secondment to the Portuguese navy. The early 1770s, however, saw Phillip again in the murky world of espionage. This was a period of peace, before the imperial conflagration of the American Revolution, yet Britain still needed to know about the potential arms-flexing of its greatest rival, absolutist France. Phillip's involvement in spying at this time is less substantiated than his stints in the mid-1780s, but some facts emerge. We know that Phillip was not engaged with obvious naval activities in the early 1770s yet he earned sufficient monies to keep himself and to make inroads on those he owed his recently separated wife, Charlott. We also know he requested leave from the navy in curiously similar language to that used in later years: twice he asked for twelve months to attend to personal matters (in this case, 'his health'). He told the navy his destinations were Saint-Amand in 1773 and Lille in 1772. Both these towns were in the then slightly more pro-British region of Flanders, near the border of less-friendly France. Phillip later compared French naval preparations in Toulon with those he'd seen 'before the [American Revolutionary] War'. Finally, Isaac Landmann, an influential Prussian professor at London's Royal Military Academy, once claimed that Phillip was his 'oldest' friend – their connection probably began when Landmann was a professor at École Militaire in Paris, between 1770 and 1776.[10]

The exhaustive research of Alan Frost adds one more suggestion to support the hypothesis. Frost notes that Phillip's long-time patron, Charles Duncombe (to whom he'd leave his 'brazil diamond ring'), had business interests in Flanders. Phillip may have been working for Duncombe at this time, but this work could also have been a front for espionage, given that Duncombe was the uncle of a rumoured spy, Robert Shafto. We know that Shafto, a member of parliament, recommended Phillip for naval promotion around 1780. Their acquaintance perhaps started long before, when both were snooping about the borderlands and port towns of the nation that most threatened Britain's saltwater supremacy.[11]

Looking back, Phillip might have felt that the fifteen years before his appointment to the governorship amounted to a ragbag of underwhelming naval campaigns and intelligence assignations. Yet for the few necessary people in the few necessary places, these accomplishments made him the ideal candidate to lead Britain's venture in New South Wales. A big naval personality like Horatio Nelson, or indeed a charismatic bureaucratic talent like Evan Nepean, would not have suited nearly so well – their egos would have got in the way, and besides, they were too important to spare. Phillip's eagerness to serve in whatever capacity asked of him, combined with a lack of any actually startling success, were his most attractive qualities.

In 1770, aged just thirty-two, Phillip could hardly have guessed that a middling naval career and some shadowy government work would one day deliver him a vice-regal position. Such a prediction would no doubt have cheered him up. In that year, he must have felt as if failure was more likely to be the dominant theme of his life. His marriage had just ended in separation, a highly unusual occurrence in the British eighteenth century. His military ambitions seemed thwarted by the rare outbreak of peace. And his humble family connections were never going to provide entree to other notable ways of serving his beloved nation. The world's horizons seemed to be contracting.

Bennelong and Cook

Ten thousand miles away, at exactly the same time, Bennelong probably felt his horizons were expanding beyond all conceivable expectation. Of course, at six years of age, the experience of being surprised by newness was not uncommon. In 1770, however, the Yiyura faced a truly extraordinary occurrence. For eight nights during the cooling season, James Cook's *Endeavour* expedition anchored at Kamay (Botany Bay). The Yiyura were saltwater people too, but no one had seen a vessel as large as Cook's. Nor had anyone seen so many humans so bleached of colour as those aboard the oversized nuwi. Perhaps most surprising, though, was the obscurity of their motive. They came into shore on smaller watercraft. They refused to be welcomed properly. They stole things, collected things, and sporadically tried to hurt the local Gweagal with firing sticks. They dumped a pile of unfamiliar debris on the beach. And then they were gone. As suddenly as they had sailed in from the south, they took off again to the north, leaving only questions, rumours, and a distinct impression of rudeness.

The first settler to write about this famed moment in history from the perspective of Bennelong as a child was Eleanor Dark. In her 1941 novel *The Timeless Land,* Dark imagined Bennelong listening to the tales of his father, who had witnessed Cook's arrival. Dark rightly assumed that a Wangal boy was unlikely to have been near Kamay, more than ten miles from his clan Country, but she did fancy that the boy's father happened to chance by when Cook approached. Dark paints Bennelong's father as a classic noble savage, immersed in a never-changing world of mythos, capable only of interpreting the strange, three-masted boat as a magical bird conveying ghosts. There is an awkward passage in the first chapter where the father senses that the *Endeavour* is a harbinger 'of peril and of change. Yet there could be no peril in this land . . . Nor was the thought of change one which dwelt easily in the mind.'[12]

A careful student of the written sources, Dark didn't just invent this Aboriginal view from thin air. She probably relied on Samuel Bennett's 1867 *History of Australian Discovery and Colonisation*. Bennett interpreted an old Gweagal man, Yadyer, as saying that the Yiyura at first thought the *Endeavour* was a 'large bird'. Bennett also wrote that most Aboriginal people called white people 'ghosts', but as later historian Maria Nugent comments, 'the reality was most likely more mundane'.[13] There is no evidence anywhere of the terror Yiyura people would have felt towards a cargo of dead men. Contrarily, there is evidence that the observing Gweagal understood the vessel to be at least modelled on their own kind of watercraft, just in outsized proportions. As current knowledge-holder Uncle Shayne Williams discusses, the local population from all the way south in Dharawal Country sent smoke signals and used message sticks to convey news of the boat's passage: they were warning of strange people in strange vessels; they were not panicking about inexplicable spirits in fantastical creatures.[14]

Both Samuel Bennett and Eleanor Dark were ensconced in a long and powerful tradition in Western history-writing which assumed that all Indigenous people understood first encounters through mythology.[15] The tradition still has wide currency today, and is not without value as a reminder for us to think beyond the usual secular frame of modern historical explanation. But the inclination only works if it is applied equally to Europeans, with an ambition to see how they also always absorbed the unknown through familiar ideas. When Indigenous people alone are made to deploy mythology, it becomes a trap instead of a universal tool. Moreover, it relegates Indigenous people to timelessness, and thus to a world without history. This in turn indicates a world without social complexity, without political nuance, and ultimately without sovereign rights. Suggesting that the *Endeavour* was seen as a magical bird carrying ghosts may seem an innocent whimsy, but on its own such notions contribute to the defanging of Aboriginal history – they are a way of stripping contact stories of their power to prompt reactions in the present.

What Bennelong the child may instead have heard in the various tellings of Cook's landing in 1770 was the following. On the last day, the massive nuwi sailed off up the coast, taking its eighty-odd men with it. The Yiyura who watched it depart probably felt less a sense of peril or impending change and more an uneasiness about rituals undone or conventions flouted. No formal welcome had been acknowledged, so no meaningful engagement had occurred. Materially, they had gained a swag of trinkets which did not appear to have any perceivable use.[16]

Earlier, the locals had watched the strange crew dig up clumps of earth and old shells to take with them. These items joined their even more mystifying collection of clearly inedible plants mixed in with some nutritious greens. What angered the Gweagal, though, was the crew's giant haul of fish and rays. They had not asked permission to take so much.[17]

The strangers carried among them several men who copied images onto thin materials. One of these men was darker than most of the others; he dressed differently and seemed to stand apart. But he didn't understand any Yiyura (Darug) words either, so was also soon ignored.[18]

One day some of the strangers went on an excursion in a smaller craft out of Yiyura Country altogether, south towards the Dharawal. These neighbours of the Yiyura's, however, had no greater success in engaging them.[19]

On the fourth day of their landing, the strangers buried one of their own on Gweagal Country. This man in death was even paler than his survivors. He had not been killed by his people but had died from some severe illness.[20]

The initial three days had seen much attempted communication, with grave defiance of protocol on the strangers' part, and various commands, shouts and threats on the Gweagal's part. Eventually the Gweagal gave up, after discovering that nearly fifty of their weapons had been stolen from their shelters. The strangers didn't even seem to use such things; they preferred heavier implements that shot fire.[21]

Eleanor Dark used the vignette of Bennelong being a child in thrall to Cook as a way of suggesting that he was destined to connect with the British sailors. It's an almost irresistible idea for a settler historian, and one not entirely negated in this book, but no colonial source actually mentions Bennelong discussing Cook's landing with Phillip's men. It's probable that the extraordinary event lived on in Yiyura storytelling through garabaras. Like everyone else in the harbour, Bennelong would have heard and watched these renditions, but he was no more or less entangled in them while growing up.

In 1770, the boy Bennelong would have been more intensely occupied with his immediate family. He knew from first consciousness that he was part of the sixty-odd Wangal living along the harbour's southwestern shore. Everyday existence, though, was shaped by his smaller band of parents, siblings and paternal relatives. A later colonial newspaper article once named Bennelong's father as Goorah-Goorah and his mother as Gagulh.[22] These names may be close to true, given the rough accuracy of the other details provided in the piece. We know that the two sisters who would go on to spend a lot of time with Bennelong were younger than him. Wariwear seems to have been born about 1767; Karangarang must have been born around the same year as Cook's arrival. To a small child, the birth of a new baby perhaps trumped news of any mysterious boat.[23]

Years on, British astronomer and linguist William Dawes wrote a list of Bennelong's siblings: 'Wariwear. Karangarang. Wurrgan.'[24] The third person was possibly Worogan, who later married the little brother of Boorong and Baludarri – a man called Yeranabe. This sister was either younger than the others or a half-sister. Worogan may have been the child of Goorah-Goorah's other wife, who was named by a colonial reporter as 'Yahanua'. The reporter thought that Yahanua was Goorah-Goorah's *next* wife, but she might simply have been the secondary wife.[25]

Romping about with little siblings and several guardians, Bennelong as a Wangal boy learned how to use a spear to fish and to fight, absorbed lessons about clan rules and histories, and played games with other children.[26] Always these activities occurred along the water's edge. Colonists later observed that Yiyura children displayed bodily adornment from a very early age. Their women carers fixed tiny teeth, bones and feathers to their hair with tree sap; male relatives scarred their chest and back with clan designs using a sharpened shell.[27] Certain hair decoration and permanent skin markings were visible on Bennelong's body for the rest of his life. These adornments perhaps became his easiest reminder in turbulent times of where he had come from.

Farmer and fighter

Lord Sydney had a further reason for thinking Phillip would make a good settler-governor, besides his skills as a sailor and spy. This was his experience as a farm manager. For four years in the 1760s Phillip had managed around forty acres of farmland in dairy country near Lyndhurst, in Hampshire, while married to his first wife, Charlott.

This unusual marriage had ended in April 1769, though the legal documents stated they had 'lately lived separate and apart'.[28] Their time on the farm was preceded by two years living in or near London. All the while, they shared their marriage with Charlott's companion, Mrs Anna Maria Cane.

Phillip knew from the start what he was getting himself into. The marriage settlement document that Charlott presented to him the day before their wedding stated that he would be responsible for allocating an annuity of £20 to Anna for the rest of his life.[29] The document also ensured that upon any permanent marital separation all her wealth would return to Charlott – a striking reversal of customary practice in eighteenth-century Britain.

Phillip's biographers have been frustrated for two centuries at not finding any remnant that suggests his feelings about this arrangement. As we have seen, however, subsequent events point to an acceptance on his part, even affectionate respect. For one thing, Phillip worked hard soon after their split to pay back the £2,000 of Charlott's money that he'd spent on their Lyndhurst estate.[30] For another, he was still conscious, twenty years later when in New South Wales, of the obligations he thought he still owed her. In 1790, Phillip believed that Charlott was dying; he therefore requested leave to return home from Sydney so he could confirm the ongoing payment of Anna's annuity, 'for which I gave security, and for which it is probable no provision will [otherwise] be made'.[31] In fact, Charlott had rewritten her will in Phillip's absence, releasing him from his commitment to guarantee the modest allowance and instead directing that nearly half of her £5,540 legacy be invested for Anna. All she required from Phillip in her final will was his signature for probate. She included a reward of £100 to him should he do so. In 1793, upon arrival home in Britain just a few months after Charlott's death, Phillip was more than happy to assist.[32]

His four years working the Lyndhurst farm were, then, really four years supervising pasture usage for two women. Phillip probably ran dairy cows on the land – possibly not even his own dairy cows. Whether or not the Phillips even generated an income from the venture is unclear. Their two prior years living near London did not seem to involve any salaried occupation for Phillip, so perhaps a financial return was the least pressing requirement of this rustic interlude.[33] We do know that while Phillip managed the farm, he undertook the office of Overseer of the Poor in Lyndhurst, an antiquated appointment demanded of most country gentlemen in the period to distribute alms to the needy under the Poor Law. His name appeared on the parish records as an overseer in 1768 and in 1766.[34]

How Phillip first met Charlott and why he entered into a relationship with her remains mysterious. They wed in 1763, a couple of months after Britain signed the peace treaty to end the world-spanning Seven Years' War. Phillip had served for six of those seven years, and came out of the war a junior lieutenant. Then suddenly, upon peace, he found himself on a miserable half-pay of fourteen shillings a week.[35] At the age of twenty-four, with a limited knowledge of Britain's contemporary warmongering capacity, he perhaps had to wonder if he'd ever see naval action again. Charlott's offer of a gentlemanly life, if a little unconventional, could have been too enticing to forgo. The portrait that Phillip commissioned of himself in 1764 certainly hinted at an ideal transition from maritime service to landed gentry.

Phillip's involvement in the Seven Years' War had been exciting – the most thrilling combat, it turned out, he'd ever experience in his long naval career. The final three years, including the epic British siege of Havana, were especially compelling. During the summer of 1762 Phillip had been part of the bombardment of Havana's harbour heads, which led to the city's fall in August.[36] Stationed in the Caribbean since 1760, Phillip was serving then as an able seaman on the *Stirling Castle*, captained by a relative of his, Michael Everitt. The vessel's orders were to join a large convoy attempting to disrupt or seize the

Caribbean assets of France and Spain, so that Britain would have something to bargain with at war's conclusion.[37]

Phillip's initial three years in this global war were spent in Europe or at home. Among his missions was the infamous failed defence of the British colony at Minorca in the Mediterranean, which involved much dramatic fighting and drew jingoistic attention from the press.[38] A mere captain's servant at this stage, Phillip was part of the British attack on the would-be French usurpers of Minorca in May 1756. A few weeks hence, though, he witnessed the surprising withdrawal of British forces under the command of the ranking Admiral, John Byng. Later, Byng was very publicly tried and executed for neglect of duty. Phillip's letter home to his sister at the time indicates that he shared the court's views. 'I need not mention,' he wrote, 'the Cowardice of the Only person Admiral Byng, that kept the French Fleet from being Distroyed, and the Island from being relieved.'[39]

This personal letter from Phillip to his sister – so rare among the surviving documents – also reveals that his anti-French sentiment was strong even at eighteen years of age. He accused the French of 'great dastardness, for not coming to a close engagemt when they had Such Odds as their Whole Fleet against [us]'. He thought it showed 'that most of them had rather Run than Fight'.

Phillip had formally entered the navy on 16 October 1755, having just turned seventeen By this stage he'd gained more than a year's seagoing experience. At fifteen he had entered a seven-year apprenticeship with merchant mariner William Readhead, a commitment he was no doubt able to break due to new national needs as Britain lurched into war, as well as the influence of his family patron, Michael Everitt, who appointed him onto his ship.[40]

If there could ever be an equivalent in Phillip's life of Bennelong's initiation by tooth evulsion, it was recruitment into Britain's maritime armed force. The British navy was considered the most manly organisation in the military, and possibly in the whole saltwater empire. It employed only men for active service, it offered sufficient pay to break any bond of dependence on parents, and it opened up access to new people beyond simply kin.[41] Like Bennelong after his yulang yirabadjang, Phillip after his voluntary enlistment attained an identity that could never be reversed.

The shadowy period of his apprenticeship to Readhead represents a transitory phase between childhood and adulthood. The arrangement was made in late 1753 by Phillip's school at Greenwich, evidently with Phillip's 'free consent'.[42] It was meant to train him to be a worthy sailor, almost certainly so that he could one day join the nation's formal seagoing arm. His brief tenure saw him on two separate stints killing whales in the Arctic and one stint trading goods in the Mediterranean. Whaling was ruthless, dangerous and hardening. Trade was cosmopolitan, commercial and contractual. No other kind of 'gap year' could have prepared Phillip better for a life of service to the British empire.[43]

Birth stories

A quarter of a century younger than Phillip, Bennelong was born around 1764. British accounts of later Yiyura births describe a scene where the mother is surrounded by other women who are easing her pains and guiding the baby into a waiting hollow of soft leaves. The mother then moves to another hollow where she births the placenta. Her attendants wash the baby and wrap them in freshly torn sheafs of paperbark, known for its antiseptic qualities.[44]

Within weeks of his birth, Bennelong would have received a name, though probably not the one he became best known by. A child's first name related to a form in nature, but was more like a diminutive or nickname than a lasting totemic name. Bennelong went by at least five names in his life, only receiving the marine-oriented 'Bennelong' upon initiation.⁴⁵ Also at a few weeks of age, his mother would have switched him from paperbark cocooning to a position on her shoulders. Most likely she nursed him herself and carried him aloft for up to two years.⁴⁶

Going by typical clan conventions, Goorah-Goorah the father would have come from the Wangal, and Gagulh the mother from an associated but different clan. Bennelong did not seem to have any older siblings. He was apparently the couple's first surviving child. If his parents were following customary life, Goorah-Goorah would have hunted for large game with spears, or gunang; fished with harpoons, or galara; and engaged in formal battles against foes with clubs (wudi) and shields (yarragung). Perhaps he was also a creator of garabaras or a healing Garadyigan, but if so all public traces of these positions are gone. Gagulh would have been a primary or everyday angler, using a gig (muding) and line (garradjun) to catch fish from her nuwi. She'd have also helped care for other small children in the kinship group.

Several colonists tried to come to terms with Yiyura hunting methods. They understood quickly that it involved far more than just attacking animals. Watkin Tench observed that the men often used traps. They might build a mound of bush scrub to lure in birds and then pierce them with implements. Or they might use fire to smoke out tree-living mammals: when the creatures fled, sometimes into tree hollows or sometimes into the bird traps, they were 'easily dislodged and taken'. John Hunter added that the Yiyura even caught kangaroo via entrapment. They would herd the animal into a tree hollow and then clamber up the trunk 'by means of notches at convenient distances, that are made with a stone hatchet'. While one man sat at the top of the tree with a weapon, another filled the hollow with smoke: 'this obliges the animal to attempt to make its escape, but . . . it is almost certain of death'.⁴⁷

Likewise Tench observed the men's maritime hunting. Mostly they fished from rocks near 'unruffled water'. For bait they chewed cockles and spat them into the water. 'Silent and watchful', they hovered their harpoons over their prey and plunged them in at the last opportunity. The men kept plunging 'so as to entangle the barbs in the flesh'. Only women fished with lines, a practice that Tench anyway believed was valued less highly than fishing with a harpoon. Whether or not Tench's own gender values were at play in this observation is hard to discern. David Collins noted that Yiyura men, in addition to harpooning fish, also hunted for eel, usually in autumn, when harbour fish stocks were lower. The men went to brackish water and trapped eels in gouged logs or elaborate nets.[48]

Less keenly or less easily, the colonists recorded the daily work of Yiyura women. The women's role as common angler, all the same, was impossible to miss. Women made their own lines from the bark of a particular shrub. They rolled shreds of it on the inside of their thighs, 'carefully inserting the ends of every fresh piece into the last made'. They made hooks from shell linings or bird talons. They then took their lines and hooks out in their nuwis. If they were breastfeeding, then the infants came too.[49]

Tench was befuddled by the women's ability to manoeuvre the nuwis, let alone manage toddlers in them. 'While she paddles to the fishing-bank, and while employed there, the child is placed on her shoulders,' he observed.

> The management of the canoe alone appears a work of unsurmountable difficulty ... [Repeated] use only could reconcile them to the painful position in which they sit in it. They drop in the middle of the canoe upon their knees, and resting the buttocks on the heels, extend the knees to the sides, against which they press strongly, so as to form a poise sufficient

to retain the body in its situation, and relieve the weight which would otherwise fall wholly upon the toes. Either in this position or cautiously moving in the centre of the vessel, the mother tends her child, keeps up her fire (which is laid on a small patch of earth), paddles her boat, broils fish and provides in part the subsistence of the day.[50]

Most of the women's childcare responsibilities went unnoticed by the British. All did, however, remark on the women's guidance of the practice that initiated female babies into girlhood. This involved tying a kangaroo sinew around the bottom joint of the baby's left-hand little finger. After a few days of interrupted blood circulation, the digit shrivelled and fell off. To a man, the colonists were aghast at this procedure and most never came to any understanding of why it was done. Collins hazarded the best guess, which was 'these joints of the little finger were supposed to be in the way when they wound their fishing lines over the hand'.[51] But all societies enact rituals to mark growth and belonging. In the colonists' society these included circumcision, corset-drawing, trouser-lengthening and beard-trimming.

As in most patrilineal societies, the Yiyura designated specific roles to the genders, although men and women of the Yiyura undertook a notable amount of activities together, too. All Yiyura participated in garabaras and other ceremonies. Each gender had a role in battles and conflict. And everyone seemed to partake in cooking. 'The wife returns to land with her booty,' wrote Tench, 'and the husband quitting the rock joins his stock to hers.' As a pair, they move to a makeshift hut nearby the shore. They fetch fire with a stick from the one already burning in the woman's canoe. Then they throw the fish, entire, onto the fire. Only after it warms, does the couple rub off the catch's scales and take out the viscera. The cooking resumes, often with the fish wrapped in fine bark. Tench noted that Yiyura partners cooked small game in the same manner, extracting feathers or fur after initial heating.[52]

Goorah-Goorah seems to have been a significant member of the Wangal. He had a special or particular custodianship of a small island just off the Wangal shoreline. Phillip heard the name of this island as Memilla. (Collins heard Me-mel; Tench heard Memel.) Collins reported, 'Bennillong, both before he went to England and since his return, often assured me, that the island of Me-mel (called by us Goat Island) close by Sydney Cove was his own property; that it was his father's.' Collins rightly found this 'strange' since he appreciated already that Yiyura people did not own Country as patrimonial freehold in the same way that Europeans did. Nevertheless, Bennelong pressed him to believe that there were also 'other people who possessed this kind of hereditary property, which they retained undisturbed'.[53]

One of the most important truths of Aboriginal people, then and now, is that they understand land in a different way to Europeans. It is exceedingly unlikely that Bennelong's claim to Memel was the one exception to Yiyura practice. Rather, Bennelong, through his father, seems to have inherited additional obligations to this island – he somehow had more dues to Memel than he owed all the other parts of Wanne, and from this he could extract more rights to Memel than he could from other parts. However configured, Bennelong was surely a proprietor of Memel in the same way that Aboriginal people today speak of being traditional owners. The distinction from Western-styled patrimony remained.[54]

Just as Bennelong and Barangaroo would twenty-five years later, Goorah-Goorah and Gagulh probably enjoyed Memel as a place for picnics and peace. Colonists noticed that Bennelong was 'much attached' to the island; he was often seen 'feasting and enjoying' himself on it. Phillip in particular clocked that it was a place where an Indigenous person could be all alone and completely without fear.[55]

Phillip's parents are nearly as hazy in the written archives as are Bennelong's. His mother was Elizabeth Breach and his father was Jacob Phillip. Elizabeth was a London-born widow in her twenties when she met Phillip's dad. Jacob, as suggested in the chapter 'London', was a German-speaking migrant of uncertain birth, age and profession.

The most solid source on Jacob, which is not solid at all, is his mention in the records of Phillip's school, the Charity School of the Royal Hospital for Seamen at Greenwich. This school existed for the 'sons of seamen, between eleven and thirteen years of age [who were] objects of charity'. Phillip entered it in 1751, aged twelve. Later, the school clarified that it was for the 'sons of *poor* seamen'.[56] Several historians have read the stricture about charity to mean that Jacob was dead by the time of Phillip's admission. But since parents were asked to indemnify the school for the value of the boys' clothing, there's a chance that Jacob was still alive at this time, just disabled or otherwise unable to make an adequate living.[57] Other sources suggest that Phillip's great facility with European languages was due to his father being also a 'teacher of languages', which indicates he was alive for some decent part of Phillip's boyhood.[58]

Most historians who believe that Jacob had died by 1751 also think that he could not have been both a seaman and a teacher. Assuming he was solely a teacher, they believe that Phillip's admittance into the Greenwich school was due rather to Elizabeth's manipulation of the rules.[59] It's true that Elizabeth had been married before Jacob to a John Herbert, able seaman for the British navy, who died in 1731. She may have appealed to the school to take in her fatherless son on the basis of

Herbert's record of service. But as we know from Phillip's own career, naval seamen in this era often worked at other jobs during peacetime. Jacob might easily have worked in education as well as for the navy. His first occupation perhaps granted his son some linguistic skills while his second maybe gave him a chance to enter the most esteemed profession in eighteenth-century Britain.

That said, from the 1750s Phillip's father does not seem to have played any role in his son's life. When Phillip wrote his letter to his sister from Minorca in 1756, he sent 'my duty to my mother' but nothing to his dad. Jacob, we assume, died before Phillip turned eighteen.

Phillip was the second-born of four children to Elizabeth and Jacob: Eliza was the last, born in 1742. Anne was born in 1740, Arthur in 1738, and Rebecca in 1737. Genealogical researcher Michael Flynn suggests that both Eliza and Rebecca died very young – maybe as children – since only Anne went on to create further life documents. Anne was undoubtedly the recipient of her brother's Minorca letter. She married and had a child, named Arthur, but both were dead by 1780, when Phillip was off serving in the American Revolutionary wars.[60]

The last child, Eliza, was born in Rotherhithe, near the esteemed British naval epicentre of Greenwich. Anne was born in Whitechapel, then home to relatively respectable businesses. But the first two, Rebecca and Arthur, were baptised in the Bread Street parish of Cheapside, well within hearing distance of St Mary-le-Bow's church by St Paul's Cathedral, making them true cockneys.[61] Tracing these moves on a map suggests that Jacob had started quite poor but became gradually wealthier.[62] Whatever riches the family had accrued by 1740, though, vanished a decade later, probably due to Jacob's death. In later school documents, Phillip was described several times as being 'poor'.[63]

Phillip's birth was more similar than different to Bennelong's. Like Gagulh, Elizabeth would have been surrounded only by other women. One of them might have been formally designated a midwife. The development of British medicine during the 1700s meant that men moved into midwifery by the late eighteenth century, but in 1738 this position was still held by a woman. Like Gagulh, too, Elizabeth birthed during a time of dire infant mortality. The average rate of death for British children under the age of ten in the early 1700s was one in two. Elizabeth's eventual loss of two of her four children matched this rate with dismal accuracy.[64]

Instead of soft paperbark, baby Arthur would have been wrapped in a special set of 'childbed linen'. Such cloths were so standard that the lack of them signalled either deep ignorance or a suspicious unpreparedness to keep the offspring.[65] Arthur, plainly, was kept, and apparently with love. He never faced the workhouse for the poor, whatever misfortunes befell the family, and he gained the best education that could be secured for the means.

Elizabeth and Jacob married sometime between 1736 and 1732.[66] As the widow of an able seaman who had died in service during a defensive imperial patrol of British Jamaica, Elizabeth would have qualified for a small government pension, but not one so generous that it detracted from the prospect of a new marriage. Elizabeth was around twenty-five when her first husband's probate came through, childless and perhaps starting to think again about a pathway to wifely status.[67]

Aside from both her husbands, Elizabeth had an intriguing tie to the British navy that turned out to advance her son's livelihood. The widow of her Uncle Benjamin Breach went on to marry into the Everitt family, which somehow remained very close to Elizabeth. The Everitt offspring were like cousins to her, even though they were not blood relatives. One of them was Michael Everitt, the captain who arranged for Phillip's initial naval appointments. These paved the way for Phillip to become a captain himself one day, then a governor, and eventually an admiral.[68]

Jacob, as noted, is today an almost completely blank slate. Given Phillip's later certainty that his family coat-of-arms was the tri-camel crest of Claude-Ambroise Philippe, Jacob could convincingly have been a descendant of Huguenot refugees who had once fled Catholic France to a German-speaking town and then fled again to an even stauncher Protestant state. Britain experienced a particularly large influx of Germanic Protestant refugees in 1709. The British government, keen to populate its new territories in North America, had advertised its commitment to settling any loyal Protestant in the New World. All the same, it was not prepared for the thirteen thousand or so refugees who consequently flooded into London. British officials managed to send only half that number to their colonial sites; the rest stayed in London. Jacob might have been one of those Germanic Protestant refugees who settled in the capital. If so, he was at least fifteen years older than Elizabeth.[69]

Jacob brought no other children or relatives to his marriage with Elizabeth, and very soon seemed not to bring much income or legacy either. One thing he did impart to his only son, however, was a taste of the Continent. Phillip's ability to understand Portuguese, German, Flemish and French gave him a marked advantage over his peers. Possibly Jacob passed on a sense of familial persecution by European history, too. None of the Protestant refugees in 1709 blamed their Germanic hosts for their statelessness; instead, they blamed France for pushing them into displacement in the first place. Whether or not Phillip was a descendant of Huguenots, he always betrayed an inveterate distrust of the French. This was not unusual among eighteenth-century Englishmen, but it was sharp in Phillip and arguably what most powered his subsequent work ethic.

In a broad sense, Elizabeth's ties to the navy and Jacob's suspected identity as a Protestant refugee represent two of the most important drivers behind the rise of the British empire in the eighteenth century.

Despite traditional claims that the British empire was rooted in private enterprise and a loose control of religious faith, what really kicked off imperial growth were the events surrounding the Glorious Revolution of 1688.

The Glorious Revolution saw the English parliament oust the old Catholic-convert king James II and install Protestant William III, brought in via marriage from the Netherlands. Parliament got the constitutional grip on the monarchy it wanted out of this Faustian pact, but the cost was having to engage with all of William's ongoing wars of survival against would-be Catholic suppressors on the Continent. William's wars of the 1690s needed a much bigger military. This required more money. Britain looked to its existing colonies for additional cashflow, but this in turn demanded more naval protection. Soon, the British government was embroiled in an escalating spiral of the military needing colonies which needed the military which needed colonies. Britain boomed after William III's ascension but it was now also caught in an endless cycle of war and expansion. Protestant fears had triggered this rise in global power, while naval dominance became one of its most defining characteristics.[70]

As a child of naval patronage as well as, perhaps, of Protestant outrage, no wonder Arthur Phillip went on to love, obey, and embody the British empire.

The Yiyura's deeper history

What the Yiyura were doing or undergoing in the late 1600s is almost entirely lost to settler view. There is a strong tendency in modern popular memory to cleave the Aboriginal past at 1788. After this date of imperial arrival there is 'history', while before this date there is 'culture'. This prior phase is often assumed to be static and textureless.

A detailed chronicle of one Yiyura man who lived across the border year of 1788, however, shows up the absurdity of this division.

Bennelong's biography, if it does nothing else for modern readers, reveals how Yiyura lives were just as peppered with grand aspirations, complex norms and volatile resentments as were European lives. That is to say, they were shaped by the clashing forces of history. For the era prior to European records, these lives are harder to describe in today's historical terms, but they were surely as mutable then as they were after the arrival of imperialists.

The current evidence, or way of assessing evidence, does not allow for estimations of exactly what forces were at play in, say, the era of Bennelong's grandparents. But between nine hundred and fifteen hundred years ago – during what Europeans call the medieval period – three particular shifts occurred in the Yiyura world which together suggest an especially notable disruption. The fact of this major social reorganisation implies further, more subtle changes over the whole millennium up to 1788.

The first shift was the introduction around nine hundred years ago of crescent-shaped shellfish hooks. The archaeological evidence indicates that these implements came into use at this time all along the southeastern coastline, from northern Sydney to the Victorian border. Scholar Val Attenbrow discounts the idea of the Yiyura using shellfish hooks any earlier, since 'their first appearance falls well within the period when organic materials survive relatively well within coastal shell middens'. It is widely accepted that these hooks were a rather sudden innovation in Yiyura Country in the early European twelfth century.[71]

Where, however, did they come from? One possibility is independent invention, though it is hard to understand how so many different and seemingly unconnected groups of Aboriginal peoples came up with the same idea at the same time.[72] Another possibility, a refinement of the first, is local invention via networks linking the 500-plus miles of distinct Aboriginal peoples. This would suggest a lot more communication between southern Indigenous groups than is currently suspected.[73] Another theory points to an introduction by Indigenous people from the far north of the continent, where shellfish hooks dating back twelve hundred years have been found. Such an idea, however, stumbles on the fact that no hooks have turned up between the Great Barrier Reef and northern Sydney, leaving a puzzling gap in usage.[74]

An increasingly popular possibility involves visitation by Pacific Islanders from Aotearoa. Māori people also used crescent-shaped shellfish hooks. Pacific Islanders settled briefly on Norfolk Island, which lies between Australia and Aotearoa, around eight hundred years ago, and were actively exploring this zone between seven hundred and twelve hundred years ago. They certainly had the technology and the cultural ambition to sail the required distances.[75]

A range of sources point to this explanation being the most convincing. Indigenous stories from both Australia and Aotearoa allude to seafarers from afar. Cook's *Endeavour* crew gathered at least two separate tales from Māori people about a large country lying to the northwest of Aotearoa. 'Some people had saild [there] in a very large canoe,' one told an associate of Joseph Banks. This passage apparently 'took them up to a month'.[76] In the mid-twentieth century, Aboriginal storytellers from regions west of Sydney remembered tales of how the morning sky was said to be propped up by eastern-lying peoples. If tributes were not sent eastwards then the props would rot and the sky would fall. Anthropologists interpreted these stories as references to European invaders coming in from the east, but they may well refer to even earlier arrivals of Pacific Islanders.[77] In addition, archaeologist Peter White and his colleagues have argued that a Pacific arrival around this era best explains how a single basalt adze from Aotearoa turned up just north of Sydney.[78] And finally, we know from very recent traumatic times that smoke from southeastern Australian bushfires can carry all the way over to Aotearoa: pre-eighteenth-century Māori perhaps saw something similar and reckoned on the existence of a landmass over their northwestern horizon.[79]

If Pacific people indeed contacted the Sydney region several centuries before Europeans did, some enduring settler ideas about the Yiyura start to dissolve. The ongoing assumption that they were an unworldly people evaporates. Had Cook known about this prior contact, would he have described the Yiyura as being 'wholly unacquainted' with the conveniences of life? Would Phillip have so readily believed he could 'civilize them' without their having 'an Idea of our great superiority over them'? Would later writers have repeatedly claimed that, to the Yiyura, the British seemed like ghosts in great birds when first appearing on Aboriginal shores?[80]

The second important shift to occur among the Yiyura during the so-called medieval era was the phasing out of certain flaked stone tools about fifteen hundred years ago. Archaeologists call these tools backed artefacts, after the method of striking the tool to flake it. The tools were used to cut, drill, scrape and incise a variety of materials, such as bone, wood, plants and skin. They also formed the tips of hunting spears. Although backed artefacts were abundant across the southeast of the continent by around five thousand years ago, the Yiyura for some reason decided to stop using them around fifteen hundred years ago. While peoples to the north and south of Sydney continued to use them, the Yiyura switched to ground-edged tools, wooden tools and non-stone fishing equipment.[81]

Because other neighbouring peoples carried on using backed artefacts, the likely reason for the Yiyura's decision was something internal to their own multi-clan society. Leadership practices may have changed, access to necessary resources or artisans may have changed, favoured foods or methods of self-adornment may have changed.[82] Pretty quickly, causes and effects in this scenario start to jumble, producing chicken-or-egg questions. Did a change in tools induce new forms of social organisation or did new forms of social organisation induce a change in tools? The chief point, again, is that variation occurred. It was an embedded aspect of the world into which Bennelong's forebears, and Bennelong himself, was born.

The third and final big shift in the Yiyura world also occurred around fifteen hundred years ago. This shift was environmental. It involved the rise in the sea level in the harbour and bays, and was caused by a warming climate. This rise of saltwater altered the borders of clan groups, and in particular those of the shore-hugging clans most often mentioned in this book: the Gadigal, Gayamaygal, Gammeraygal, Wallumedegal, Burramattagal and Wangal. This was not the first time that their shorelines had changed, either. Between fifteen hundred and seven thousand years ago, the water's edge was also low, due to the cooler and drier climate of the late Holocene freezing more ice sheets at the earth's poles. And before that, the Yiyura's world had seen a period of some eight millennia of gradual inundation. Between seven thousand and fifteen thousand years ago, in fact, the waters rose to such an extent that Bennelong's Wanne would have been completely submerged.[83]

Even though Aboriginal people have lived in the vicinity of the Yiyura's lands for at least twenty-five thousand years and probably sixty thousand years, it is likely, therefore, that the clan boundaries Bennelong knew were fifteen hundred years old at most.[84] Clan identity was core to the way Bennelong's generation interpreted their place in the harbour, in ancestral time, and in the cosmos, but its definition was not archaic. It was affected by changes in that one supreme phenomenon – land – that was so central to the Yiyura's understanding of both life and the past.

Bennelong's Yiyura world, then, while often thought to be unchanging, was dynamic in its geography, in its social order, and probably in its experience of other people. This dynamism was critical to the Yiyura's immense longevity before settlers invaded. It is also essentially what allowed them to carry on through the later assaults of empire. As anthropologist Nicholas Peterson once wrote, 'it is inconceivable that any culture could remain totally unchanging over such long periods and still survive. Survival requires flexibility and adaptability . . . The cumulative effects of hundreds of years of coping with natural disasters and accommodating different personalities alone would ensure this.'[85] Dynamism explains both the length of Aboriginal history and the fact of an Aboriginal future.

Ending a history back in earlier times helps us see anew the groundings of the two men's lives. Having traced the full outline of Phillip's experiences, we can recognise in a different way just how much he reflected his nation's era and his personal circumstances. We can understand just how aggressive was that era and just how political were those circumstances, adding further nuance to our picture of the one-time governor. This is not to say that Phillip was wholly hostage to his heritage, because he did enact that inheritance in a uniquely careful, even aloof, manner. But it is to grasp the significance of his famed naval and rational persona in a freshly contextualised way.

And having detailed Bennelong's attachment to kin and country, we can see that he too was very much a product of his times and family. Importantly, those times were not static and that family was not simple. Bennelong was evidently exceptional to have accepted the opportunity to be a negotiator for his people, but he was also in many senses representative of how a dynamic and complex society such as the eighteenth-century Yiyura faced novel intrusion. Approaching the dynamism and complexity of Bennelong's world from the other end, so to speak, illuminates these qualities as an additional explanation for his behaviour.

CONCLUSION

Stories and Futures

Reversing through the whole lives of Phillip and Bennelong tells a new story about the explosive incursion of European empires into Indigenous lands. If Phillip somehow represents the foundation of one particular modern nation – Australia – his full, unravelled life demonstrates that the country began as an extension of a multi-pronged and reactionary global empire. Australia still carries within it the legacy of ferocious eighteenth-century rivalry with other powers – mostly Catholic ones and always democratic ones – as well as an irregular deployment of laws regarding slavery and dispossession. Nations that emerge from such a past cannot reckon with the implications of their histories if they remain immersed in myths about them, especially myths entangled in loose understandings of the Enlightenment. It should go without saying that Britain, too, as the nucleus of Phillip's empire, has as much to reckon with as any settler satellite.

If Bennelong represents the many First Nations people who faced European invasion during the birthing era of modernity, his long life, when unspooled, reveals that they did so actively, with a range of strategies and attitudes. Through Bennelong's actions it's possible to see how Indigenous peoples played critical roles in the course of imperial transformation, even while they were the more afflicted party. They exacted retribution, demanded concessions, appropriated customs, deflected enquiries, withheld information or otherwise confused imperial plans. Modern societies will only begin to address the problems wreaked by empire if they know the complex story of interaction between those who came and those who were already there.

The upturned twinned biographies of Phillip and Bennelong also shed light on the individuals themselves, as well as on the notion of firsts and lasts in settler-Indigenous history. Starting with Phillip's final years in counter-revolutionary Britain prompts us from the beginning to place his governorship in a global context. The real centre of his life was fighting other Europeans, wherever needed, for the advancement of British supremacy. To him, the shape or form of rival Europeans never mattered more than their threat to Britain's international influence. Nine years opposing French revolutionary democracy were virtually the same as fifteen years countering French Catholic absolutism. The point was to help secure the singular superpower status of his father's adopted nation. To view Phillip's relatively brief term establishing New South Wales as just one more way to defend British power highlights the colony's international circumstances. It also emphasises that the colony fitted within ambitions and ideologies already in train, rather than being the first of anything.

An investigation into Phillip's networks and choices shows that the empire he served was powered by patronage, with a highly segregated form of patriarchy and a rationality peculiar to its time and place. All these features were core expressions of the British version of the Enlightenment. Phillip was indeed an Enlightenment figure, but this did not remotely boil down to being transparent, liberal or consistently fair.

More idiosyncratically, Phillip's life attests to how patronage worked in sometimes mysterious ways in the eighteenth-century British empire. His very ordinariness may have been the key to his highest appointment, though he himself perhaps felt frustrated that he didn't achieve more in the navy. Phillip's relations with women, both intimates and subordinates, displayed an even stiffer sense of gender regulation than was typical for his times. The flipside of this stiffness was a similarly exacting sense of Enlightenment reasoning. To a greater extent than his contemporary governors, Phillip tried to approach the takeover of Indigenous lands in as rational a way as his society allowed. That is, he acted to ensure the most direct path to the legal possession of territory which was only dubiously possessable according to Britain's own laws. This paradoxical task demanded that he combine diplomacy with bursts of brute force, eschew slave labour but seize certain key individuals, and make plans for a treaty while laying mass claims to sovereignty. The contradictions in Phillip's behaviour speak of a patriotic fervour trumping all other instincts. They say even more about the limitations of British Enlightenment.

For his part, Bennelong's fifty-odd years of life practising Yiyura customs places his decade or so of engaging with colonists into some much-needed perspective. Being a negotiator with the British colony was not his most defining accomplishment, it was merely a continuation of the work he'd undertaken since adulthood to help nurture his culture. The fact that the majority of this work occurred after he stepped away from colonial business underscores how imperial intrusion disordered but never extinguished the Yiyura. Bennelong's usual reputation as a man lost between two worlds has always implied the ascendancy of one of those worlds and the fall of the other. To see instead that Bennelong remained connected to his Yiyura society, indeed thrived in it when away from colonial eyes, is to think again about endpoints. Bennelong's generation was not the last of an unworldly people. They faced empire with the same determination to persist as they'd brought to other challenges over the previous millennium.

Bennelong's life story confirms that, like Phillip, he enjoyed some male privilege, although men and women of the Yiyura world were not as segregated as they were in Britain at the time, and particularly not within the realm of politics. Glimpses of Bennelong's interactions with his fellow Yiyura reveal a rich and dynamic society. His ritual battles, conventions around death and birth, love of theatre, skills as an angler and swimmer, observance of strict though mutable clan boundaries, and his possible role as a healer all point to an intricately layered social order. His ready talents as a negotiator, and the fact that his deployment of these changed over time, reflect a culture experienced in managing both transgressions and the unexpected.

The range of Bennelong's negotiating tactics is the most notable aspect of his relationship with the colonists. He was not a conventional go-between, for which many have labelled him a sell-out or turncoat. Instead, he negotiated sometimes via strategic compromise, sometimes via physical punishment and sometimes via refusal. Perhaps his most important tactic was, finally, to walk away from the colony, in his quest for Yiyura preservation. Just as his own society did, Bennelong changed his approach according to the conditions at hand.

In 2021 the Wiradjuri writer Stan Grant wrote about some of the problems entailed in discussing key Aboriginal characters of colonial history. 'The noble savage or the doomed race or the resistance warrior,' he notes – these stereotypes are so often rolled out in descriptions about them: 'but to reduce us to a simple narrative steals our souls'.[1]

It's possible that all history-writing has an element of soul-stealing. I have tried in this work, nonetheless, to inject as much detail and subtlety into Bennelong's life story as my sources could yield. I have done so not only to reverse common misunderstandings about Bennelong (most of them invented in the early 1800s), but also to revise prevailing assumptions about Aboriginal society being simple or ill-fated through the initial period of colonisation. I have tried to portray Phillip with equally novel complexity. Like Bennelong, though to far less cost, he has often been remembered in basic ways – in his case, as Founding Father, or Enlightenment Paragon, or even Renegade Humanitarian. To expand on his global, rationalist, conservative and complicated paternal contexts casts him as a more interesting, and more telling, symbol of early settler history.

Narrating these lives back to front has helped me make my chief points. It has allowed the general disturbance I wanted to bring to the standard histories of my subjects. Putting the end first has pushed me to recognise throughout that it was empire, rather than New South Wales, that was at the heart of Phillip's life. It has also highlighted how Bennelong always focused on his own world, never seeing himself as the other side of an encounter story.

I was first inspired to think about writing this history in reverse by a moment in a novel. Claire Fuller's *Swimming Lessons* (2017) includes a character who wonders whether his prospective romance might be better if inverted. He wishes it could start with the rage of divorce and then proceed through decreasing unpleasantries, so that the giddy hope of new love would be what remained longest: 'If I could, I would turn our love on its head: we would get the anger, the guilt, the blame, the disappointment, the irritation, the work-a-day and the humdrum over and done with first. We would have everything to look forward to.'² The 'everything' of this passage does the most work. It conjures not just the baleful future that the rather pessimistic character imagines, but also all the other possible ways his love might run.

It's of course silly, and inappropriate, to compare a romance with settler–Indigenous relations; moreover we stand at the end of the relationship between Phillip and Bennelong while Fuller's character stands at the start of his relationship. Nevertheless, the fictional moment prompted me to unfurl in my mind the comparable lives of Phillip and Bennelong, and through them those of the British empire and the Yiyura. It seemed obvious to begin such an exercise in the present, with its still glaring lack of conciliation between settlers and First Nations. But where to end it was much less clear, as I travelled quickly past 1788, past 1770, and even past each man's birthdate. It reminded me of philosopher Michel Foucault's remark that 'what is found at the historical beginning of things is not the inviolable identity of their origin; it is the dissension of other things'.[3]

Reversing through time also allowed me to glimpse in fresh ways some of the futures – the 'everything' – that the meeting of Bennelong and Phillip could have produced but did not. This isn't to muse wistfully about an imperial connection with Indigenous people that somehow avoided violence and inequality. It is, though, to contemplate seriously the influence of, say, the smallpox epidemic in reducing Indigenous numbers. Or what the effect on British behaviour might have been if the French had competed for New South Wales. Or what would have ensued if Phillip and Bennelong had not diverted more clashes. It is even to wonder about what needed to occur, during Britain's various confrontations with Indigenous peoples around the world, to crack open its famed Enlightenment values sufficiently to adjust the definition of reasonable possession.

Without doubt, the most significant future that could have happened but didn't was a treaty between British and Aboriginal leaders. Phillip seemed to assume that such an agreement would eventuate within his, or at least Bennelong's, lifetime. We see Phillip's assumption in his extensive efforts to cultivate Bennelong as a link to the Yiyura, in the time and cost of those efforts, and in the various minor humiliations he bore as a governor standing before subordinates. We see it in the itinerary he gave Bennelong in London, the same one undertaken by most Indigenous treaty-signatories before him, and in the buying of clothes fit for an audience with the king. Some officials may have already decided that New South Wales was going to break Britain's legal tradition and forgo a formal contract with its prior inhabitants. But the fact that the governor himself was mindful of precedent reminds us that the lack of treaty was not inevitable – it was not given by nature.

These contemplations are not just fanciful mind-games that fall outside the proper business of history. They are, in the end, what history is all about. They are what turn the mere accounting of times gone by into a provocation for seeing that times in the future can or must be different. I hope this history of Phillip and Bennelong reveals that conciliation between settlers and First Nations has never truly occurred, despite a brief attempt to establish terms. I hope it shows how this circumstance was produced by much longer histories of Indigenous experience and imperial reaction than has been appreciated. Most of all, I hope it prompts some understanding of why conciliation, ultimately, can and must happen.

Notes

All italics and spelling in quotes are as per the originals. In the interests of accessibility, I have tried wherever possible to use searchable online transcriptions of eighteenth-century and other sources. In many cases this means that only chapter numbers can be given, since there are no page numbers on some digital editions. The chief editions and locations used (and cited in short form hereafter) are:

Joseph Banks, The Endeavour Journal of Sir Joseph Banks, 1768–1771, at gutenberg.net.au

Louis Becke and Walter Jeffrey, *Admiral Phillip: The Founding of New South Wales* (London: Fisher Unwin, 1899), at gutenberg.net.au

F.M. Bladen, Alexander Britton and James Cook, eds, *Historical Records of New South Wales*, seven volumes (hereafter HRNSW) (Sydney: Government Printer, 1892–1901), accessible via Trove at nla.gov.au

William Bradley, Journal of a Voyage to New South Wales, December 1786—May 1792, compiled 1802, at gutenberg.net.au

David Collins, *An Account of the English Colony in New South Wales, Vol. 1* (London: Cadell & Davies, 1798), at gutenberg.org

——*An Account of the English Colony in New South Wales, Vol. 2* (London: Cadell & Davies, 1802), at gutenberg.net.au

James Cook, *Captain Cook's Journal . . . a Literal Transcription*, ed. W.J.L. Wharton (London: Elliot Stock, 1893), at gutenberg.net.au

William Dawes, Notebooks, at williamdawes.org

Historical Records of Australia, vol. 1 (hereafter HRA) (Commonwealth Parliament, 1914), accessible via Trove at nla.gov.au

John Hunter, *An Historical Journal of the Transactions at Port Jackson and Norfolk Island* (London: Stockdale, 1793), at gutenberg.org

Watkin Tench, *A Narrative of the Expedition to Botany Bay* (London: Debrett, 1789), at gutenberg.org

——*A Complete Account of the Settlement at Port Jackson* (London: Nicol and Sewell, 1793), at gutenberg.org

Daniel Southwell, *Journal and Letters* (1788-92) at gutenberg.net.au
Thomas Watling, *Letters from an Exile at Botany Bay* (first pub. 1794), at gutenberg.net.au

Abbreviations

ADM	Admiralty (National Archives, UK)
NLA	National Library of Australia
PCC, PROB	Prerogative Court of Canterbury, Probate (National Archives, UK)
SLNSW	State Library of New South Wales
SOAS	School of Oriental and African Studies, University of London
UP	University Press

Introduction: The Past Two Hundred Years

1. Paul Daley, 'Bennelong's Grave', *The Guardian*, 19 Nov. 2018. The site is now pinpointed at 25 Watson Street in the suburb of Putney (lot 9/-/DP24056).
2. 'Heritage Advisory Committee – Minutes of Meeting' (Meeting, City of Ryde, 21 February 2018), 4.
3. Maxine McKew, 'Maiden Speech', Federal Parliament, Canberra, 14 February 2008, cited in Emma Dortins, *The Lives of Stories: Three Aboriginal–Settler Friendships* (Canberra: ANU Press, 2018), 141.
4. Cited in Dortins, *The Lives of Stories*, 109.
5. Geoffrey Robertson, *Dreaming Too Loud: Reflections on a Race Apart* (Sydney: Random House, 2013), 17–20.
6. *Courier Mail*, 21 June 1937; *Daily News*, 19 June 1937. See also Michael Flynn, 'A Diminutive Enigma: New Perspectives on Arthur Phillip, first Governor of New South Wales', *Sydney Journal* 5/1 (2016).
7. *Sydney Morning Herald*, 21 Dec. 1907.
8. I am using the term Yiyura in this way even though a linguist would argue that these coastal clans shared the same language, if not dialect, as the hinterland Darug-speaking people. The word Yiyura means simply 'people of this place', which is how they described themselves to the first British settlers: as such it is technically incorrect as a group descriptor. Nonetheless, it is preferred by many Sydney-based Aboriginal people today. 'Yiyura' is also a helpful way to avoid using retrospective British phrases like 'the Sydney clans'. Its usage in this book refers to research about only the coastal clans; some inland Darug-speaker customs or experiences may be slightly different. See chiefly Jakelin Troy, *The Sydney Language* (Canberra: ASP, 2019). See also City of Sydney Barani

site: <https://www.sydneybarani.com.au/sites/aboriginal-people-and-place/>, and James Kohen, *The Darug and their Neighbours: The Traditional Aboriginal Owners of the Sydney Region* (Blacktown: BDHS, 1993), 1, 10.
9. Yves Rees in C. Holbrook, D. Lowe, & L. McGarrity, eds, *Lessons of History* (Sydney: NewSouth, 2022), ch. 4.
10. Priya Satia, *Time's Monster: History, Conscience, and Britain's Empire* (London: Allen Lane, 2020), 296.
11. Ibid., 289. See also the earlier work of Dipesh Chakrabarty, 'Postcoloniality and the Artifice of History', *Representations* 37 (1992): 1–26. In historiography, the kind of history that tends to believe that events move always towards greater liberty is termed whiggish.
12. Jean O'Brien, *Firsting and Lasting: Writing Indians out of Existence in New England* (Minneapolis: University of Minnesota Press, 2010).
13. Grace Karskens, *The Colony: A History of Early Australia* (Sydney: Allen & Unwin, 2009), 422. See also a discussion of Kim Scott on this issue in Maria Nugent, *Captain Cook Was Here* (Cambridge: Cambridge UP, 2009), 70–71.
14. See Kate Fullagar, 'Remembering Cook, Again: The State of the Mixed Media Field', *Australian Historical Studies* 52/4 (2021): 9.
15. See, for examples, Stephen Gibb in *The Daily Mail*, 26 Jan. 2020, and a summary by Joe Hinchliffe in *The Guardian*, 24 May 2022.
16. <https://www.westminster-abbey.org/media/3178/arthur-phillip-unveiling-2014.pdf>; Marie Bashir in *The Sydney Morning Herald*, 10 July 2014.
17. Michael Pembroke, *Arthur Phillip: Sailor, Mercenary, Governor, Spy* (Richmond & London: Hardie Grant, 2014). Pembroke's book was one of the very few that noted Phillip's life beyond New South Wales. Also in 2014, the Governor Phillip Scholarship Trust, under the patronage of both private and public contributors, convened in honour of Phillip's 'wonderful Enlightenment quality of humanity' – see <governorphillip.org>.
18. Lyn Fergusson, *Admiral Arthur Phillip: The Man* (Killara: Pilar, 2009), 136, 235–37. This new data is explored in the chapter 'London'.
19. Inga Clendinnen, *Dancing with Strangers* (Melbourne: Text, 2003), 23, 181.
20. Alan Frost, *Arthur Phillip 1738–1814: His Voyaging* (Melbourne: Oxford UP, 1987), 260.
21. Ibid., 261. One year earlier, Australia's biggest selling history work of all time appeared, Robert Hughes' *The Fatal Shore: The Epic of Australia's Founding* (New York: Knopf, 1986), which carried little analysis of Phillip at all.

22. M. Barnard Eldershaw, *Phillip of Australia: An Account of the Settlement at Sydney Cove* (London: Angus and Robertson, 1938), 26, 292.
23. Ibid., 342.
24. George Mackaness, *Admiral Arthur Phillip: Founder of New South Wales 1738–1814* (Sydney: Angus and Robertson, 1937), 465–74.
25. Karskens, *The Colony*, 14, 398. See also Grace Karskens, 'Phillip and the Eora: Governing race in New South Wales', *The Sydney Journal* 5 (2017): 39–55.
26. W.E.H. Stanner, 'The History of Indifference Thus Begins', *Aboriginal History* 1/1 (1977): 10, 18, 25 [the journal noted that this was drafted back in 1963].
27. Alan Atkinson, *The Europeans in Australia: Volume One the Beginning* (Sydney: UNSW Press, 2016 [first pub. 1997]), 80–89, 138–47.
28. On the history of British attitudes towards human rights and the human, see Samuel Moyn, *The Last Utopia: Human Rights in History* (Cambridge: Harvard UP, 2012), esp. ch. 1; and J. Damousi, T. Burnard, and A. Lester, eds, *Humanitarianism, Empire and Transnationalism, 1760–1995* (Manchester: Manchester UP, 2022).
29. Emma Dortins has compiled the fullest analysis of Bennelong's story: *The Lives of Stories*, 91-156.
30. Keith Smith, *Wallumedegal: An Aboriginal History of Ryde* (Ryde: City of Ryde, 2005). By 2009, Karskens, for one, was convinced. Contrary to popular assumptions, she wrote, Bennelong, after his sojourn with Phillip in England, 'got his life back together': Karskens, *The Colony*, 422. Peter Read is the other historian who thought similarly: in the SBS TV series *The First Australians*, he voiced the opinion that Bennelong actively chose his own life after England and reintegrated back into his old world: prod. Louis Nowra & Rachel Perkins, *The First Australians: Episode 1* (Blackfella Films and SBS, 2008), DVD.
31. Wesley Enoch & Anita Heiss, *I am Eora*, played at Carriageworks Theatre, Sydney, January 2012. Another influential Indigenous commentator who celebrates Bennelong as an esteemed leader is John Paul Janke; see his words on the National Indigenous Television blogsite: 'Today marks the 250th anniversary of modern day Australia', NITV, <https://www.sbs.com.au/nitv/feature/today-marks-250th-anniversary-modern-day-australia-and-heres-why-i-think-we-should-celebrate> accessed September 2021.
32. Andrews in Dortins, *The Lives of Stories*, 106–7. A similar story is suggested by Dennis Foley, a Gai-mariagal man, who recalled in 2020 that 'my uncles spoke about [Bennelong] in hushed tones. To them he was an image of sadness': Dennis Foley and Peter Read, *What the Colonists Never Knew: A History of Aboriginal Sydney* (Canberra: NMA, 2020), 10.

33. Eric Willmot, *Pemulwuy: The Rainbow Warrior* (Sydney: Weldon, 1987). There were shards of 'Competent Bennelong' in the 1980s, but these existed in the slimmest of conjectures. In 1989 archaeologist Isabel McBryde wondered if Bennelong's crumbling reputation reflected changes in European attitudes rather than changes in him. [Isabel McBryde, *Guests of the Governor: Aboriginal Residents of the First Government House* (Sydney: Friends of the First Government House, 1989), 27.] Seven years prior, historian Richard Broome asserted in two lone sentences that after his split from Phillip, Bennelong 'went back to his own people and culture. It was the Aboriginal way of life that persisted through all the upheavals.' [Richard Broome, *Aboriginal Australians: Black Responses to White Dominance* (Sydney: Allen & Unwin, 2001 [first pub. 1982]), 69.]
34. See quotes at <https://www.bangarra.com.au/learning/resources/classroom-resources/bennelong/excerpts/>. See also Kate Fullagar, 'The Story of Bennelong is potent and evocative – but it is being contested', *The Guardian*, 8 July 2017.
35. Ibid.
36. Thomas Keneally, *The Commonwealth of Thieves: The Sydney Experiment* (Sydney: Random House, 2005), 446.
37. Lucy Hughes Turnbull, *Sydney: Biography of a City* (Sydney: Random House, 1999), 35–54.
38. Clendinnen, *Dancing with Strangers*, 271–72.
39. Bernard Smith, *The Spectre of Truganini: The Boyer Lectures* (ABC, 1980), 37–39.
40. H.C. Coombs, foreword to John Kenny, *Bennelong: First Notable Aboriginal* (Sydney: RHAS, 1973), 1. A similar view was expressed in Bruce Elder's widely influential *Blood on the Wattle: Massacres and Maltreatment of Aboriginal Australians since 1788* (Sydney: Child and Associates, 1988).
41. Manning Clark, *A History of Australia I: From the Earliest Times to the Age of Macquarie* (Melbourne: Melbourne UP, 1991 [first pub. 1962]), 145.
42. Eleanor Dark, *The Timeless Land* (New York: Macmillan, 1941), part 5.
43. Matt Murphy, *Rum: A Distilled History of Colonial Australia* (Sydney: HarperCollins, 2021).
44. Isadore Brodsky, *Bennelong Profile: Dreamtime Reveries of a Native of Sydney Cove* (Sydney: University Co-op, 1973), 76–78.
45. *Sydney Gazette*, 9 Jan. 1813.
46. D. John Mulvaney, *A Good Foundation: Reflections on the Heritage of the First Government House* (Canberra: AGPS, 1985), 14.
47. W.E.H. Stanner, *White Man Got No Dreaming: Essays 1938–73* (Canberra: ANU Press, 1979), 182, 231.

48. These are the odds I roughly calculated after searching through TROVE: <https://trove.nla.gov.au/>, accessed September 2021. It is worth noting that in the 1930s Phillip won some small recognitions in Britain. In 1932 his London birthplace was commemorated with a bronze bust on the side of a nearby church and in 1937 his retirement place was commemorated with a plaque in Bath Abbey. The latter noted Phillip's 'indomitable courage, prophetic vision, forbearance, faith, inspiration and wisdom'. See Fergusson, *Admiral Arthur Phillip*, 216–17.
49. Becke & Jeffery, *Admiral Phillip*. For a typical review, see *The Queenslander*, 4 Nov. 1899.
50. The best discussion and description comes from <https://publicart aroundtheworld.com>, accessed September 2021. The same burgeoning nationalist energy that led to Simonetti's commission pushed to have Phillip's grave ascertained in 1897, after a lack of interest in the subject for over seventy years: see Flynn, 'A Diminutive Enigma', 10.
51. Richard Sadleir, *The Aborigines of Australia* (Sydney: Richards, 1883), 24.
52. Ibid., 25.
53. Brian Fletcher confirms there is next to no material on Phillip before the 1880s: 'Discovering a Colonial Governor, Arthur Phillip, 1888–1938', in D. Shreuder, ed., *Imperialisms* (Sydney: University of Sydney Press, 1991), 153–75. W.E.H. Stanner may have stretched the truth when he observed a 'Great Australian Silence' about Aboriginal people since the 1780s, but he was not wrong to see it practised with regards to Aboriginal *history* through much of the 1800s: see *White Man Got No Dreaming*, 207; see also Ann Curthoys' cogent critique, 'W.E.H. Stanner and the historians', in M. Hinkson and J. Beckett, eds, *An Appreciation of Difference: W.E.H. Stanner and Aboriginal Australia* (Canberra: Aboriginal Studies Press, 2008), 233–51.
54. Mackaness, *Admiral Arthur Phillip*, 454.
55. The same sentence seemed to appear in roughly a hundred British newspapers found on <www.britishnewspaperarchive.co.uk>, e.g. *The Norfolk Chronicle*, 15 March 1823.
56. It was only found after a request from Louis Becke, the 1899 biographer of Phillip, sent a vicar looking for it. Fergusson, *Admiral Arthur Phillip*, 215; Flynn, 'A Diminutive Enigma', 10.
57. Charles Wilton, review of Peter Cunningham's *Two Years in New South Wales* (1827), *The Australian Quarterly Journal of Theology, Literature, and Science* (1828): 137. See also Keith Smith, 'Bennelong among his people', *Aboriginal History* 33 (2009): 21.
58. Wilton, review, 137.

59. Wife's burial noted in Joseph Arnold, Journal MS SAFE/C 720/4 (Safe 1/269) SLNSW, 13 July 1815; burial of Nanbarree and wife noted in *Sydney Gazette*, 8 Sept. 1821.
60. Alexander Strachan, *Remarkable Incidents in the Life of the Rev. Samuel Leigh* (London: Hamilton, Adams & Co, 1873), 147.

Endings: Kin and Country, 1823–1796
1. Mackaness, *Admiral Arthur Phillip*, 454–55.
2. As Frost notes, Isabella's baptismal records are dated 2 January 1751, so she was likely born at the end of 1750: Frost, *Arthur Phillip*, 225.
3. Joseph Arnold's Journal, 1815, page 401. SAFE/C 720/4 (Safe 1/269), SLNSW. The syntax of this line makes it unclear who died first, but since no other report mentioned that Bennelong joined his wife's grave, it is assumed that Boorong joined her husband's grave.
4. My assumption that Bennelong's Wangal clan followed patrilineal customs, if not patriarchal ones, follows Val Attenbrow, *Sydney's Aboriginal Past* (Sydney: NewSouth, 2010), 57. Bennelong did not seem to move to his wives' lands or believe that his children would belong ultimately to his wives' clans. Patrilineality as a general rule among the Yiyura has been contested, however: see Foley & Read, *What the Colonists Never Knew*, 16.
5. Frederick Chapman, *Governor Phillip in Retirement* (Sydney: Halstead Press, 1962), 35, 37, 39–41.
6. See letters owned by Chapman and cited in *Governor Phillip in Retirement*, 24, 33.
7. Arthur Phillip to Isabella Phillip, 24 April 1803, Bath and North East Somerset Record Office, cited in Michael Flynn, 'The Women in Arthur Phillip's Life,' *JRHAS* 105 (2019): 20.
8. Arthur Phillip to Isabella Phillip, 4 October 1801, Bath and North East Somerset Record Office, cited in Flynn, 'The Women', 19.
9. On Isabella, see Frost, *Arthur Phillip*, 224–25. On singles in this era, see Alexandra Shepard, *Meanings of Manhood in Early Modern England* (Oxford: Oxford UP, 2003), 168.
10. For details on Charlott Phillip, see Flynn, 'The Women', 7–15.
11. Douglas Hay & Nicholas Rogers, *Eighteenth-Century English Society* (Oxford: OUP, 1997), 43. See also Sybil Wolfram, 'Divorce in England 1700–1857', *Oxford Journal of Legal Studies* 5/2 (1985): 155–86. The Phillips' judicial separation meant that Charlott's wealth was returned to her, as it had only been granted to Arthur under the marriage settlement in trust. The separation did not, however, free either to remarry until one of them died. Suitably for Phillip, Charlott did so in 1792.

12. Flynn, 'The Women', 14–15.
13. See marriage settlement and will at ML B1143, SLNSW. See also HRA 1/1, 172.
14. Smith discovered that Bennelong's sister had a dream about who caused Digidigi's death, discussed in Rev. William Walker, *Methodist Magazine* (1825): 344–45. Smith then realised that Boorong's brother also believed the same person caused his nephew's death in the same way at the same time, and acted accordingly. Only Digidigi could be the nephew of both Bennelong's sibling and Boorong's sibling. I thank Keith Smith for explaining this trail to me. See Jules Dumont d'Urville, *Two Voyages to the South Seas ... 1826–29*, trans. & ed. Helen Rosenman (Melbourne: Melbourne UP, 1992), 88.
15. Keith Smith, 'Bennelong among his people', *Aboriginal History* 33 (2009): 10.
16. Smith, *Wallumedegal*, 16–17.
17. On Boorong as star see Anonymous [Phillip and Collins], 'Vocabulary of the language of N.S. Wales', SOAS MS 41645; *The Journal of Daniel Paine*, ed. R. Knight and A. Frost (Sydney: LAH, 1983), 42; Troy, *The Sydney Language*, 51. On the incident, see Tench, *Complete Account*, ch. 17, and Collins, *Account*, vol. 1, appen. VII.
18. Phillip in Hunter, *Historical Journal*, ch. 18; Collins, *Account*, vol. 1, appen. VI.
19. Tench, *Complete Account*, ch. 9.
20. Phillip in Hunter, *Historical Journal*, ch. 19, and Tench, *Complete Account*, ch. 17.
21. Tench, *Complete Account*, ch. 9.
22. Phillip in Hunter, *Historical Journal*, ch. 18, and Collins, *Account*, vol. 1, appen. XI.
23. Clendinnen, *Dancing with Strangers*, 165.
24. Will of Arthur Phillip 1814, PCC, PROB 10/4172. See also will of Isabella Phillip 1823, PCC, PROB 11/1668/122.
25. Alastair Owens, David Green, Craig Bailey, and Alison Kay, 'A Measure of Worth: Probate Valuations, Personal Wealth and Indebtedness in England, 1810–40', *Historical Research*, 79/205 (2006).
26. The auction occurred on 19 July 1815: see Jane Lennon, 'Second Thoughts on First Views: The Port Jackson Circle, 1788–1800', *Australian Journal of Art*, 14/1 (1998): 35, 49. See also Louise Anemaat, *Natural Curiosity: Unseen Art of the First Fleet* (Sydney: NewSouth, 2014), 79, 248, which suggests that the story of the lot's dispersal is 'unknown'. Frost thinks that some of it may be in the Natural History Museum's vast collection on first fleet art: *Arthur Phillip*, 268.

27. Pembroke, *Arthur Phillip*, 75.
28. See Duncombe's will, PCC, PROB 11/1399/276, cited in Pembroke, *Arthur Phillip*, 75.
29. As suggested in Frost, *Arthur Phillip*, 55. See also M.E. Scorgie & Peter Hudgson, 'Arthur Phillip's Familial and Political Networks', *JRHAS* 82/1 (1996): 23–39.
30. On Nepean and Phillip, see Frost, *Arthur Phillip*, 100–101, 131, 139.
31. Everitt was the child of a woman who had previously been married to Benjamin Breach, who was the uncle of Phillip's mother; Everitt's mother in other words *had* been Phillip's mother's aunt, but was no longer, technically, after she married Everitt's father. On John Lane and Michael Everitt, see Frost, *Arthur Phillip*, 3–7; Pembroke, *Arthur Phillip*, 7–8; and Fergusson, *Admiral Arthur Phillip*, 12–13. See also Dan Byrnes, The Cozen/Byrnes Merchants Networks Project, <http://www.danbyrnes.com.au/networks/periods/1775after/lanesonfraser.htm>, accessed September 2021.
32. See Attenbrow, *Sydney's Aboriginal Past*, 140–41; Denise Donlon, 'Mortuary Practices and the Sex Ratio of Australian Aboriginal Skeletal Remains in the Sydney Basin', in Mary Casey, ed., *Redefining Archaeology* (Canberra: ANU Press, 1998), 221–26; Judith Littleton, 'Time and Memory: Historic Accounts of Aboriginal Burials in South-eastern Australia', *Aboriginal History* 31 (2007), 103–21; Paul Irish and Tamika Goward, 'Where's the Evidence? The Archaeology of Sydney's Aboriginal History', *Archaeology in Oceania* 47 (2012): 63, 65; & Sue Feary, 'An Aboriginal Burial with Grave Goods near Cooma, New South Wales', *Australian Archaeology* 43 (1996): 40–42.
33. For a general discussion see Wendy Anderson, 'Badarian Burials: Evidence of Social Inequality in Middle Egypt During the Early Predynastic Era', *Journal of the American Research Center in Egypt* Vol. 29 (1992): 51–66; C. Rodning, 'Mortuary Practice, Gender Ideology, and the Cherokee Town', *Journal of Anthropological Archaeology* 30 (2011): 145–73.
34. Edward Duffy, *Rousseau in England* (Berkeley: University of California Press, 1979).
35. *Sydney Gazette*, 27 Sept. 1822.
36. *Sydney Gazette*, 6 Feb. 1823. Note that the NSW Births Deaths and Marriages Death Certificate (1349/1823) shows 1804, <https://familyhistory.bdm.nsw.gov.au>.
37. *Sydney Gazette*, 6 Feb. 1823.
38. Strachan, *Remarkable Incidents*, 119.
39. On the extraordinary history of Maria, later Maria Lock, see Michelle Lea Locke, 'Wirrawi Bubwul – Aboriginal Women Strong', *Australian*

Journal of Education 62/3 (2018): 299–310. See also Grace Karskens, who names her Maria Lutrell in *People of the River: Lost Worlds of Early Australia* (Sydney: Allen & Unwin, 2020), 376, 389–92.

40. 'Establishment of the Native Institution 1814 – Government and General Order', 10 Dec. 1814: NRS 1046 [SZ759, pages 11–14; Reel 6038], NSW Records, <https://www.records.nsw.gov.au>.
41. Aboriginal Elders quickly stopped sending their children to the Institution. By the 1820s, they (including Yarramundi) recognised it as a dangerous and alienating place. Today, it looms as the original mechanism for stealing children from Aboriginal families, which escalated to crisis levels by the twentieth century. See Joanna Cruickshank and Patricia Grimshaw, *White Women, Aboriginal Missions and Australian Settler Governments: Maternal Contradictions* (Leiden: Brill, 2019), 19–30; and Anne O'Brien, 'Creating the Aboriginal Pauper: Missionary Ideas in Early 19th Century Australia', *Social Sciences and Missions* 21 (2008): 6–30.
42. Attenbrow, *Sydney's Aboriginal Past*, 139.
43. Shino Konishi, 'Crossing Boundaries: Tracing Indigenous Mobility and Territory in the Exploration of South-Eastern Australia', *Indigenous Mobilities: Across and Beyond the Antipodes*, ed., R. Standfield (Canberra: ANU Press, 2018), 47–48. See also W. Spiers & W. Patrick, 'Thoughts on the Law of the Land: The Persistence of Aboriginal Law', in J. Hendry, M.L. Tatum, M. Jorgensen & D. Howard-Wagner, eds, *Indigenous Justice: New Tools, Approaches, and Spaces* (London: Palgrave, 2018*)*. A good description of the role of dreams is found in D'Urville, *Two Voyages to the South Seas*, 88.
44. See Margaret Catchpole to Dr Strebbens, 21 Jan. 1802, cited in Karskens, *The Colony*, 443.
45. *The Caledonian Mercury*, 26 May 1813, reporting 'an extract of a letter from a free merchant of India, dated on board the Henrietta schooner, off Bass's Straits, 17th April 1813.'
46. See John Turnbull, *A Voyage around the World*, vol. 1 (Gillet: London, 1805), 69; and Paine, *The Journal*, 39-40.
47. Thomas W. Laqueur, *The Work of the Dead: A Cultural History of Mortal Remains* (Princeton: Princeton UP, 2015), 8.
48. Thomas Lewis, *Churches not Charnel Houses* (London: A Bettesworth, 1726), 54–55.
49. Tench, *Complete Account*, ch. 12.
50. See Collins' description of Bennelong leading the mourners in the funeral for Baludarri, Boorong's brother, in 1791: *Account*, vol. 1, appen. XI.
51. Rachel Wilson, 'A General State of Mourning', *History Today* 67/3 (2017).

52. See Littleton, 'Time and Memory', 110, and M.F. Oxenham, T. Knight, and M. Westaway, 'Identification of Australian Aboriginal Mortuary Remains', in M. Oxenham, ed., *Forensic Approaches to Death, Disaster and Abuse* (Bowen Hills: Australian Academic Press, 2008), 41.
53. See Mackaness, *Admiral Arthur Phillip*, 453–54; on 'simple linen', see Isabella Phillip, PCC, PROB11/1668/173.
54. See Attenbrow, *Sydney's Aboriginal Past*, 140–41; Donlon, 'Mortuary practices', 221–26; and Oxenham et al., 'Identification of Australian Aboriginal Mortuary Remains', 40. On Bennelong at a cortège in 1791, see Collins, *Account*, vol. 1, appen. XI.
55. Laqueur, *The Work of the Dead*, 112–13.
56. Collins, *An Account*, vol. 1, appen. VI. On Yiyura burials generally, see Littleton, 'Time and Memory'; Oxenham et al., 'Identification of Australian Aboriginal Mortuary Remains', 39.
57. Landmann cited in Mackaness, *Admiral Arthur Phillip*, 462.
58. Phillip to Dundas, 23 July 1793, cited in Becke & Jeffery, *Admiral Phillip*, ch. 16.
59. See R.S. Neale, *Bath 1680–1850: A Social History* (London: Routledge, 1981).
60. Frost, *Arthur Phillip*, 226.
61. P.J. Corfield, *The Impact of English Towns 1700–1800* (Oxford: Oxford UP, 1982), 10–25.
62. Pierce Egan, *Walks Through Bath* (Bath: Meyler & Son, 1819), 69. On the new phenomenon of display, see Lawrence Klein, 'Politeness for Plebes: Consumption and Social Identity in Early Eighteenth-century England' in A. Bermingham & J. Brewer, eds, *Consumption of Culture* (London: Routledge, 1995).
63. Before his final promotion, Phillip had been made Vice Admiral of the Red in 1810, Vice Admiral of the White in 1809, Vice Admiral of the Blue in 1806, Rear Admiral of the Red in 1805, Rear Admiral of the White in 1804, and Rear Admiral of the Blue in 1799: Pembroke, *Arthur Phillip*, x.
64. Fanny Chapman's diaries owned by and cited in Chapman, *Governor Phillip*, 33–44.
65. Both *Persuasion* and *Northanger Abbey* were published in 1817 but the latter was written around 1803.
66. Chapman, *Governor Phillip*, 33–41.
67. King cited in Becke & Jeffrey, *Admiral Phillip*, ch. 16.
68. Assignment of 19 Bennett Street, 20 Nov. 1806, Bath and North East Somerset Record Office, Bath (ref: BC 153/2453/5). Described in *Bath Chronicle and Weekly Gazette*, 3 April 1823. See for both, Flynn, 'A Diminutive Enigma', 8–9.

69. Cited in Mackaness, *Admiral Arthur Phillip*, 460. See also Isabella's will cited in Flynn, 'Diminutive', 9.
70. The print evidenced in Mackaness, *Admiral Arthur Phillip*, 460. See also Kate Fullagar, 'Remembering Sydney Cove' in *The Mantis Shrimp: A Simon Schaffer Festschrift*, eds, D. Margocsy and R. Staley (Cambridge: HPS Collective, 2022).
71. Stephen Gapps, *The Sydney Wars: Conflict in the Early Colony 1788–1817* (Sydney: NewSouth, 2018), 127.
72. See Smith, 'Bennelong among His People', 10.
73. Smith, *Wallumedegal*, 12–13. See also Kohen, *The Darug and Their Neighbours*, 16, 19.
74. Rev. William Walker to Rev. Richard Watson, Parramatta, 15 Nov. 1821, cited in Smith, *Wallumedegal*, 21.
75. *The Memoirs of Joseph Holt*, ed. T.C. Croker (London: Colburn, 1838), 148–54. The settler William Lawson in 1838 remembered Bennelong as belonging to the Kissing Point Tribe (a group he thought had by this time become 'nearly extinct'): 'Mr. Lawson's account of the Aborigines of New South Wales', NSW Records, 5/1161, Item No 82: 554–555.
76. See Attenbrow, *Sydney's Aboriginal Past*, 60. My spelling follows Troy, *The Sydney Language*, 38.
77. Hunter, *Historical Journal*, ch. 20; Collins, *Account*, Vol. 2, ch. 7.
78. Attenbrow, *Sydney's Aboriginal Past*, 60. Note Isabelle Merle's problem with this anomaly in her review of Clendinnen's *Dancing with Strangers* in *Aboriginal History* 28 (2004): 268. I owe this speculation to discussions with Bill Gammage, 2021.
79. Ellis Bent, Letter 1810 in Letterbook by Ellis Bent, to his mother and J.H. Bent, NLA MS 195, folio 127; D.D. Mann, *The Present of New South Wales* (London: Booth, 1811), ch. 3; George Howe, 'Chronology of Local Occurrences', *New South Wales Pocket Almanac* (1806): 60; J.W. Price, Journal 1800, in Pamela Jane Fulton, ed., *The Minerva Journal of John Washington Price* (Miegunyah Press: Melbourne, 2000), 146–49.
80. W.P. Crook to J. Hardcastle, Parramatta, 5 May 1805, BT Box 49 ML, folio 251, SLNSW.
81. Turnbull, *A Voyage*, 73, 75–78. Turnbull's diatribe served as the basis for the excoriating obituary of Bennelong that appeared in the *Sydney Gazette*, 9 Jan. 1813, which in turn shaped so much of his public reputation through the nineteenth century.
82. See Jennifer Mori, 'The Political Theory of William Pitt the Younger', *History* 83/270 (1998): 234–48; and J.J. Sack, 'The Memory of Burke and the Memory of Pitt: English Conservatism Confronts its Past 1806–1829', *The Historical Journal* 30/3 (1987): 623–40. Pitt served as prime

minister 1783–1801 and then 1803–1806, but he was followed by like-minded conservatives until 1830.

83. Phillip to Lord Sydney, 7 Oct. 1798, in private possession, transcribed in Mackaness, *Admiral Arthur Phillip*, 430.
84. Frost, *Arthur Phillip*, 231–33.
85. Ibid.
86. Impressment is almost as controversial in modern scholarship as it was in eighteenth-century practice. Several revisionists have tried to argue that it was not as horrendous as earlier claimed. See for instance N.A.M. Rodger, *The Wooden World: An Anatomy of the Georgian Navy* (Norton: New York, 1986); and J. Ross Dancy, *The Myth of the Press Gang* (Woodbridge: Suffolk, 2015). For a reclamation of the original critique, see Nicholas Rogers, 'British Impressment and Its Discontents', *The International Journal of Maritime History* 30/1 (2018): 52–73. Rogers quotes Phillip's own report to suggest that nearly 50 per cent of sailors were pressed by the French Revolutionary wars.
87. See Frost, *Arthur Phillip*, 240–45.
88. Phillip, Report of 5 December 1801, ADM 1/579; and Phillip, Reports of 21 & 26 February 1805, ADM 1/581. See also Frost, *Arthur Phillip*, 244–45.
89. Nicholas Rogers, 'The Sea Fencibles, Loyalism and the Reach of the State' in Mark Philp, ed., *Resisting Napoleon: The British Response to the Threat of Invasion, 1797–1815* (London: Ashgate, 2006), 43.
90. See Frost, *Arthur Phillip*, 244–45; and Rogers, 'Sea Fencibles', 44–46.
91. This is in the end what the government decided to do. See Phillip, Report of 26 February 1805, ADM 1/581, cited in Frost, *Arthur Phillip*, 245.
92. Phillip to Admiralty, 17 Feb. 1798, transcribed in Mackaness, *Admiral Arthur Phillip*, 428–29.
93. On Phillip's dismissal see Mackaness, *Admiral Arthur Phillip*, 429. On the younger men who took over, see Frost, *Arthur Phillip*, 238.
94. See Frost, *Arthur Phillip*, 234–38.
95. Detailed in Mackaness, *Admiral Arthur Phillip*, 420–24. Phillip did see some movement briefly in July 1796 when he escorted a merchant fleet headed for the East Indies as far as Lisbon.
96. See Frost, *Arthur Phillip*, 243, 247.
97. Phillip to Lord Sydney, 7 Oct. 1798, cited in Mackaness, *Admiral Arthur Phillip*, 430.
98. For one account of what Aboriginal Law meant to nearby Aboriginal people, see Karskens, *People of the River*, 142–43.
99. Collins, *Account*, vol. 1, ch. 23. See also D'Urville, *Two Voyages*, 87.
100. *Sydney Gazette*, 2 Feb. 1806.

101. See Karskens, *The Colony*, 440–41 for Hyde Park inference. The report comes from the *Sydney Gazette*, 15 Dec. 1805.
102. *Sydney Gazette*, 13 Jan., 7 April, 14 July 1805.
103. See Mark Finnane 'Payback, Customary Law and Criminal Law in Colonised Australia', *International Journal of the Sociology of Law* 29 (2001): 293–301; and Lisa Ford, *Settler Sovereignty: Jurisdiction and Indigenous People in America and Australia, 1788–1836* (Cambridge: Harvard UP, 2010).
104. *Sydney Gazette*, 2 Oct. 1803.
105. Samuel Smith, Journal, ML C222/CY581, cited in Karskens, *The Colony*, 443; Collins, *Account*, vol. 1, general remarks before appendices; Macquarie's decree in *Sydney Gazette*, 4 May 1816.
106. Gapps, *The Sydney Wars*, chs 4–5. The Newcastle Colonial Massacres Map lists three conflicts in this period that amounted to a massacre (more than 6 dead): <https://c21ch.newcastle.edu.au/colonialmassacres/map.php>, accessed Oct. 2021.
107. See especially Mulvaney, *A Good Foundation*, 14; & Stanner, *White Man Got No Dreaming*, 182, 231.
108. Benjamin Bowen Carter, Journal on Anne & Hope, 1798–1799, MSS 769, Pacific Manuscripts Bureau, Canberra. For other battles like this, see Collins, *Account*, Vol. 2, chs 1, 5, 12.

Journeys: At Home and Abroad, 1796–1794
1. Letter from Bennelong to Mr Phillips, MS4005, NLA.
2. John Paul Janke interviewed by Louise Maher, 'Treasure Trove: Bennelong's letter', ABC Radio, 8 August 2013, <https://www.abc.net.au/local/stories/2013/08/08/3821136.htm>. Tahjee Moar, 'A life between two worlds: Woollarawarre Bennelong of the Wangal', 1 June 2014, <https://www.artlink.com.au/articles/4172/a-life-between-two-worlds-woollarawarre-bennelong-/ 2014>. Both accessed Oct. 2021.
3. Just two examples of Phillip as Phillips: *The Times*, 22 May 1793, and Hervey to Pinto de Souza, 25 Aug. 1774, transcribed in Becke & Jeffery, *Admiral Phillip*, appen. 2. For further discussion on the letter see Rita Metzenrath, 'Bennelong's Letter', AIATSIS website, <https://aiatsis.gov.au/blog/bennelongs-letter>, accessed Oct. 2021.
4. Penny van Toorn, 'Bennelong's Letter', *Writing Never Arrives Naked: Early Aboriginal Cultures of Writing in Australia* (Canberra: AIATSIS, 2006), 106–18.
5. Anonymous [Phillip and Collins], 'Vocabulary of the Language of N.S. Wales', SOAS Ms 41645, stated Wog-ul-trowe, Bannellon, Boinba, Bunde-bunda; P.G. King in *An Historical Journal of the Transactions at Port Jackson . . .* (London: Stockdale, 1793), 405, stated Bannelon,

Wollewarre, Boinba, Bunde-bunda, Wogletrowey; Collins, *Account*, 1, ch. 29: engraving caption stated Ben-nil-long, Wolarra-bar-ray, Wo-gul-trow-e, Boinba and Bun-de-bun-da.
6. See Shino Konishi, 'Bennelong and Gogy: Strategic Brokers in Colonial New South Wales' in S. Konishi et al., eds, *Brokers and Boundaries: Colonial Exploration in Indigenous Territory* (Canberra: ANU Press, 2016), 21.
7. Phillip to Banks, 7 Sept. 1796, SAFE/Banks Papers/Series 37.29, SLNSW.
8. King to Portland, 15 June 1797, HRNSW 3, 221–22.
9. The correspondence with Waterhouse is noted in Waterhouse to his father, 20 Aug. 1797, HRNSW 3, 288 – there is nothing else by or noted to be by Phillip in the proceeding volumes, other than letters regarding King. We know Phillip visited and entertained private correspondence with both King and Hunter into the 1800s: see for instance Mackaness, *Admiral Arthur Phillip*, 446; Frost, *Arthur Phillip*, 226. On the Greenway rumour see Alasdair McGregor, *A Forger's Progress: The Life of Francis Greenway* (Sydney: NewSouth, 2014), 62.
10. Phillip to Home Affairs Office, 23 July 1793, transcribed in Becke & Jeffery, *Admiral Phillip*, ch. 16.
11. See Tench, *Complete Account*, ch. 13; William Bradley's Journal, 245; Collins, *Account*, vol. 1, ch. 14; Keith Smith, *Bennelong* (Sydney: Kangaroo Press, 2001), 117.
12. Norfolk Island Victualling Book 1792–1796, SAFE/A (Safe 1/266), SLNSW.
13. Dawes, Notebook C, 9.
14. Collins, *Account*, vol. 1, ch. 30.
15. Gapps, *The Sydney Wars*, 126.
16. Collins, *Account*, vol. 1, ch. 29. Admittedly, the hut was said to be 'tumbling down' by this point.
17. Collins, *Account*, vol. 1, ch. 27.
18. Shortland to Lord Sydney, 26 Oct. 1795, DLMSQ 522/Item 1, SLNSW.
19. Waterhouse to Phillip, 24 Oct. 1795, Banks Papers Series 37.28, SLNSW.
20. Mary Johnson to Henry Fricker, 21 Dec. 1795, MLMSS 6722, SLNSW. Paul Irish claims this patch was by now indeed the land of the Burramattagal: *Hidden in Plain View* (Sydney: New South, 2017), 23–24.
21. Glen Humphries, *James Squire: The Biography* (Woonona: LDS, 2017).
22. See Collins, *Account*, vol. 1, ch. 29.
23. Collins, *Account*, vol. 1, ch. 29 and appen. 5.
24. Milius, *The Journal*, 170.
25. See Wilfrid Prest, *Albion Ascendant: English History 1660–1815* (Oxford: Oxford UP, 1998), 292–93; and Frank O'Gorman, *The Long Eighteenth*

Century: British Political and Social History (London: Arnold, 1997), 242–48.
26. Richard Price, *A Discourse on the Love of our Country* (London: T. Cadell, 1789).
27. Atkinson, *The Europeans in Australia 1*, 58–79.
28. See Hamish Maxwell-Stewart & Emma Christopher, 'Convict Transportation in Global Context' in A. Bashford & S. Macintyre, eds, *The Cambridge History of Australia* 1 (Cambridge: Cambridge UP, 2013), 85–86.
29. *Morning Chronicle*, 3 & 14 & 21 Oct. 1786. See also Kate Fullagar, 'The British Empire after Revolution: Swings to the East, Swings to the Right' in *The Cambridge History of the American Revolution III*, eds. M. Kars, M.A. McDonnell, & A. Schocket (Cambridge: Cambridge UP, forthcoming).
30. On convict task work, advocating convict agency in this decision, see John Hirst, *Convict Society and Its Enemies: A History of Early New South Wales* (Sydney: Allen & Unwin, 1983), ch. 2.
31. See Phillip to Under Secretary, 26 Nov. 1793 & 4 May 1795, HRNSW 2, 99, 290–91.
32. Ibid.
33. Phillip to Whitehall, 16 Oct. 1793, HRNSW, vol. 2.
34. See Manuel Covo & Megan Maruschke, 'The French Revolution as an Imperial Revolution', *French Historical Studies* 44/3 (2021): 371–97.
35. Stuart Banner, *Possessing the Pacific* (Cambridge: Harvard UP, 2007), 1–46.
36. Phillip to Nepean, 9 July 1788, HRNSW 1/2, 153.
37. See John Stevenson, *Popular Disturbances in England 1700–1832* (London: Routledge, 2014), ch. 5; O'Gorman, *The Long Eighteenth Century*, 266–67; and Jenny Uglow, 'Famine and Food Riots,' *Who Do You Think You Are?* magazine (2015).
38. Frost, *Arthur Phillip*, 145–48.
39. The convict ship the *Matilda* took only four and a half months in 1791.
40. Hunter to Under Secretary King, 7 March 1795, HRNSW 2, 284.
41. Daniel Paine, *The Journal of Daniel Paine, 1794–1797*, eds. R.J.B. Knight & Alan Frost (Sydney: Library of Australian History, 1983), 14–20.
42. Paine, *The Journal*, 42. Bass in William Marsden, 'On the Polynesian or East Insular Languages', *Miscellaneous Works of William Marsden* (London: Parbury, Allen, 1838), 111–12. See also Keith Smith, *Mari Nawi: Aboriginal Odysseys* (Dural: Rosenberg, 2010), 37.
43. See Jack Brook, 'The Forlorn Hope: Bennelong and Yemmerrawannie Go to England', *Australian Aboriginal Studies* 1 (2001): 39.
44. Hunter to Under Secretary King, 25 Jan. 1795, HRNSW 2, 281.
45. Hunter to Under Secretary King, 20 May 1795, HRNSW 2, 296; Arthur

Phillip *The Voyage of Governor Phillip to Botany Bay* (London: John Stockdale, 1789), 33.
46. Paine, *The Journal*, xviii, 11–13.
47. Tench, *Complete Account*, chs 3 & 13.
48. On demographics, see Angelo Carrara, 'The population of Brazil, 1570–1700: A Historiographical Review', *Tempo* (2014); and Dauril Alden, 'The Population of Brazil in the Late Eighteenth Century', *The Hispanic American Historical Review* 43/2 (1963): 173–205.
49. See Paine, *The Journal*, 2; and Hunter's complaint to Under Secretary King, 20 May 1795, HRNSW 2, 296–97.
50. Smith, *Mari Nawi*, 37.
51. Hunter to Under Secretary King, 25 Jan. 1795, HRNSW 2, 281.
52. See Mackaness, *Admiral Arthur Phillip*, 422–23.
53. Gazeta de Lisboa, 27 July 1793, found and transcribed by Keith Smith at <https://www.eorapeople.com.au/uncategorized/in-memorium-2/>.
54. Phillip to Nepean, 2 Sept. 1787, HRNSW 1/2, 112. Tench, *Narrative*, ch. 5, Collins; *Account*, vol. 1, 'section 2'.
55. Phillip to Nepean, 3 Sept. 1787, HRNSW 1/2, 116.
56. See a cogent account in Frost, *Arthur Phillip*, 113–17.
57. Phillip reminisces to Nepean about it, 2 Sept. 1787, HRNSW 1/2, 114.
58. See Frost, *Arthur Phillip*, 116.
59. *St. James's Chronicle*, 1 Feb. 1787.
60. Frost, *Arthur Phillip*, 112.
61. Hervey to Pinto de Souza, 25 Aug. 1774, transcribed in Becke & Jeffery, *Admiral Phillip*, appen. 2.
62. Journal of Capt. Arthur Phillip, Sydney Papers, vol. 17, William Clements Library; Frost, *Arthur Phillip*, 88–90.
63. Lavradio to Castro, 10 May 1778, transcribed in Becke & Jeffery, *Admiral Phillip*, appen. 2.
64. Attenbrow, *Sydney's Aboriginal Past*, 139–40. See also Paine, *The Journal*, 41.
65. Attenbrow, *Sydney's Aboriginal Past*, 139–40.
66. Collins, *Account*, vol. 1, chs 6 & 27.
67. *Oxford Journal*, 31 May 1794. *Morning Post*, 29 May 1794. *Morning Chronicle*, 28 May 1794.
68. Hunter to Under Secretary King, 25 Jan. 1795, HRNSW 2, 281.
69. Smith, *Mari Nawi*, 34. On keba, see Troy, *The Sydney Language*, 47; see also G.F. Angas, *Savage Life in Australia and New Zealand* 1 (London: Smith, Elder & Co., 1847), 222.
70. See Treasury Board Papers 1793–94, Public Records Office, T1/733, NSW Archives, reels 3555–56.
71. Weather recorded in *Gentleman's Magazine* 75 (1794): 394.

London: Journal of a Metropolitan Year, 1794–1793

1. *Gentleman's Magazine* 64 (1794): 394.
2. Joseph Brand, *Observations on Popular Antiquities Chiefly Illustrating the Origin of Our Vulgar . . . 2* (Rivington: London, 1813), 20–38.
3. Frost, *Arthur Phillip*, 226. On circulating libraries, see I. McCalman, gen. ed., *Oxford Companion to the Romantic Age* (Oxford: Oxford UP, 1999), 453–54.
4. Treasury Board Papers, Public Records Office, T1/733: AJCP Reel No: 3555–56 in Trove, NLA.
5. Daniel Lysons, 'Eltham' in *The Environs of London: Volume 4, Counties of Herts, Essex and Kent* (London: Cadell & Davies, 1796), 394–421.
6. *Oracle & Public Advertiser*, April 19, 1794; *The World*, April 19, 1794; T1/733.
7. See Daniel O'Neill, *Edmund Burke and the Conservative Logic of Empire* (Berkeley: University of California Press, 2016), 92–93.
8. Edmund Burke, *The Works of the Right Honorable Edmund Burke* vol. 9 (London: Nimmo, 1887), 337. See also Richard Bourke, *Empire and Revolution: The Political Life of Edmund Burke* (Princeton: Princeton UP, 2015), 840–50.
9. *The History of the Trial of Warren Hastings, Esq* (London: J. Debrett at al., 1796), 94–97.
10. *The World*, 19 April 1794. See also Kate Fullagar, *The Savage Visit: New World People and Popular Imperial Culture in Britain, 1710–1795* (Berkeley: University of California Press, 2012).
11. *Oracle & Public Advertiser*, 19 April 1794.
12. T1/733; *Gentleman's Magazine* 64 (1794): 94.
13. See McCalman, *Oxford Companion to the Romantic Age*, 627–28.
14. Phillip to Banks, 13 March 1794, SAFE/Banks Papers/Series 37.27, SLNSW.
15. Note that Parramatta was called Rose Hill until 1791.
16. See Stephen Cuneen, 'From Phillip to Grose: Leadership in New South Wales from 1788 to 1794' (PhD Thesis, University of New England, 2012), 114–18.
17. Cuneen, 'From Phillip to Grose', 102–105. See also Matthew Allen, 'Alcohol and Authority in Early New South Wales: The Symbolic Significance of the Spirit Trade, 1788–1808', *History Australia* 9/3 (2012): 7–26.
18. See Richard d'Apice, 'Heraldry of the Governors of New South Wales', *Heraldry News* 67 (2014): 8, confirmed by correspondence with the College of Arms' Chester Herald, Christopher Vane, 9 Feb. 2022.
19. Phillip *The Voyage of Governor Phillip to Botany Bay*, 3.

20. Becke & Jeffrey, *Admiral Phillip*, ch. 1; Pembroke, *Arthur Phillip*, 3; Frost, *Arthur Phillip*, 3; Fergusson, *Admiral Arthur Phillip*, 3.
21. See Michael Flynn, 'New Perspectives on Arthur Phillip . . . Part 2: The French Connection', *Descent* (2013): 201–03.
22. Phillip scholars owe this discovery to David V. White, *Somerset Herald*, discussed in Flynn, 'New Perspectives', and d'Apice, 'Heraldry'.
23. *Fürstsches Wappenbuch* (1703), discussed in Flynn, 'New Perspectives', 210. See both coats reproduced in Jacques Meurgey, *L'Ex-Libris de Claude Ambroise Philippe* (Paris: Société Française des Collectionneurs d'Ex-Libris, 1931).
24. Meurgey, *L'Ex-Libris de Claude Ambroise Philippe*, 5–23. See also F.I. Dunod de Charnage, *Mémoires pour servir à l'histoire du comté de Bourgogne* (Besançon: Charmet, 1740), 661; and Jules Finot, *Les Anoblissements en Franche-Comté* (Paris: Angers, 1868), 9.
25. Charnage, *Mémoires*, 661.
26. Fergusson, *Admiral Arthur Phillip*, 5–8. Charnage claims that Philippe had no male progeny but his will cites two sons: Meurgey, *L'Ex-Libris de Claude Ambroise Philippe*. See also Myriam Yardeni, *Le Refuge Huguenot: Assimilation et Culture* (Paris: Champion, 2002). Special thanks to Bryan Banks for talking with me about names, locations, and professions of the early-modern Huguenot diaspora.
27. Flynn, 'New Perspectives', 207.
28. *Gentleman's Magazine* 64 (1794), 2.
29. T1/733. Brook, 'The Forlorn Hope', 40.
30. T1/733. Caroline Hamilton, Honours thesis, Goldsmith's, University of London, confirmed by correspondence, Feb. 2022.
31. Grace Karskens, 'Red Coat, Blue Jacket, Black Skin: Aboriginal Men and Clothing in Early New South Wales', *Aboriginal History* 35 (2011): 9, 11, 14–17.
32. Frank McLynn, *1759: The Year Britain Became Master of the World* (London: Pimlico, 2005), 64.
33. On fire in Yiyura festivities, see Hunter, *Historical Journal*, ch. 8. On English Christmas traditions, see Clement A. Miles, *Christmas in Ritual and Tradition, Christian and Pagan* (London: Fisher Unwin, 1912).
34. See James Harriman Smith on *The Suspicious Husband* (2013): <https://museoffire.hypotheses.org/373>; and Paul Menzer, 'The Devil and Dr Faustus' in *Christopher Marlowe, Theatrical Commerce, and the Book Trade*, eds, Kirk Melnikoff, Roslyn L. Knutson (Cambridge: CUP, 2018), 218–20. See also *Songs etc in the Pantomime of Harlequin and Faustus; or The Devil Will Have His Own* (London: T. Cadell, 1794).
35. Hunter, *Historical Journal*, ch. 8. See also Collins, *Account*, vol. 1, appen. II; and Tench, *Complete Account*, ch. 17.

36. See Clint Bracknell, 'Kooral Dwonk-katitjiny (listening to the past)', *Aboriginal History* 38 (2014): 6, 9; and Janice Newton, 'Two Victorian Corroborees: Meaning Making in Response to European Intrusion', *Aboriginal History* 41 (2017): 124; and Jill Stubington, *Singing the Land: The Power of Performance in Aboriginal Life* (Sydney: Currency House Inc, 2007).
37. Robert Jordan, *The Convict Theatres of Early Australia* (Sydney: Currency House, 2002), ch. 2.
38. Ibid.
39. R.I. McCallum, 'Observations upon Antimony', *Proc. Roy. Soc. Med.* 70 (1977): 759.
40. Brook, 'The Forlorn Hope', 46. See also Margaret DeLacy, *Contagionism Catches On: Medical Ideology in Britain, 1730–1800* (New York: Palgrave Macmillan, 2017), 5.
41. Collins, *Account*, vol. 1, appen. 11.
42. Frost, *Arthur Phillip*, 32, 218. See also Becke & Jeffery, *Admiral Phillip*, 317; and Mackaness, *Admiral Arthur Phillip*, 159.
43. Phillip to Home Affairs Office, 23 July 1793, transcribed in Becke & Jeffery, *Admiral Phillip*, ch. XVI.
44. Personal letter cited in <https://fannychapmansdiary.wordpress.com/tag/john-hutton-cooper/>.
45. Richard D. Altick, *The Shows of London* (Cambridge, MA.: Harvard UP, 1978), 32.
46. Ibid.
47. *Catalogue of the Leverian Museum* (London: Hayden, 1806), NLA NK765, fully digitised on TROVE. See also Troy Bickham, 'A Conviction of the Reality of Things', *Eighteenth-Century Studies* 39/1 (2005), 29–47.
48. Transcript in Jessie M. Sweet, 'Robert Jameson in London, 1793', *Annals of Science* 19/2 (1963): 102.
49. Phillip to Banks, 3 Dec. 1791, Banks Papers, Series 37.20, SLNSW. See also Phillip to Banks, 26 July 1790, Banks Papers, Series 37.12, SLNSW.
50. Phillip to J.F. Blumenbach, 16 Aug. 1793 and Banks to S.J. Brugmans, 22 Sept. 1793, both cited in Matthew Fishburn, 'The Field of Golgotha: Collecting Human Skulls for Sir Joseph Banks', *Meanjin* (2017): 107–16.
51. Fishburn, 'The Field of Golgotha', 110. Note this is a different person to John Hunter in NSW.
52. See Alexander Anderson and Edward Riou, both from 1789, both cited in Fishburn, 'The Field of Golgotha', 107.
53. S. Deas & R. O. Bucholz, 'Household of Prince Henry Frederick, Duke of Cumberland c. 1760–1790', <https://courtofficers.ctsdh.luc.edu>.
54. Phillip to Middleton, 16 March 1791, Henry Waterhouse papers, MLMSS 6544/3/132-33, SLNSW.

55. Edward Jones, *Musical and Poetical Relicks of the Welsh Bards* (London: for the Author, 1784). See also Jeff Strabone, *Poetry and British Nationalisms in the Bardic Eighteenth Century* (London: Palgrave, 2018), 226.
56. Keith Smith, '1793: A Song of the Natives of New South Wales', *Electronic British Library Journal* (2011). See also Edward Jones, *Musical Curiosities* (London: for the Author, 1811); William Dawes, Notebook B, 31; David Collins, *An Account of the English Colony in New South Wales*, 2nd edition (London: Cadell & Davies, 1804), 394.
57. Clarence Slockee cited in Steve Meacham, 'Right Back at Us: Bennelong's Song for 1793 London', *Sydney Morning Herald*, 20 Sept. 2010. See also Ewen McDonald, ed., *Site* (Sydney: Museum of Contemporary Art, 2012), 97.
58. David Henry, *An Historical Description of the Tower of London and Its Curiosities* (London: J. Newberry, 1753), 14–24. The kangaroos arrived in 1792 from a returning ship: *Lloyd's Evening Post*, 31 May 1792. See also Markman Ellis, 'That Singular and Wonderful Quadruped' in *Intangible Natural Heritage*, ed. Eric Dorfman (London: Routledge, 2011), 73.
59. *True Briton*, 2 June 1793.
60. The history of this tradition is the focus of my first book, *The Savage Visit* (2012).
61. Alan Frost, 'New South Wales as *Terra Nullius*: The British Denial of Aboriginal Land Rights', *Australian Historical Studies*, 19/77 (1981): 513–523. For further on my reasoning for thinking it was still unresolved for Phillip see my *The Savage Visit*, 174–75.
62. Instructions, 25 April 1787, in HRNSW 1/2, 90; Proclamation, 10 Nov. 1791, HRNSW 1/2, 576.
63. See for an Aboriginal summation, James Millar, *Koori: A Will to Win* (London: Angus and Robertson, 1985), 18-19.
64. Dennis Foley in Foley & Read, *What the Colonists Never Knew*, 19, 27. Shino Konishi, *The Aboriginal Male in the Enlightenment World* (London: Pickering & Chatto, 2012), 10. See also Tony Swain, *A Place for Strangers* (Cambridge: Cambridge UP, 1993); and Julie Dibdin, *Drawing in the Land: Rock Art in the Upper Nepean* (Canberra: ANU Press, 2019), 47–49.
65. Collins, *Account*, vol. 1, appen. 1.
66. Fullagar, *The Savage Visit*, chs 2–6.
67. Phillip to Banks, 3 Dec., 1791, Banks Papers, Series 37.20, SLNSW.
68. Banner, *Possessing the Pacific*, ch. 1.
69. *The Oxford Journal*, 8 June 1793.
70. Collins, *Account*, vol. 1, ch. 25.
71. T1/733.
72. *General Evening Post*, May 28–30, 1793. Like many newspaper notices cited in this chapter, this article was reprinted elsewhere: see for this

one the *London Chronicle, St. James's Chronicle or the British Evening Post* and *The London Packet*, 28–30 May 1793.

Détente: Forging Order, 1793–1790
1. John Easty journal, 1786-1793, MS SAFE/DLSPENCER 374, SLNSW.
2. Collins, *Account*, vol. 1, ch. 19.
3. Grimes to Grimes, 21 Oct. 1792, HRNSW 1/2, 672. On better times from this point on, see also Easty journal.
4. Tench, *Complete Account*, ch. 6; Harris (1791) cited in J.A. Newling, 'Foodways Unfettered: Eighteenth-Century Food in the Sydney Settlement', MA thesis, University of Adelaide, 2007, 51. Watling, 13 Dec. 1791 in his *Letters from an Exile*.
5. Lois Davey, Margaret Macpherson & F.W. Clements, 'The Hungry Years: 1788–1792: A chapter in the History of the Australian and his Diet', *Historical Studies: Australia and New Zealand* 3:11 (1945): 187–208; amplified as the 'starvation years' in Hughes, *The Fatal Shore*.
6. Newling, 'Foodways Unfettered', 21. See also Alan Frost, 'New South Wales' in A. Frost and G. Williams, eds, *Terra Australis to Australia* (Melbourne: Oxford UP, 1988), 168.
7. Ibid.
8. Newling, 'Foodways Unfettered', 29.
9. Collins, *Account*, vol. 1, ch. 1; William Bradley, 30 April 1788, Journal; George Worgan to his brother, June 1788, MS Safe 1/114, SLNSW. See also several mentions of game in Elizabeth Macarthur, Journal and Correspondence, 1789–1840, MS A 2906 (Safe 1 / 398), SLNSW.
10. Tench, *Complete Account*, ch. 10.
11. See the monument erected by the Australian government in Bath Abbey in 1937, which proclaims that to Phillip's 'indomitable courage, prophetic vision, forbearance, faith, inspiration, and wisdom was due the success of the First Settlement in Australia at Sydney'.
12. See Collins, *Account*, vol. 1, appen. 5, discussed in Ann McGrath, 'The White Man's Looking Glass: Aboriginal–Colonial Gender Relations at Port Jackson', *Australian Historical Studies*, 24:95 (1990): 195.
13. Phillip's Instructions, 25 April 1787, HRNSW 1/2, 84–91.
14. Grenville, 5 Nov. 1791, HRNSW 1/2, 539. See also Atkinson, *The Europeans in Australia 1*, 104.
15. Irish, *Hidden in Plain View*, 17–18. See also Attenbrow, *Sydney's Aboriginal Past*, 55–59; Peter Sutton & Keryn Walshe, *Farmers or Hunter Gatherers? The Dark Emu Debate* (Melbourne; Melbourne UP, 2021), 125–44.
16. Phillip to Sydney, 28 Sept. 1788, HRNSW 1/2, 192; and Bradley, 1 Oct. 1788, Journal.

17. David Christian, *Maps of Time: An Introduction to Big History* (Berkeley: University of California Press, 2004), ch. 8.
18. Phillip to Sydney, 15 May 1788, HRNSW 1/2, 123 & 134–35. See also Hunter, *Historical Journal*, ch. 3.
19. Hunter, *Historical Journal*, ch. 19.
20. Ibid.
21. Collins, *Account*, vol. 1, ch. 6. See also Karskens, *The Colony*, 368.
22. Collins, *Account*, vol. 1, ch. 12.
23. Tench, *Complete Account*, ch. 6.
24. On roots, see Hunter, *Historical Journal*, chs 3 & 6; on fish, see Tench, *Complete Account*, ch. 17.
25. Audra Simpson, *Mohawk Interruptus: Political Life Across the Borders of Settler States* (Durham, NC: Duke UP, 2014), ch. 4.
26. The following account of Baludarri comes from Collins, *Account*, vol. 1, ch. 13.
27. Hunter, *Historical Journal*, ch. 22.
28. Ibid.
29. Collins, *Account*, vol. 1, app. XI.
30. The following account of Bangai comes from Tench, *Complete Account*, ch. 12; and Hunter, *Historical Journal*, ch. 22.
31. Hunter, *Historical Journal*, ch. 19.
32. Smith, *Bennelong*, 82.
33. Tench, *Complete Account*, chs 8 & 9.
34. Collins, *Account*, vol. 1, ch. 12.
35. Tench, *Complete Account*, ch. 12.
36. Hunter, *Historical Journal*, ch. 19.
37. Ibid.; Tench, *Complete Account*, ch. 12.
38. Stanner, *White Man Got No Dreaming*, 186; Clendinnen, *Dancing with Strangers*, 180–181 (nine years later influential critic Ross Gibson agreed with her: *26 Views of the Starburst World: William Dawes at Sydney Cove 1788–91* [Perth: UWAP, 2012], 160); Smith, *Bennelong*, 85; Karskens, *The Colony*, 398.
39. Clendinnen, *Dancing with Strangers*, 179.
40. Smith, *Bennelong*, 89; and Karskens, *The Colony*, 396–97. Warungin's name is given and spelt by William Dawes, Notebook B, 45. This man was known as 'Botany Bay Colebee' because he had exchanged names with the Gadigal Colebee.
41. See Willmot, *Pemulwuy, the Rainbow Warrior*. Pemulwuy was decapitated and his head sent to Joseph Banks, who deposited it in the Hunterian Museum – I discuss this in the chapter 'London'.
42. Dawes, Notebook B, 9. Dawes also lists Wurrgan as a sister, though she seems to have been a half-sister – discussed in the final chapter.

43. Marian Aveling, 'Imagining New South Wales as a Gendered Society, 1783–1821', *Australian Historical Studies*, 25:98 (1992): 1–12; and McGrath, 'The White Man's Looking Glass', 189–206.
44. My interpretation of Barangaroo's death comes mostly from Collins, *Account*, vol. 1, appendices 6 & 11.
45. Attenbrow, *Sydney's Aboriginal Past*, 140.
46. Collins, *Account*, vol. 1, appen. 11.
47. Daniel Southwell to his mother, 12 Oct. 1791, *Journal and Letters*.
48. Collins, *Account*, vol. 1, appen. 1 & ch. 2. See also Shino Konishi, 'The Father Governor: The British Administration of Aboriginal People at Port Jackson, 1788–1792', in M. McCormack, ed., *Public Men: Masculinity and Politics in Modern Britain* (London: Palgrave Macmillan, 2007), 54–72.
49. Collins, *Account*, vol. 1, appen. 11. On the 'ringing' bird, scholars are divided over whether this was the 'tinking' bellbird, as Collins believed (*Account*, vol. 2, ch. 15), or the 'spinking' brown treecreeper, as L.E. Threlkeld thought in his *Australian Grammar* (Sydney: Stephens and Stokes, 1834), 92. Dawes showed that Dil or Til meant ring: Dawes, Notebook B, 20.13.
50. My interpretation of Dilboong's birth comes mostly from Hunter, *Historical Journal*, ch. 22.
51. Collins, *Account*, vol. 1, appen. 6. See also Patricia Grimshaw et al., *Creating a Nation 1788–1990* (Ringwood: McPhee Gribble, 1994), 7–9; for the Aboriginal English word 'borning', see <https://www.commonground.org.au/learn/pregnancy-and-birthing>.
52. Ibid. See also Grimshaw et al., *Creating a Nation*, 9–12.
53. Ibid.
54. Hunter, *Historical Journal*, ch. 19.
55. Ibid.; and Tench, *Complete Account*, ch. 11. Hunter reported that Bennelong used 'a boy's wooden sword ... made of very light wood'.
56. Hunter, *Historical Journal*, ch. 19.
57. Tench, *Complete Account*, ch. 11.
58. Hunter, *Historical Journal*, ch. 19; and Tench, *Complete Account*, ch. 11.
59. Hunter, *Historical Journal*, ch. 19.
60. Clendinnen, *Dancing with Strangers*, 151. Shino Konishi largely endorses Clendinnen in her 'Bennelong and Gogy', 15–38.
61. Phillip to Nepean, 17 June 1790, HRNSW 1/2, 346. This is in fact in keeping with general trends in the British empire then. Nancy Paxton reveals that fear of native rape only surged from the 1850s: *Writing Under the Raj: Gender, Race, and Rape in the British Colonial Imagination, 1830–1947* (New Brunswick, N.J.: Rutgers UP, 1999). For the lack of Indigenous rape fears

in North America, see Nancy Shoemaker, 'An Alliance between Men: Gender Metaphors in Eighteenth-Century American Indian Diplomacy East of the Mississippi', *Ethnohistory* 46/2 (1999): 239–63.
62. Sydney to Treasury, 18 Aug. 1786, HRNSW 1/2, 15.
63. Order for Transportation, Dec. 1786, HRNSW 1/2, 31.
64. Phillip's Views, 1787, HRNSW 1/2, 50, 51, 59. See also Atkinson, *Europeans in Australia 1*, 179.
65. Atkinson, *Europeans in Australia 1*, 180.
66. Marian Aveling, 'Gender in Early New South Wales Society', *The Push from the Bush* 24 (1987): 31–4. See also Karskens, *The Colony*, 315–21.
67. Daniels, *Convict Women*, ch. 4.
68. See Aveling, 'Imagining New South Wales'. See also Kay Daniels, *Convict Women* (Sydney: Allen & Unwin, 1998), ch. 4.
69. Daniels, *Convict Women*, ch. 4.
70. Atkinson, *Europeans in Australia 1*, 188.
71. McGrath, 'The White Man's Looking Glass', 195; Collins, *Account*, vol. 1, appen. 8.
72. Frank Bongiorno, *The Sex Lives of Australians* (Melbourne: Black Inc., 2012), 26.
73. See Aveling's thesis about the familial structures that Phillip sought to establish as a way of ruling through patriarchy at every level: 'Imagining New South Wales', 5.
74. Jan Kociumbas, *The Oxford History of Australia* (Oxford: Oxford UP, 1992), 20.
75. HRNSW 1/2, 128, 130–31, 191, 309.
76. Phillip's Views, 1787, HRNSW 1/2, 52.
77. For Karskens' discussion of the likelihood that what the colonists called Sydney Cove had already been left alone by Gadigal for religious reasons, see *The Colony*, 55–56.
78. Journal of George Thompson, May 1792 in HRNSW 2, 797.
79. Collins, *Account*, vol. 1, ch. 11; Hunter, *Historical Journal*, ch. 18.
80. Tench, *Complete Account*, ch. 10.

Gayamay: Drama at Manly Cove, 1790–1789
1. My account comes chiefly from Waterhouse's eyewitness telling in William Bradley, Journal. It is also informed by Tench, *Complete Account*, ch. 8; Jacob Nagle, 'His Book A.D. One Thousand Eight Hundred and Twenty Nine May 19th. Canton. Stark County Ohio' (1829) SAFE/ MLMSS 5954 (Safe 1/156) SLNSW; James Scott, 'Remarks on a Passage Botnay [sic] bay 1787', 1787–1792, SFAE/DLMSQ_43 SLNSW; John Harris, Papers 1791–1837, A 1597 SLNSW; Collins, *Account*, vol. 1, ch. 11;

and Hunter's understanding of Phillip's personal rendition in Hunter, *Historical Journal*, ch. 8.
2. Instructions transcribed in HRNSW 1/2, 89.
3. Clendinnen, *Dancing with Strangers*, 111–29. See also Inga Clendinnen, 'Spearing the Governor,' *Australian Historical Studies*, 33/1118 (2002), 157–74.
4. Smith, *Bennelong*, 51–59.
5. McBryde, *Guests of the Governor*, 15; Stanner, *White Man Got No Dreaming*), 184. See also Kociumbas, *The Oxford History of Australia*, 53.
6. Isabelle Merle, 'Watkin Tench's Fieldwork: The Journal of an "Ethnographer" in Port Jackson, 1788–1791' in *Oceanic Encounters: Exchange, Desire, Violence*, eds, Margaret Jolly, Serge Tcherkezoff, Darrell Tryon (Canberra: ANU Press, 2009), 211–212; Philip Jones, *Ochre and Rust: Artefacts and Encounters on Australian Frontiers* (London: Hurst, 2019), 42. See also Gapps, *The Sydney Wars*, 77.
7. Clendinnen, *Dancing with Strangers*, 113. Despite Clendinnen's more Indigenous-centred perspective she still took at face value the colonists' assumptions about why Bennelong's body was now more weathered.
8. Hunter, *Historical Journal*, ch. 8.
9. T. Burrows and C. Johnson, eds, *Collecting the Past: British Collectors and their Collections* (London: Routledge, 2019); Tiffany Shellam, *Shaking Hands on the Fringe: Negotiating the Aboriginal World at King George's Sound* (Crawley: UWA Press, 2009).
10. Tench, *Complete Account*, ch. 8; Collins, *Account*, vol. 1, ch. 11.
11. Hunter, *Historical Journal*, ch. 20. See also Smith, *Bennelong*, 94.
12. Hunter, *Historical Journal*, ch. 8; Collins, *Account*, vol. 1, ch. 11.
13. Hunter, *Historical Journal*, ch. 20. And see my discussion in the chapter 'Détente'.
14. Tench, *Complete Account*, ch. 9.
15. Ibid.
16. Ibid.
17. Ibid.
18. Phillip to Grenville, 17 July 1790, HRNSW 1/2, 359.
19. Johnson to Thornton, July 1790, HRNSW 1/2, 386–89.
20. Phillip to Grenville, 13 July 1790, HRNSW 1/2, 354–55.
21. Phillip to Grenville, 17 July 1790, HRNSW 1/2, 359.
22. Phillip to Nepean, 17 June 1790, HRNSW 1/2, 346–50.
23. Ibid.
24. Phillip to Grenville, 20 June 1790, HRNSW 1/2, 352.
25. Southwell to his mother, 7 Aug. 1790, HRNSW 2, 722.
26. Johnson to Fricker, 21 Aug. 1790, MSS - Safe 1/121 - Letter 5, SLNSW.

27. Hill to Wathen, 26 July 1790, HRNSW 1/2, 370.
28. Tench, *Complete Account*, ch. 7.
29. Phillip to Nepean, 17 June 1790, HRNSW 1/2, 347.
30. On go-betweens in general, see Simon Schaffer, Lissa Roberts, Kapil Raj & James Delbourgo, *The Brokered World: Go-Betweens and Global Intelligence, 1770–1820* (Sagamore Beach, MA: Watson Publishing International, 2009). On the eighteenth-century British history of this phenomenon, see Fullagar, *The Savage Visit*.
31. Phillip to Banks, 26 July 1790, SAFE/Banks Papers/Series 37.12, SLNSW.
32. Collins, *Account*, vol. 1, appen. 11.
33. Bradley, Journal.
34. Collins thinks they were actually married by 1789, though Bennelong never indicates as much in the other records for that period. *Account*, vol. 1, appen. 5.
35. Hunter, *Historical Journal*, ch. 18.
36. Ibid.; and Philip Gidley King, Remarks and Journal, 1786–1790, SAFE/C 115 (Safe 1/246), SLNSW.
37. Hunter, *Historical Journal*, ch. 18.
38. Bill Gammage, *The Biggest Estate on Earth: How Aborigines made Australia* (Sydney: Allen and Unwin, 2011), 25–38; Attenbrow, *Sydney's Aboriginal Past*, 129; Lynette Russell, *Roving Mariners: Australian Aboriginal Whalers and Sealers in the Southern Oceans, 1790–1870* (Albany: SUNY Press, 2012), 23–29. Wallangang Elder Glen Timbery discusses online how whales were common around the Yiyura's harbour in Bennelong's day: <https://www.sl.nsw.gov.au/stories/eight-days-in-kamay/chapter-6-place-plenty/8>.
39. Claude Lévi-Strauss, *Totemism* (London: Merlin Press, 1964 [1962]).
40. Tench, *Complete Account*, ch. 6.
41. Hunter, *Historical Journal*, ch. 7.
42. Collins, *Account*, vol. 1, ch. 9.
43. Both letters dated 15 April 1790, in HRNSW 1/2, 329–30.
44. Bennelong had actually mentioned this earlier; see Phillip to Sydney, 13 Feb. 1790, HRNSW 1/2, 309.
45. Philip Gidley King, Remarks and Journal, 1786–1790, SAFE/C 115 (Safe 1/246), SLNSW. This line was later appropriated in Hunter's 1793 *Historical Journal*, ch. 15.
46. Gammage, *The Biggest Estate*, 15. On the La Niña cycle in this period, see J. Gergis, D. Garden & C. Fenby, 'The Influence of Climate on the First European Settlement of Australia: A Comparison of Weather Journals, Documentary Data and Palaeoclimate Records, 1788–1793', *Environmental History* 15/3 (2010): 485–507.

47. King, Remarks and Journal.
48. Southwell to Butler, 14 April 1790, HRNSW 2, 709.
49. Smith, *Bennelong*, 44.
50. Tench, *Complete Account*, ch. 6.
51. Collins, *Account*, vol. 1, ch. 9.
52. Bradley, Journal.
53. Southwell to Butler, 14 April 1790, HRNSW 2, 709. On the colonists disliking any substitute for salt pork, see Phillip to Grenville, 17 July 1790, HRNSW 1/2, 362.
54. Marcia Langton, 'Rum, Seduction and Death: "Aboriginality" and Alcohol', *Oceania* 63/3 (1993): 200.
55. John Turnbull, *A Voyage around the World*, vol. 1 (Gillet: London, 1805), 73, 75–78.
56. Langton, 'Rum, Seduction and Death', 196.
57. Bradley, *Journal*.
58. Phillip to Lord Sydney, 13 Feb. 1790, HRNSW 1/2, 309.
59. Ibid.
60. Phillip to Lord Sydney, 13 Feb. 1790, HRNSW 1/2, 308.
61. Tench, *Complete Account*, ch. 5; Hunter, *Historical Journal*, ch. 6.
62. Phillip to Nepean, 15 May 1788, HRNSW 1/2, 130. Collins on tooth evulsion: *Account*, vol. 1, appen. 6.
63. Hunter, *Historical Journal*, ch. 7. Collins, *Account*, vol. 1, chs. 2–3.
64. Tench, *Complete Account*, ch. 5.
65. Bradley, Journal.
66. Hunter, *Historical Journal*, ch. 6.
67. Tench, *Complete Account*, ch. 6.
68. Hunter, *Historical Journal*, ch. 6. See also Bradley, Journal.
69. Tench, *Complete Account*, ch. 5. Bradley, Journal.
70. Tench, *Complete Account*, ch. 5.
71. Tench, *Complete Account*, ch. 4. See also Collins, *Account*, vol. 1, ch. 7; and Bradley, Journal.
72. Phillip to Lord Sydney, 13 Feb. 1790, HRNSW 1/2, 308.
73. Hunter, *Historical Journal*, ch. 6.
74. Collins, *Account*, vol. 1, ch. 8; and Bradley, Journal.
75. Bradley, Journal.
76. My account derives chiefly from Bradley, Journal. It is also informed by Philip Gidley King, Remarks and Journal; Hunter, *Historical Journal*, ch. 6; Jacob Nagle, 'His Book'; Tench, *Complete Account*, ch. 5; and Collins, *Account*, vol. 1, ch. 8.

Decisions: Enduring History, 1789–1783
1. Hunter, *Historical Journal*, ch. 6.
2. Peter Dowling, *Fatal Contact: How Epidemics Nearly Wiped Out Australia's First Peoples* (Melbourne: Monash University Publishing, 2021), 23.
3. For an overview, see Dowling, *Fatal Contact*, 23; and Alan Frost, *Botany Bay Mirages: Illusions of Australia's Convict Beginnings* (Melbourne: Melbourne UP, 1994), 190–210.
4. Collins, *Account*, vol. 1, ch. 7.
5. Dowling, *Fatal Contact*, 18–21.
6. Phillip to Sydney, 9 Feb. 1790, HRNSW 1/2, 299.
7. See Christopher Warren, 'Smallpox at Sydney Cove – Who, When, Why?', *Journal of Australian Studies*, 38:1 (2014): 76; Michael Bennett, 'Smallpox and Cowpox under the Southern Cross: The Smallpox Epidemic of 1789 and the Advent of Vaccination in Colonial Australia', *BHM* 83/1 (2009): 45–46; Noel G. Butlin, *Our Original Aggression: Aboriginal Populations of Southeastern Australia 1788–1850* (Sydney: George Allen & Unwin, 1983); Judy Campbell, *Invisible Invaders: Smallpox and Other Diseases in Aboriginal Australia, 1780–1880* (Melbourne: Melbourne UP, 2002); John Maynard in 'Devil Devil', <https://www.abc.net.au/news/health/2021-06-07/patient-zero-smallpox-outbreak-of-1789/100174988>.
8. Tench, *Complete Account*, ch. 4.
9. Warren, 'Smallpox', 76; and Bennett, 'Smallpox and Cowpox', 47.
10. Collins, *Account*, vol. 1, ch. 7.
11. See overview in Warren, 'Smallpox', 68.
12. Elizabeth A. Fenn, 'Biological Warfare in Eighteenth-Century North America: Beyond Jeffery Amherst', *Journal of American History* 86/4 (2000). On Pontiac's War in general, see Michael A. McDonnell, *Masters of Empire: Great Lakes Indians and the Making of America* (New York: Hill and Wang, 2015), ch. 6.
13. J.R. Smith, *The Speckled Monster: Smallpox in England, 1670–1970* (Chelmsford: Essex Record Office, 1987).
14. Hunter, *Historical Journal*, ch. 6; Bradley, Journal.
15. Collins, *Account*, vol 1, appen. 8; and Troy, *The Sydney Language*, 36.
16. Paul Kelton, 'Cherokee Medicine and the 1824 Smallpox Epidemic' in D.M. Gordon & Shepard Krech, eds, *Indigenous Knowledge and the Environment in Africa and North America* (Athens: Ohio UP, 2012), 154.
17. Tench, *Complete Account*, ch. 5.
18. King in Hunter, *Historical Journal*, chapter titled 'Norfolk Island'.
19. Tench, *Complete Account*, ch. 4.
20. Ibid.
21. Ibid.

22. Ibid.
23. Collins, *Account*, vol. 1, appen. 8.
24. Hunter, *Historical Journal*, ch. 6; and Collins, *Account*, vol. 1, ch. 7.
25. Phillip to Sec. Stephens, 16 November 1788, HRNSW 1/2, 214.
26. David Blackburn, 15 Nov. 1788, Blackburn Papers, ab163, SLNSW; Tench, *Complete Account*, ch. 2. See also Smith, *Bennelong*, 28–30.
27. Hunter, *Historical Journal*, ch. 3.
28. Newton Fowell to John Fowell, 31 July 1790, MSS 4895/1/21, SLNSW; Clendinnen, *Dancing with Strangers*.
29. Collins, *Account*, vol. 1, ch. 4.
30. Ibid.
31. Mackaness, *Admiral Arthur Phillip*, 118; S. Maloney and C. Grosz, 'Arthur Phillip and Jean-François de Galaup, Comte de La Pérouse', *The Monthly* (2011).
32. Saliha Belmessous, 'Commemorating French Colonialism in Australia: On the Lapérouse monument in Sydney', *History Australia*, 17/3 (2020): 475.
33. Margaret Cameron-Ash, *Beating France to Botany Bay: The Race to Found Australia* (Sydney: Quadrant, 2021), 349, 369.
34. Arthur Bowes Smyth, 'An Officer's Journal', in HRNSW 2, 394.
35. Phillip to Sydney, 15 May 1788, HRA 1, 24. See also other sources cited in Cameron-Ash, *Beating France*, 394 & 397.
36. Alec Protos, *The Road to Botany Bay* (Sydney: Randwick and DHS, 1988), 7.
37. John White, *Journal of a Voyage to New South Wales* (London, 1790), 125; Doug Munro & Ivan Barko, 'Dagelet and Dawes', *Historical Records of Australian Science* 20/1 (2009), 1–40; Hunter, *Historical Journal*, ch. 3; Collins, *Account*, vol. 1, ch. 1; Tench, *Narrative*, ch. 7. See also for an excellent summary, Cameron-Ash, *Beating France*, 391–93.
38. See John Dunmore, *Pacific Explorer: The Life of Jean-Francois de La Pérouse 1741–1788* (Palmerston: Dunmore Press, 1985).
39. Ivan Barko, 'The Case Against the Allegation that Lapérouse's Men Killed 20 Aborigines on 26 January 1788', *French Australian Review* 41 (2006): 45.
40. Tench, *Narrative*, ch. 7.
41. Tench, *Narrative*, ch. 12; Bradley, 9 Feb. 1788, Journal; *The Journal of Jean-François de Galaup de la Pérouse 1785–1788*, vol. 2, ed. and trans. John Dunmore (London, Hakluyt Soc. 1995), 540–41. See also F.R.L. Carleton, 'An Eighteenth-Century Conventual Franciscan Naturalist on the Lapérouse Expedition', *The Great Circle* 15/1 (1993): 18–29, which goes against the contemporary reports that Receveur died from Samoan-inflicted injuries.

42. Bowes Smyth, 7 Feb. 1788, Journal; Tench, *Narrative*, ch. 10.
43. Bowes Smyth, 21 Jan. 1788, Journal; Bradley, 21 Jan. 1788, Journal.
44. See Cameron-Ash, *Beating France*, 282.
45. See Bill Gammage, 'Early Boundaries of New South Wales', *Australian Historical Studies* 19/77 (1981): 524-31.
46. Tench, *Narrative*, ch. 10.
47. Collins, *Account*, vol. 1, ch. 1; *The Journal of Lapérouse*, vol. 2, 446-48.
48. Bowes Smyth, 25 Jan. 1788, Journal.
49. Clark, 26 Jan. 1788, Journal.
50. Bowes Smyth, 24 Jan. 1788, Journal.
51. Clark, 7 Feb. 1788, Journal; Bowes Smyth, 7 Feb. 1788, Journal.
52. Margaret Cameron-Ash, *Lying for the Admiralty: Captain Cook's Endeavour Voyage* (Dural: Rosenburg, 2018) argues that Cook knew the harbour well but kept it secret, for only a few Admiralty eyes, to prevent the French from learning about it. See, though, a doubtful review: Geoffrey Blainey, *Captain Cook's Epic Voyage: The Strange Quest for a Missing Continent* (North Sydney: Penguin, 2020), 160.
53. Phillip to Sydney, 15 May 1788, HRNSW 1/2, 122.
54. Hunter, *Historical Journal*, ch. 3; Collins, *Account*, vol. 1, ch. 1. See also Tench, *Narrative*, ch. 8.
55. See the first and second commissions of Arthur Phillip in HRNSW 1/2, 24-25 & 61-67. See also Frost, *Arthur Phillip*, 148.
56. Memorandum, n.d., transcribed in HRNSW 1/2, 50-54.
57. Pembroke, *Arthur Phillip*, 158. See also Cassandra Pybus, *Black Founders: The Unknown Story of Australia's First Black Settlers* (Sydney: UNSW Press, 2006), 94, 97.
58. Frost, *Arthur Phillip*, 45.
59. Howe to Sydney, 3 Sept. 1786, HRNSW 1/2, 22.
60. Frost, *Arthur Phillip*, 113, 141-42; and Atkinson, *The Europeans in Australia Vol. 1*, 65, 76.
61. Atkinson, *The Europeans in Australia Vol. 1*, 68-74.
62. Frost, *Arthur Phillip*, 138; and Atkinson, *The Europeans in Australia Vol. 1*, 74-75.
63. Beauchamp Committee Report, cited in Atkinson, *The Europeans in Australia Vol. 1*, 75.
64. For an overview of these leading motivations, see Fullagar, 'The British Empire after Revolution'. See also *Morning Chronicle*, 3, 14, & 21 Oct. 1786; and Maxwell-Stewart & Christopher, 'Convict Transportation in Global Context', 90.
65. Testimony by Joseph Banks, *Report of the Select Committee on Convicts 1779*, trans. & ed. John Currey (Melbourne: Colony Press, 1992).

66. Collins, *Account*, vol. 1, chapter entitled 'Customs and Manners'.
67. See Hunter, *Historical Journal*, ch. 20.
68. Ibid.
69. Ibid.
70. Hunter, *Historical Journal*, ch. 3.

Beginnings: Saltwater People

1. Roger Carrick, 'Admiral Arthur Phillip Address 2020: Recent Insights and Events', <https://britozwest.org.uk/arthur-phillip-history/>.
2. *Secret Service Ledger*, Nepean entries 11 Nov. 1784 & 2 Nov. 1785, both viewable only in person at Clements Library, University of Michigan: cited thankfully in Frost, *Arthur Phillip*, 131–33. See also ADM 1/2307 & ADM 6/207.
3. S.E. Maffeo, *Most Secret and Confidential: Intelligence in the Age of Nelson* (Annapolis, Md.: Naval Institute Press, 2000).
4. On the Wolters agency, see Matthijs Tieleman, 'No Intrigue is Spared: Anglo-American Intelligence Networks in the Eighteenth-Century Dutch Republic', *Itinerario* 45/1 (2021): 99–123. See also Frost, *Arthur Phillip*, 130, though Frost refers to Marguerite as Mevrow Wolters (simply, Mrs Wolters).
5. Wolters correspondence in ADM 1/3969. See also Dundas to Sydney, 1 Nov. 1784, Public Record Office 30/8/157.
6. *Secret Service Ledger*, Nepean entry 11 Nov. 1784, Clements Library, University of Michigan, cited in Frost, *Arthur Phillip*, 130. See also ADM 1/2307.
7. Phillip to Nepean, Jan & March 1785, FO 95/4/6, cited in Frost, *Arthur Philip*, 133 (which noted that the March report was numbered '5').
8. ADM 6/207.
9. See Pembroke, *Arthur Phillip*, 77–108; Mackaness, *Admiral Arthur Phillip*, 19–35; Frost, *Arthur Phillip*, 113–25.
10. See anonymous account of Phillip in *Observer*, 22 Dec. 1793 (not 15 Dec., as cited in Mackaness, *Admiral Arthur Phillip*, 9, and repeated elsewhere); ADM 106/2972; G.T. Landmann, *Adventures and Recollections of Colonel Landmann vol. 1* (London: Colburn and Co., 1852), 121–26. See also Henri Volpert, 'Édit portant création de l'École militaire', FranceArchives website (2001), <https://francearchives.fr/fr/commemo/recueil-2001/38816>.
11. Frost, *Arthur Phillip*, 98, 112, 130. Robert Shafto seems also to have been the eponymous subject of the well-known nursery rhyme, 'Bobby Shafto'.
12. Eleanor Dark, *The Timeless Land* (New York: Macmillan, 1941), part 1 in Kindle edition.

13. Samuel Bennett, *The History of Australian Discovery and Colonisation* (Sydney: Hanson & Bennett, 1867), 83, 259; Maria Nugent, *Captain Cook was Here* (Cambridge: CUP, 2009), 56.
14. See Senior Gweagal knowledge-holder Elder Shayne Williams at <https://www.sl.nsw.gov.au/stories/eight-days-in-kamay/chapter-1-we-saw-them-coming/2>.
15. For some of the more thoughtful discussions on this tradition, see Olivia Harris, 'The Coming of the White People: Reflections on the Mythologisation of History in Latin America', *Bulletin of Latin American Research* 14/1 (1995): 9–24; Marshall Sahlins, *How Natives Think, About Captain Cook, for example* (Chicago: University of Chicago Press, 1995); Eric R. Wolf, *Europe and the People without History* (Berkeley: University of California Press, 1982).
16. On trinkets, see Banks, Endeavour Journal, 28 April 1770; Cook, *Captain Cook's Journal*, 1 May 1770.
17. On plant collecting and fishing, see Banks, Endeavour Journal, 3–4 May 1770.
18. This man was Tupaia, the Ra'iatean man who had joined Cook's *Endeavour* some months earlier at Tahiti. He served as a translator for Cook in many Pacific Islands but could not fathom Darug.
19. Cook, *Captain Cook's Journal*, 3 May 1770.
20. The man was poulterer Forbes Sutherland, who died of 'consumption', possibly a tubercular disease associated with coughing up blood. Richard Pickersgill's Journal, 1 May 1770, in HRNSW 1/2, 214.
21. Cook, *Captain Cook's Journal*, 29–30 April 1770; Banks, Endeavour Journal, 29–30 April 1770.
22. Atticus, 'To the Printer', *Sydney Gazette*, 29 March 1817.
23. On Wariwear, see Collins, *Account*, Vol. 1, ch. 22, and on Karangarang, see <https://dictionaryofsydney.org/entry/carangarang>.
24. William Dawes, Notebook B, 9, 4–5.
25. Atticus, 'To the Printer'. On Worogan and Yeranabe, see Smith, *Mari Nawi*, 97–101.
26. Collins, *Account*, vol. 1, appen. 6; Tench, *Complete Account*, ch. 17.
27. Collins, *Account*, vol. 1, appen. 2; Patricia Grimshaw et al., *Creating a Nation*, 4.
28. See Probate for Charlott in ML B1143, SLNSW.
29. See Flynn, 'The Women in Arthur Phillip's Life', 9.
30. *Observer*, 22 Dec. 1793.
31. Phillip to Nepean, 15 April 1790, HRNSW 1/2, 330.
32. Flynn, 'The Women', 13. See also Charlott's documents at ML B1143, SLNSW.

33. Frost, *Arthur Phillip*, 50.
34. Mackaness, *Admiral Arthur Phillip*, 10.
35. ADM 25/64–66. See also Frost, *Arthur Phillip*, 49.
36. Ibid., 37–43. See also Elena Schneider, *The Occupation of Havana: War, Trade, and Slavery in the Atlantic World* (Chapel Hill: UNC Press, 2018), 113–218.
37. A year later, during peace negotiations, Havana was traded back to Spain for the cost of Florida. Whether or not Phillip believed this was a profitable exchange for the British empire is unknown. It would have been a difficult calculation to make after factoring in the 25% death rate that Britain sustained during the siege. Paul Langford, *A Polite and Commercial People* (Oxford: OUP, 1989), 351; and Stephen Brumwell, *Redcoats: The British Soldier and War in the Americas, 1755–1763* (Cambridge: Cambridge UP, 2002), 46.
38. Langford, *Polite and Commercial People*, 231; Sarah Kinkel, 'Saving Admiral Byng: Imperial Debates, Military Governance and Popular Politics at the Outbreak of the Seven Years' War', *Journal for Maritime Research* 13/1 (2011): 3–19.
39. Phillip to Phillip, 26 June 1756, Australian Joint Copying Project part 9, PRO 30/8/52.
40. Mackaness, *Admiral Arthur Phillip*, 4.
41. Banister, *Masculinity, Militarism and Eighteenth-Century Culture*.
42. ADM 73/390. See also Frost, *Arthur Phillip*, 13.
43. See Mackaness, *Admiral Arthur Phillip*, 3.
44. See Collins, *An Account*, vol. 1, appen. 6; Clarence Slockee, 'Understanding Plant Uses', <https://www.abc.net.au/gardening/factsheets/understanding-plant-uses/9430794>.
45. See genealogical advice from AIATIS, <https://aiatsis.gov.au/family-history/you-start/indigenous-names>; see also the Indigenous collaborative guide for the Dharawal (close neighbours of the Darug): L. Bursill, M. Jacobs, D. Lennis, B. Timbery-Beller & M. Ryan, *Dharawal* (Sydney: Kurranulla, 2007), 13–14; Grimshaw et al., *Creating a Nation*, 13.
46. See Collins, *Account*, vol. 1, appen. 6; and Bursill, et al., *Dharawal*, 13.
47. Tench, *Complete Account*, ch. 5; Hunter, *Historical Journal*, ch 3.
48. Tench, *Complete Account*, ch. 17; Collins, *Account*, vol. 1, appen. 4.
49. Tench, *Complete Account*, ch. 17; see also Hunter, *Historical Journal*, ch. 3.
50. Tench, *Complete Account*, ch. 17.
51. Collins, *Account*, vol. 1, appen. 2. See also Hunter, *Historical Journal*, ch. 3; Tench, *Complete Account*, ch. 14.
52. Tench, *Complete Account*, ch. 17. See also 'Eight Days in Kamay', <https://www.sl.nsw.gov.au/stories/eight-days-in-kamay>.

53. Collins, *Account*, vol. 1, appen. 9. See also Tench, *Complete Account*, ch. 17; and Hunter, *Historical Journal*, ch. 18.
54. See the discussion of Yiyura ownership of Memel by the Walker family in Stephen Rice, 'This Island', *The Australian*, 21 July 2022. See also Val Attenbrow, who similarly concludes that Bennelong had 'greater rights' to Memel than did others, rather than a patrimonial claim: *Sydney's Aboriginal Past*, 60.
55. Collins, *Account*, vol. 1, appen. 9; Phillip in Hunter, *Historical Journal*, ch. 18.
56. John Cooke, *An Historical Account of the Royal Hospital for Seamen at Greenwich* (London: Nichol et al., 1789), 125, 128.
57. Cooke, *Historical Account*, 126.
58. 'Anecdotes of Governor Phillip' in Arthur Phillip *The Voyage of Governor Phillip to Botany Bay* (London: John Stockdale, 1789), 3.
59. On Elizabeth's possible manipulation, see Frost, *Arthur Phillip*, 3; on Jacob not being a teacher, see Flynn, 'The Women in Arthur Phillip's Life', 7.
60. See for all these documents and excellent recent research into the London Metropolitan Archives, Flynn, 'New Perspectives on Arthur Phillip', 197.
61. Ibid.
62. Although Whitechapel became poor later, it was a better neighbourhood than Cheapside in the early 1700s: A. Diniejko, 'Slums and Slumming in Late-Victorian London', *The Victorian Web*, 3 Oct. 2013.
63. Greenwich school documents of Phillip's later apprenticeship state that he had been admitted as a 'poor' pupil, see Mackaness, *Admiral Arthur Phillip*, 3.
64. On obstetrics, see Adrian Wilson, *The Making of Man-Midwifery: Childbirth in England, 1660–1770* (Cambridge: Harvard UP, 1995). On infant mortality see Peter Razzell & Christine Spence, 'The History of Infant, Child and Adult Mortality in London, 1550–1850', *The London Journal*, 32:3 (2007): 271–292.
65. Sarah Fox, 'The Woman was a Stranger: Childbirth and Community in Eighteenth-Century England', *Women's History Review*, 28:3 (2019): 421–436.
66. No marriage certificate has been found: see Frost, *Arthur Phillip*, 3; and Flynn, 'New Perspectives,' 199.
67. ADM 36/4179; PCC, PROB 11/653. Elizabeth's marriage to John Herbert in 1728 stated that she was 'twenty one years', making her birth year around 1707: Fergusson, *Admiral Arthur Phillip*, 3.
68. Frost cites the will of the widow, Mary Breach, who became Mary Everitt. Mary's will stated that she had three children by Benjamin and

two by Everitt, the last being Michael: *Arthur Phillip*, 4. Flynn notes that Michael Everitt was also the only personal signatory on Phillip's document of separation from Charlott: 'The Women', 10.

69. Harry Dickinson, 'The Poor Palatines and the Parties', *The English Historical Review* 82/324 (1967): 464–85; and Julian Hoppitt, *A Land of Liberty? England 1689–1727* (Oxford: OUP, 2000), 69, 215. If Jacob had reached majority age by the time he travelled, he must have been born by at least 1691.
70. For other summaries of this version of events, see Kate Fullagar, *The Warrior, the Voyager, and the Artist: Three Lives in an Age of Empire* (New Haven: Yale UP, 2020), 49–50; John Brewer, *The Sinews of Power: War, Money, and the English State 1688–1783* (Cambridge: Harvard UP, 1988), ch. 5; and David Armitage, *The Ideological Origins of the British Empire* (Cambridge: Cambridge UP, 2000), ch. 7.
71. Attenbrow, *Sydney's Aboriginal Past*, 98; see also Ian Walters, 'Fish Hooks: Evidence for Dual Social Systems in Southeastern Australia?' *Australian Archaeology* 27 (1988): 98–114.
72. Ibid.
73. See Ian McNiven, 'Colonial Diffusionism and the Archaeology of External Influences on Aboriginal Culture' in B. David, B. Barker and I.J. McNiven, eds, *The Social Archaeology of Australian Indigenous Societies* (Canberra: Aboriginal Studies, 2006), 103; and D.J. Mulvaney, 'The Chain of Connection: The Material Evidence' in N. Peterson, ed., *Tribes and Boundaries in Australia* (Canberra: Australian Institute of Aboriginal Studies Press, 1976), 72–94.
74. Attenbrow, *Sydney's Aboriginal Past*, 98; Walters, 'Fish Hooks', 100.
75. See G.J. Irwin, *The Prehistoric Exploration and Colonisation of the Pacific* (Cambridge: Cambridge UP, 1992), 100; Kate Fullagar, 'Voyagers from the Havai'i Diaspora: Polynesian Mobility, 1760s–1850s' in Lynette Russell and Ann McGrath, eds, *The Routledge Companion to Global Indigenous History* (London: Routledge, 2021), 221–22.
76. Banks, 9 Dec. 1769; and Cook, 7 Feb. 1770.
77. D. Johnson, *Night Skies of Aboriginal Australia: A Noctuary* (Sydney: Oceania Monograph, 1998), 125–26; see also E.A. Bryant, G. Walsh and D. Abbott, 'Cosmogenic Megatsunami in the Australia Region: Are They Supported by Aboriginal and Maori legends?' in L. Piccardi and W.B. Masse, eds, *Myth and Geology* (London: Geological Society, 2007), 203–14.
78. Peter White, Christian Reepmeyer and Geoffrey Clark, 'A Norfolk Island Basalt Adze from Coastal New South Wales', *Australian Archaeology*, 79:1 (2014): 131–136; see also Alison Bashford, 'World History and the Tasman Sea', *American Historical Review* 126/3 (2021): 922–48.

79. 'Australian Fires', 2 Jan. 2020, BBC News, <https://www.bbc.com/news/world-asia-50969488>; see also M.J. Rowland and R.C. Kerkhoveb, 'Evidence of External Contact Between the Pacific Basin and the East Coast of Australia During the Holocene: A Review', *Queensland Archaeological Research* 25 (2022): 47–66.
80. Cook, Journals I, 399. HRNSW 1/2, 52; and Bradley, Journal.
81. Attenbrow, *Sydney's Aboriginal Past*, 85–103; Karskens, *People of the River*, 36. See also Jo McDonald, Wendy Reynen and Richard Fullagar, 'Testing Predictions for Symmetry, Variability and Chronology of Backed Artefact Production in Australia's Western Desert', *Archaeology in Oceania* 53 (2018): 179–190; and M.E. Sullivan, who explains that fishing took over from mollusc-hunting roughly around this time too: 'The Recent Prehistoric Exploration of Edible Mussel in Aboriginal Shell Middens in Southern New South Wales', *Archaeology in Oceania* 22 (1987): 97–106.
82. Attenbrow, *Sydney's Aboriginal Past*, 156.
83. Karsken, *The Colony*, 30; Attenbrow, *Sydney's Aboriginal Past*, 157.
84. Attenbrow, *Sydney's Aboriginal Past*, 157.
85. Nicholas Peterson, 'Open Sites and the Ethnographic Approach to the Archaeology of Hunter Gatherers' in D. Mulvaney and J. Golson, eds, *Aboriginal Man and Environment in Australia* (Canberra: ANU Press, 1971), 243; see also Bryant et al., 'Cosmogenic Megatsunami in the Australia Region'.

Conclusion: Stories and Futures
1. Stan Grant, *On Thomas Keneally* (Melbourne: Black Inc., 2021), 44.
2. Claire Fuller, *Swimming Lessons* (London: Penguin Fig Tree, 2017).
3. Michel Foucault, 'Nietzsche, Genealogy, History' in his *Language, Counter-Memory, Practice: Selected Essays and Interviews*, ed. D.F. Bouchard (Ithaca: Cornell UP, 1977), 142.

Acknowledgements

I may as well continue with my unravelling mode and start at the end. My final thanks are to my publisher, Simon & Schuster, and especially to Ben Ball for his faith and interest, and for always pushing me to say more. Thank you also to my wonderful copy-editor Meredith Rose, who engaged with my prose so carefully.

I am grateful to my agent David Godwin for reaching out to me at just the right time. His interest in my work from the UK has been a motivation through the drearier times. Thanks, too, to his associate, Philippa Sitters, with whom I discovered an unlikely prior connection.

Leanne Watson at the Darug Custodial Aboriginal Corporation generously extended important advice about certain terms. Lynette Russell served as the book's expert Indigenous reviewer. That she found the time to encourage and help me while undertaking her mammoth research endeavours into the past one thousand years of contact in Australia is humbling to say the least. Grace Karskens served as another expert reviewer, a favour I can only hope to repay forwards. Her volume *The Colony* (2009) is what turned my interests in the eighteenth century towards Australia in the first place: it continues to inspire.

Many friends stepped up to read parts of this book while it was in progress and to save me from some errors. I am deeply grateful to, though entirely exonerate, Amy Way, Killian Quigley, Yves Rees, Lisa O'Connell, Kristie Flannery, Leigh Boucher and Warwick Anderson. Historians Mark McKenna, Mike McDonnell, Bill Gammage and Marina Bollinger read the whole first draft and offered incisive comments and counsel, to which

ACKNOWLEDGEMENTS

I have probably not done adequate justice but on which I will meditate for years. (Mark also delivered an emergency pep talk and Marina shared timely suggestions, affirmations and coffee – thank you so much.)

I initially broached the idea of writing this history in reverse to Tim Rowse. His surprising encouragement of the idea gave me the confidence to try it. I refer all complaints thereof to him. For general or moral support, I thank Angela Woollacott, Zora Simic, Sarah Pinto, Steve Pincus, Tamson Pietsch, Ann McGrath, Rohan Howitt, Tom Griffiths, Joanna Gilmour, Emma Cullen, Clare Corbould, Anna Clark, Alisa Bunbury, Bruce Buchan, Frank Bongiorno, Jillian Beard, Michelle Arrow, and my new ACU colleagues not otherwise mentioned, particularly Ellen Warne, Mary Tomsic, Amanda Nettelbeck, Ben Mountford, Shino Konishi, Jessica Lake, Paul Giles, Sheila Fitzpatrick, Lorinda Cramer and Sarah Bendall. I was inspired early on by Annemarie McLaren and the marvellous Omohundro virtual 'coffeehouse' group we led together in 2021, including Robert Wellington, Richard Price, Sarah Pearsall, Michael Oberg, Hannah Murray, Karen Marrero, Bennett Jones, Nikki Hessell and Melanie Burkett.

For responding so promptly and warmly to some specific enquiries, I thank Michael Rosenthal, Peter Read, Richard Neville, Caroline Hamilton, Matthew Fishburn, Emma Dortins and Bryan Banks.

I am unable to express adequately my appreciation of my new boss, Joy Damousi, for her intellectual enthusiasm and graceful leadership, and for that call to me which transformed my research life. Joining the Institute of Humanities and Social Sciences at ACU has been a blast; all kudos to my new university for its initiative.

It was an honour to meet Alan Frost after enjoying his scholarship for two decades. My work on Arthur Phillip plainly builds upon the bedrock he established.

It has also been a huge privilege to engage with many Indigenous leaders on the history of Bennelong. For their constancy of support and interest, I thank Lynette Russell, Shino Konishi and John Paul Janke. For sharing their stories about Bennelong's place in their world, I am indebted to, and always moved by, Jo Rey, Dennis Foley and Pauline Clague. For early advice and assistance, I acknowledge Marcus Hughes. My sincere thanks, in

ACKNOWLEDGEMENTS

addition, for the kind words, and permission to quote from, Uncle Shayne Williams, Tahjee Moar, John Maynard and Gavin Andrews.

I have long enjoyed chats about Bennelong with enthusiasts Adam Joseph, Peter Mitchell, and especially the late Keith Vincent Smith. Keith passed away just as I finished drafting this book: he never got to read it but he knew it was under way and said he looked forward to its arrival. He remains the most dogged, and most generous, researcher I've ever met.

Writing a book through pandemic lockdowns would have been nigh impossible without the research assistance of Paige Gleeson, whose initiative and reliability made all the difference. I am grateful, too, for my three-month fellowship at the National Library of Australia, taken in between lockdowns, which enabled deeper research into the legacy and counterparts of Bennelong.

In the end, of course, is my beginning. My last, and first, thanks go to my family. I am buoyed by the love of my dad Peter, my brother David, my sister-in-law Leslie and my nephew James.

My greatest debt is to my partner Iain McCalman, who reads and cheers on everything I do (including every chapter draft, research byway or eventually failed idea). I note that I began my immersion in the period of Bennelong and Phillip twenty-five years ago when working on the *Oxford Companion to the Romantic Age* (1999), edited by Iain. The experience revealed to me an imperial world not of unthinking consensus but one convulsing with political division and outlandish ideas. I have tried to inject the complexity of this world into all my writings ever since, not as an apology for the British empire but to show that power will never be deeply understood if it is dismissed as simple-minded.

Iain has brought into my life many wonderful McCalmans and para-McCalmans. I treasure every day the company of Andrew, Eileen, Lachy, Jac, Annika, Gaël and Bruce. This book is dedicated to our beautiful, thoughtful, teenaged son, Rohan Fullagar McCalman – a history for your future.

All royalties from this book go to the Uluru Dialogue education campaign. To donate yourself please visit ulurustatement.org.

Picture Credits

Text

PAGE 4   Phillip's burial place at St Nicholas's Church, Bathampton, c. 1845. Bath & North East Somerset Council, image ref 14873.

PAGE 5   Joseph Lycett, *Kissing Point*, aquatint, c. 1825. National Library of Australia, nla.obj-135701358.

PAGE 108   Engraving of the rotunda in the Parkinson Museum, 1790s, British Museum.

Insert

PAGE 1   Charlott Phillip by George James, 1764, State Library of New South Wales, DG235; Boorong, painted by 'Port Jackson Painter', Natural History Museum, Watling Drawing, No. 45.

PAGE 2   Engraving by Francis Jukes, *A View of Sydney Cove*, c. 1804. TROVE, PIC Drawer 16 #S4; Rio in the 1790s: Maritime procession in front of Hospital dos Lázaros, by Leandro Joaquim, Collection of the National Historical Museum/Ibram. Public domain, no. 003179.

PAGE 3   Colebee, from a sketch by Thomas Watling, 1790s, State Library of New South Wales, PXB49; Claude-Ambroise Philippe, engraving, 1667, with coat of arms in bottom left corner, University of Melbourne Library, 996.2060.000.000; Bennelong, pen and wash on light board, by 'W.W', 1793, State Library of New South Wales, DGB10.

PAGE 4   Bennelong, pen and wash on light board, by 'W.W.', 1793, State Library of New South Wales, DGB10; Silhouette of Yemmerrawanne, unsigned, pen and wash on light board, 1793, State Library of New South Wales, DGB10.

PAGE 5   Phillip's Government House, 1790, Natural History Museum, Raper Drawing, No. 16; Bennelong (front nuwi) meeting Phillip, October 1790, Natural History Museum, Watling Drawing No. 40; Pencil sketch showing Bennelong's hut on the Sydney Cove promontory, with Phillip's Government House about midway, 1790, [Thomas Watling?], Watling Drawing No. 41, State Library of New South Wales, DG V1/14.

PAGE 6   Native name Ben-nel-long, as painted when angry after Botany Bay Colebee was wounded, watercolour, c. Dec 1790, Natural History Museum; *Captain Arthur Phillip*, oil painting by Francis Wheatley, 1786, National Portrait Gallery of Australia, 2010.54.

PAGE 7   Scenes from a yulang yirabadjang, engravings by James Neagle, 1790s, TROVE, PIC Volume 26 #S11111.

PAGE 8   Tupaia's sketch of three Indigenous fishermen at Kamay, 1770, British Library, add MS 15508, f 10; Lieut. Arthur Phillip, by George James, 1764, State Library of New South Wales, DG166.

Index

Aboriginal people, *see specific group names (most are mapped on p. xv)*: Burramattagal, Dharawal, Gadigal, Gammeraygal, Garigal, Gayamaygal, Gweagal, Kamaygal, Wallumedegal, Wangal, Yiyura

Admiralty, British, 24, 39, 46–48, 75, 78–79, 213–14
  see also navy

Africa, 70, 74–75, 79, 185, 207–08

alcohol, 14, 44, 93–94, 174–75

American Revolution, 4, 20, 30, 77–80, 90, 117, 195, 207–209, 213–15, 231

Americans, Native, 112, 116, 131, 186–88, 195

Andrews, Gavin, 14

Arabanoo (Gayamaygal), 189–91

Atkinson, Alan, 12, 126

Attenbrow, Val, 34, 235

Austen, Jane, 39

Baludarri (Burramattagal), 27, 133–36, 141, 150, 221

Bangai (Yiyura), 135–37, 150

Bangarra Dance Theatre, 15

Banks, Joseph, 36
  and collecting, 59, 104, 106–107, 194
  and Cook, 57, 123, 209, 236
  and Phillip, 57–58, 93–94, 106–107, 119, 166

Barangaroo (Gammeraygalleon), 175, 188
  as Bennelong's wife, 25, 27–28, 65, 121, 130, 141–47, 160–62, 166–68, 229

Barnard Eldershaw, M., 11

Barnard, Marjorie, 11

Bashir, Marie, 10

Bass, George, 72, 75

Bath, 1, 3, 22, 29, 37–40, 58, 60, 66, 87, 100, 102, 104

Bathampton, 2–4, 19

Becke, Louis, 18

Belmessous, Saliha, 194

Bennelong (Wangal)
  appearance, 99, 171
  birth and childhood, 217–221, 225
  in Britain, 81–119
  children, 20, 28, 32–33, 141–45, 180
  death and burial, 1–5, 19–21, 31, 34–37
  initiation, 209–11

291

INDEX

journey home from England,
  54–57, 60–66, 71–76
kidnapping, 181–82
last years, 40–44, 49–53
names, 56
as negotiator with Phillip,
  120–22, 127–41, 152–53,
  160–62, 166–81
reputation, 6–9, 13–17, 19–20,
  43–44, 50–51, 64, 240–45
and spearing of Phillip, 154–60
totem, 37, 168
and women, 21–22, 25–29, 53, 65,
  141–48
Bennelong, modern parliamentary
  seat of, 2, 15
Bennelong Point, *see* Dubuwagulya
Bennett, Samuel, 218
Bent, Ellis, 43
Bidgee Bidgee (Yiyura), 19–20,
  25–26
Blackburn, David, 191
Bligh, William, 43
Bondel (Aboriginal man), 61
Boorong (Burramattagalleon)
  as girl in colony, 65, 133, 150, 161,
    166, 179–80, 190
  as wife of Bennelong, 4, 20–21,
    25–28, 32–33, 121, 221
Botany Bay (Kamay), xi, 49, 138,
  184, 197–202, 211, 217
  see also Gweagal, Kamaygal, New
    South Wales
Bradley, William, 166–67, 173,
  178–82, 188, 197
Brazil, Portuguese colony of, 29–30,
  71, 73–81, 206, 215–16
Breach, Benjamin, 232

British society
  death conventions, 35–36, 82–83
  gender conventions, 21–25, 86–87,
    141, 148–52
  kin conventions, 29–31, 94,
    230–34
  imperialism, 3–4, 13, 29–32, 38, 45,
    57–60, 68, 77, 80–81, 89–91,
    107, 109, 111–12, 116–17,
    194–95, 199–202, 204–09,
    213–16, 225
  theatre, 38, 86, 92, 100–102, 111,
    115–16, 118
  see also Christianity;
    Enlightenment
Britain-Australia Society, 10
Brodsky, Isadore, 16–17
Brook, Jack, 97
Burke, Edmund, 36, 90–91, 107
Burramattagal, 26, 41, 62–63, 65, 93,
  129–30, 133–34, 161, 168, 170–71,
  180, 238
Byng, John, 224

Cane, Anna Maria, 24–25, 222
Caribbean region, 48, 76, 214,
  223–24, 232
Caruey (Gadigal), 66
Chapman, Fanny, 39
Chapman, Henry, 39, 59, 104
Chapman, William, 59
China, 172
Christianity, 32–33, 36, 74, 92,
  95–96, 113–15, 118, 195, 201, 205,
  233–34
Christmas, 100, 176
Clark, Manning, 16
Clark, Ralph, 203

INDEX

Clendinnen, Inga, 10–12, 16, 27, 139–40, 147, 157, 192
Coke, Thomas Walker, see Digidigi
Colebee (Gadigal)
  with Bennelong, 52, 61–62, 65, 155–56, 158, 188, 210
  captivity of, 155, 177–82
  and Warungin ('Botany Bay Colebee'), 140–41
Collins, David
  and Bennelong, 37, 62, 65, 114–15, 117, 121, 142–46, 168–70, 176, 180–81, 229
  on the colony, 64, 99, 172, 186–87, 196, 198
  on the Yiyura, 49, 110, 130, 135, 190, 192–93, 204, 209–10, 227–28
convicts
  in plans for colonisation, 67–69, 195–96, 207–09
  in the colony, 9, 19, 93, 98, 102, 121–27, 133–37, 144, 147–52, 162–65, 172–73, 186–87, 191–92, 203, 205
  Portuguese, 78
Cook, James, 9–10, 77, 123, 176, 194, 196, 204, 217–220, 237
Cooke, George, 99
Coombs, H.C., 16
Cooper, John Hutton, 104
Cornwallis, Lord, 90
corroboree, see garabara
Crook, William Pascoe, 44

Dagelet, Joseph, 196
Dark, Eleanor, 16, 217–18, 220

Darug (language), xi, 72, 92, 144, 219
Dawes, William, 110, 192, 196, 221
Denison, Charlott, see Charlott Phillip
Dharawal, 14, 218–19
Dickensen, David, 43
Dicky, see Digidigi
Digidigi (Bennelong's son), 20, 32–35, 180
Dilboong (Bennelong's daughter), 28, 141, 143–45
disease, see smallpox
Doyle, Matthew, 110
Dubuwagulya, 2, 15, 63, 110, 145, 152
Duncombe, Charles, 29–30, 216
Dutch people, 185, 201, 213–14

Easty, John, 120
Eldershaw, Flora, 11
Eltham, 72
Enlightenment values, 6, 9–13, 122, 139, 159, 205–06, 240–42, 244–45
Enoch, Wesley, 14
Eora, see Yiyura
Everitt, Eleanor, 31
Everitt, Michael, 31, 223–24, 232

Falmouth, 118–19
Fergusson, Lyn, 10–11, 96
Fishburn, Matthew, 106–107
Flanders, 30, 215–16
Flynn, Michael, 96, 231
Foley, Dennis, 114
food, 219, 226–29
  in Britain, 67, 70
  in the colony, 63, 74, 120, 123–32, 145, 150, 162, 169, 173–75, 177, 181–82

INDEX

Foucault, Michel, 245
Fowell, Newton, 192
France, 66, 95, 183–86, 193–203, 208, 212, 214–15, 224, 241, 245
see also French Revolution
French Revolution, 4, 6, 20, 45–48, 58, 60, 66–67, 69–71, 108, 165, 241
Frost, Alan, 11, 78, 206, 216
Fuller, Claire, 244

Gadigal, x, 20, 41, 49, 52, 63, 66, 144, 152, 175, 177–78, 182, 188, 191, 198, 238
see also Colebee; Nanbarree
Gagulh (Bennelong's mother), 220, 226, 229, 231–32
Gammage, Bill, 171
Gammeraygal, 27, 161, 166–67, 175
Gapps, Stephen, 41, 51
garabara, 92, 101–102, 220, 226, 228
Garadyigans (healers), 42, 103, 159, 210–11, 226
Garigal, 155, 159–60
Garradah (Gammeraygal), 27
Gayamay, 154–55, 168, 181–82, 190, 211
Gayamaygal, 189, 192, 238
George III, King, 70, 106, 108–09, 115–17, 165, 174, 246
German lands, 76, 94–96, 214, 230, 233
Glorious Revolution, 234
Gnunga Gnunga (Bennelong's brother-in-law), 143, 145
Goorah-Goorah (Bennelong's father), 220–21, 226, 229

Government House (Sydney), 55, 57, 62–63, 73, 133, 144, 155, 160, 167, 169, 172–73, 179, 189–90
Grant, Stan, 243
Great Barrier Reef, 236
Greenway, Francis, 59
Greenwich (hospital and school), 76, 94, 225, 230–31, 233
Grenville, William, 163–64
Grimes, Charles, 123
Grose, Francis, 65, 93–94
Gweagal, 49–50, 65, 140–41, 146–47, 175, 192, 199, 217–20

Hamilton, Caroline, 98
Handel, G.F., 92–93, 101
Harris, John, 123
Hastings, William, 89–91, 111, 118
Heiss, Anita, 14
Henry Frederick, Prince, 109
Hervey, Admiral, 79
Hill, William, 164
history in reverse, 5–9, 22, 88–89, 240–45
Holt, Joseph, 42
Howe, George, 43–44
human remains collected, 106–107
Hunter, John, anatomist, 107
Hunter, John, naval captain
 with Bennelong, 71–76, 81, 83–84, 90, 93, 101–102, 129–30, 136–37, 153, 169, 176–77, 211
 as governor, 43, 54–55, 57, 59, 62–63, 126
 as lieutenant-governor, 179, 188, 191, 196, 201–204, 226

INDEX

impressment, British naval, 46–47, 71
India, 76, 90, 123

James II, King, 234
Jameson, Robert, 105
Janke, John Paul, 54–55
Jeffrey, Walter, 18
Johnson, Mary, 64, 161, 166, 179
Johnson, Richard, 113, 160–64, 166, 179
Jones, Edward, 109–110, 118
Jordan, Robert, 102
Jukes, Francis, 40–41

Kamaygal, 49, 51–52, 140, 192–93, 197–99
Karangarang (Wangalleon), 141–42, 146, 220
Karskens, Grace, 8, 11–12, 98, 139
Kebarrah (initiate), 84, 210
Keneally, Thomas, 15
Kent, Edward, 72–73, 84–85, 87–88, 100, 118
Kent, William, 72, 84
King, Philip Gidley, 40, 43, 58–61, 141, 170–74, 189, 196
Kissing Point, 5, 21, 41–42, 57, 63, 65
Konishi, Shino, 34, 114
Kurubarabula (Gweagalleon), 25, 54, 65–66, 121, 140–41, 145–48, 150

Landmann, Isaac, 215
Lane, John, 31
Langton, Marcia, 174
Lapérouse, Jean-François, 193–97, 200–204

Laqueur, Thomas, 35
Lavradio, Marquess of, 80
Lennis, John, 14
Lever, Ashton, 105
Lévi-Strauss, Claude, 168–69
Lille, 215
Lock, Maria, 32–33
London, 10, 196, 230, 233
    Bennelong in, 72–73, 82, 87–94, 97–102, 104–18, 245
    Phillip in, 54, 57, 60, 66, 68–70, 86–87, 94–96, 102, 104–18, 222–23, 245
Louis XVI, King, 45, 165

McBryde, Isabel, 157
McEntire, John, 137–40
Mackaness, George, 11
Macquarie, Lachlan, 43
Makassar, 185–86
Manly Cove, *see* Gayamay
Maugoran (Burramattagal), 27
Memel, 161, 229
Milius, Pierre, 66
Minorca, 76, 224, 231
Mitchell, Peter, 2
Moar, Tahjee, 55
Mulvaney, John, 17
Murphy, Matt, 16

Nanbarree, 4, 20, 156, 179–80, 190, 210
navy, British, 30–31, 38, 46, 84, 108, 123, 198, 204, 206, 224–25, 230–32, 234
    and Phillip, 19, 24, 46–48, 58, 60, 66, 76–79, 94, 104, 141, 212–16, 223–24, 242

INDEX

see also Admiralty; impressment;
  sea fencibles
Neagle, James, 99
Nelson, Horatio, 38, 47, 216
Nepean, Evan, 29–30, 77, 164–65,
  170, 173, 207, 213–14, 216
New Holland, xi, 66, 105–107, 118,
  198–99
  see also New South Wales colony
New South Wales colony, xi, 18–19,
  30, 44, 50, 58–59, 69, 84, 87,
  245–46
  and Phillip, 1, 3, 6–7, 11–12, 37, 40,
    45, 58–60, 67–70, 81, 83, 89,
    91, 94, 102, 104–10, 113,
    116–17, 119–20, 122, 149, 162,
    173, 183, 195, 203–09, 216, 241,
    244
New South Wales state
  government, 2–3, 10
Newling, Jacqui, 124
Norfolk Island, 57–58, 60, 62, 65, 93,
  171–72, 196, 236
Nugent, Maria, 218

O'Brien, Jean, 8

Pacific Islanders, 116, 149, 197,
  236–37
Paine, Daniel, 71–72, 74
Parkes, Henry, 18
Parkinson Museum, 104–108, 118
parliament in London, 45, 89–91,
  116, 207–09, 216, 234
Parramatta, 1, 93, 129–30, 170
Parramatta Native Institution,
  32–33
Pembroke, Michael, 10, 29

Pemulwuy (Bidjigal), 14, 17, 51,
  137–41, 150, 210
Peterson, Nicholas, 239
Philippe, Claude-Ambroise, 95–96,
  233
Phillip, Anne, 224, 231
Phillip, Arthur
  and American Revolution, 215
  ancestors, 94–96, 230–34
  appearance 37
  with Bennelong in Britain, 81–84,
    89–93, 104–10, 113–19
  with Bennelong in the colony,
    132–41, 152–53, 160–62, 169–78
  birth, 230–32
  in Brazil, 76–81
  death and will, 1–4, 19, 21, 28–31,
    35–37
  final years, 37–40
  first years in the colony, 183–93
  and the French, 6, 44–48, 66–71,
    79, 95–96, 195–96, 212, 214–15,
    224, 233, 241
  governorship, 1, 57–60, 67–70,
    93–94, 102, 120–32, 162–66,
    204–206
  ill–health, 37–40, 103–104
  reputation, 6–13, 17–19, 125,
    240–45
  and Seven Years' War, 223–25
  spearing, 154–60
  spying, 30, 212–16
  and women, 21–26, 52–53, 86–87,
    142–52, 221–23
Phillip, Charlott Tibbott Denison,
  24–25, 27, 30, 87, 121, 170, 215,
  221–23
Phillip, Eliza, 231

296

INDEX

Phillip, Elizabeth, 230–33
Phillip, Isabella
  and Bennelong, 54–55, 81
  death, 19, 21, 40
  and Phillip, 22–27, 29–30, 38, 48, 58, 60, 86–87, 121
Phillip, Jacob, 31, 94, 230–33
Phillip, Rebecca, 231
Pitt, William, 45, 71, 90–91, 107, 213
Pontiac's War, 187
Portugal, 30, 47–48, 74, 76–80, 201, 215
  see also Brazil
Price, John Washington, 43
Price, Richard, 67
Prospect Hill, 170
Protos, Alec, 196

rape, 148, 151–52
Readhead, William, 224–25
Receveur, Laurent, 197
Richmond, Duke of, 111
Rio de Janeiro, see Brazil
Robertson, Geoffrey, 2–3, 6, 9–10
Rose Bay (Banarung), 166–67, 175
Rose Hill, 170
Rousseau, Jean-Jacques, 32

Sadleir, Richard, 19
Saint-Amand, 215
Satia, Priya, 7
scientific voyaging, 10, 59, 194, 196
sea fencibles, 46–48, 71
Seven Years' War, 3, 223–24
Shafto, Robert, 216
Shortland, John, 64
Simonetti, Archille, 18
Simpson, Audra, 131

slavery, 12, 46, 68, 74, 79, 81, 171, 205–206, 240
Slockee, Clarence, 110
smallpox, 176, 178–79, 184–89, 245
Smith, Bernard, 16
Smith, Keith Vincent, 13–14, 25, 84, 138, 157, 172
Solomon Islands, 197
Southwell, Daniel, 144, 164, 172–73
Spain, 48, 77–80, 166, 201, 214–15, 224
Squire, James, 65
Stanner, W.E.H., 11–12, 17, 139, 157
statues, 9, 18
Sydney botanic gardens, 3, 14, 18
Sydney Cove (Warrane), 40–43, 59, 65, 71–72, 93, 130, 134, 138, 144, 152, 185, 196, 198–99, 203, 229
  see also New South Wales colony
Sydney, Lord (Thomas Townshend), 45, 54–55, 64, 67, 69, 84, 104, 149, 170, 176, 185, 204–207, 212–13, 221

Tench, Watkin
  and Bennelong, 136, 146–47, 153, 160–61, 167, 169, 174, 176–79, 181
  and the colony, 123, 125, 131, 140, 165, 172, 186, 190–91, 196–97, 226–29
Thompson, George, 152–53
Tories, 45, 91
totems, 37, 114, 127, 168–69, 177, 225
Toulon, 212–15
treaty, idea of, 69, 112, 117, 119, 132, 166, 204, 209, 242, 245–46

INDEX

Turnbull, John, 44, 174
Turnbull, Lucy Hughes, 15

Van Toorn, Penny, 56
Vasconcelos, Luis de, 78

Walker, William, 20, 33
Wallumedegal, x, 37, 41–42, 62–63, 65, 168, 238
Wangal, 3, 20, 26, 37, 41–42, 62–63, 73, 128, 137, 168, 175, 178, 180, 183, 192–93, 211, 217, 220–21, 226, 229, 238
  see also Bennelong
Wariwear (Wangalleon), 141–43, 145–46, 220–21
Warrane (in Gadigal Country), 198–99
  see also Sydney Cove
Warungin (Gweagal, 'Botany Bay Colebee'), 140
Waterhouse, Henry, 59, 64, 72, 108–109, 154–56
Waterhouse, William, 72–73, 87–88, 91, 93, 97–99, 108–109, 115, 118
Watling, Thomas, 123
Westminster Abbey, 10, 36, 212
whales, 142, 156, 158, 168, 225
Whigs, 45, 89
White, John, 142, 179, 196
Whitehead, Isabella, see Isabella Phillip
Whitehead, Richard, 23, 38, 86–87
Willemering (Garigal), 155, 159–60
William III, King, 234
Williams, Uncle Shayne, 218
Willmot, Eric, 14
Wolters, Marguerite and Richard, 213
Worogan (Wangalleon), 26, 221

Yadyer (Gweagal), 218
Yarramundi (Aboriginal man), 33
Yemmerrawanne (Wangal)
  and Britain, 87–92, 97–100, 103–20, 133, 210
  death, 73, 76, 82–85
Yeranabe (Burramattagal), 26, 221
Yiyura
  battle conventions, 34–35, 48–52, 138
  cosmology, 36–37, 82, 127–32, 168, 188, 218–20, 238–39
  death conventions, 31–37, 82–83, 143
  gender conventions, 21, 26–28, 52, 101, 121, 136, 141–48, 167, 227–28
  kin conventions, 26, 225–30
  male initiation, x, 176, 209–11
  words, xi, 5, 55
  see also Darug; food; garabaras; and specific clan names
yulang yirabadjang, 209–11, 225